My Life among the Deathworks

Volume I

 SACRED ORDER/SOCIAL ORDER

KENNETH S. PIVER, GENERAL EDITOR

Publication of this volume was assisted by a generous grant from the Institute for Advanced Studies in Culture at the University of Virginia.

PHILIP RIEFF

My Life among the Deathworks

ILLUSTRATIONS OF THE
AESTHETICS OF AUTHORITY

Introduction by James Davison Hunter

UNIVERSITY OF VIRGINIA PRESS CHARLOTTESVILLE AND LONDON

University of Virginia Press

© 2006 by Philip Rieff

Introduction © 2006 by James Davison Hunter

All rights reserved

Printed in the United States of America on acid-free paper

First published 2006

9 8 7 6 5 4 3 2 1

Library of Congress Cataloging-in-Publication Data

Rieff, Philip, 1922–

My life among the deathworks : illustrations of the aesthetics of
authority / Philip Rieff ; introduction by James Davison Hunter.

p. cm.—(Sacred order / social order; v. 1)

Kenneth S. Piver, general editor.

Includes bibliographical references and index.

ISBN 0-8139-2516-9 (cloth : alk. paper)

1. Culture. 2. Civilization, Modern. 3. Postmodernism—Social
aspects. 4. Freud, Sigmund, 1856–1939—Influence. 5. Authority.
6. Religion and sociology. 7. Social ethics. 8. Moral conditions.
I. Piver, Kenneth S., 1965– II. Title.

HM621.R534 2006

306'.09182'109045—dc22

2005024384

Susan Sontag
in remembrance

A. A violent order is disorder; and
B. A great disorder is an order. These
Two things are one. (Pages of illustrations.)

Wallace Stevens, "Connoisseur of Chaos"

Contents

Editor's Acknowledgments

I have often heard Philip Rieff comment on the length to which acknowledgments sections have grown in recent years, to the extent that anyone with whom the writer had even the remotest contact receives mention. To Rieff's mind, this trend illustrates an attitude symptomatic of the contemporary "iron law of gratitude": *ingratitude*. Nevertheless, I would be truly remiss if I did not mention a small list of essential principals. Of course, I am especially indebted to Professor Rieff for the trust he has placed in me as general editor of his lifework, *Sacred Order/Social Order*, and the great honor of this occasion to continue under his master tutelage. Rieff's devotion to his students is deservingly legendary.

In addition, I want to extend my deep thanks to James Davison Hunter for his enthusiasm and guidance regarding this project, his superior introduction to this first volume, and the generous financial support he helped secure as director of the Institute for Advanced Studies in Culture at Virginia. I also am most grateful to Penelope Kaiserlian, director of the University of Virginia Press, for her guidance, patience, and commitment to this endeavor. And I am very thankful for the editorial help of Ellen Satrom, Mary MacNeil, and Ruth Melville. In addition, I want to express special thanks to Arnold Eisen, Alan Woolfolk, Gordon Marino, Joel Friedlander, Mira Kautzky and Keith Flaherty, Mark and Bella Green, and David Rieff for their help and support. I am also grateful to the various museums, galleries, and estates for allowing the reproduction of their important works, with particular thanks to Anne d'Harnoncourt, president of the Philadelphia Museum of Art. Finally, I am eternally indebted to my wonderful wife, Danielle, and marvelous family for their unwavering support, patience, love, and faith.

Introduction

JAMES DAVISON HUNTER

With the publication of *Sacred Order/Social Order: My Life among the Deathworks*, we have the long-awaited first volume of the summation of Philip Rieff's sociological theory and cultural analysis. Though a wonderfully edited collection of his essays and reviews was published in 1990 as *The Feeling Intellect*, and bits and pieces of key scholarship specifically relating to this volume have surfaced in the meantime, this is his first major work to appear since *Fellow Teachers* was published in 1973.[1]

Philip Rieff had long ago established himself as the most enduringly insightful interpreter of Sigmund Freud and his cultural legacy. In the effort to understand the intellectual origins of psychoanalysis, its emergent and competing schools, and its unintended if not tragic cultural consequences, *Freud: The Mind of the Moralist* (1959; 3rd ed. 1979) and then *The Triumph of the Therapeutic* (1966) were rightly acclaimed as critical masterpieces—works as profound in their moral implications as they were illuminating in their exegesis. With the present work, Rieff extends his reputation as one of the most innovative theorists of culture and cultural authority of the last half century. *Sacred Order/Social Order: My Life among the Deathworks* is stunning in its originality, breathtaking in its erudition and intellectual range, and astonishing in the brilliance of its insights into our historical moment. It penetrates settled conceptual conventions to open up new ways of thinking about culture, religion, morality, character, identity, social movements, and a pantheon of intellectuals, novelists, poets, and artists. In the discipline of social theory, there is nothing quite like this.

As a work of cultural analysis, it is also inherently provocative, controversial, and, in parts, incendiary. Rieff will surely sting as many as he astounds, incense as many as he inspires. There is some intention here. Against the analytic detachments of his earliest scholarship, Rieff now concludes that "there is no meta-culture, no neutral ground, from which the war of the worlds can be analyzed." As such, his examination leads to criticism of some of the most cherished pieties of our time.

I

Reading *My Life among the Deathworks* is no easy task. The book is difficult, intentionally so.[2] His is a strategy of concealment. In a culture where everything is on display yet so little of substance actually revealed, Rieff tends to write with deliberate and often clever obscurity as a means of veiling his contentions and insights. Simply following a line of argument, much less understanding the layers of nuance, indirection, paradox, irony, witticism, simile, and satire, requires determined effort. The difficulty of his prose is, by no means, carelessness on Rieff's part. One senses that the wide range of familiar and unfamiliar illustrations, puzzling references, and numerous neologisms are chosen with precision. Rieff wants the reader to work for the insight he has to offer; to read and then reread. There is, in this, a similarity to the kind of lyrical but tortured thinking one finds in Nietzsche's later work. And as it is with Nietzsche, the labor is worth it. The slow trudging through thickets of literary and artistic allusion nearly always leads to clearings of profound lucidity and discernment about the nature of culture and the character of our times.

Part of what makes Rieff's work distinctive—at least as an exercise in social theory—is the way he uses "image entries" from poetry, literary texts, the visual arts, and music interwoven with other texts that range from the writings of Freud to television interviews and newspaper stories. On the face of it, this approach comports with the interpretive practices fashionable within cultural studies, but there are some differences that have significant consequence for the analysis that follows. Most obviously, against the radical contemporaneity of much of what one finds in cultural studies, Rieff historicizes relentlessly and in this demonstrates an uncommon depth of familiarity with the text or object he cites. The work, then, suffers from none of the hermeneutic superficiality so common among the academic dilettantes.

Far more important is the ontology he imputes to these objects and texts. The arts and literature have not been created and do not exist in a separate realm of the social world, autonomous from life and moral meaning. Neither are they "mere" representations or logical abstractions. For Rieff, image entries are crystallizations of real action, and through them we see "shadows of truth." In his words, "These image entries are in their appearance an entry into the reality itself. They are not the parallels of abstract and static selves. They themselves relate to actualities, actual actions—they themselves are reality." In short, these image entries *are* what they represent.

The ontological turn he takes with regard to these image entries he also takes in his entire understanding of culture. Identity and morality, for example, are not infinitely pliable fictions but are real precisely because they exist as enactments of body and mind in relation to sacred order. The same can be said for gender, authority, and God not least. Even Freud, according to Rieff, unwittingly acknowledges the irreducibly metaphysical properties of culture in his master concept of repression—which is, in Rieff's words, the "unconscious . . . playing out of the authority that once belonged consciously to revelation." Freud's acknowledgment is both negational and unintended, to be sure, but repression has no significance except in disguised service to enduring truths. In these affirmations, one finds no quotation marks signaling an ironic detachment from words and assertion, no wink or nod suggesting the insincerity of the worldly-wise. This take on culture is unusual, to say the least. It is true that of late one can find certain gestures toward ontology in political theory, but these movements affirm a weak version at best.[3] Rieff's is considerably stronger. As such, in his approach toward culture Rieff stands foursquare against the reductive and deconstructive analytical strategies that have been central to modern social science over the last two centuries. The implications are arresting.

II

Rieff's theory of culture proceeds from an analytical posture that he has long called "the feeling intellect." This is an understanding born out of intimacy; a personal knowledge, to use Polanyi's phrase, of subject, text, artifact, author. At the same time, it is an understanding particularly aware of the higher truths and the structure of authority within which those truths are embedded that give meaning to identity and action, object and subject, indeed life itself. It is not only those with some present or distant attachments to living tradition or creedal community who intuitively understand what Rieff is about here. As he notes, even "Nietzsche has such a feeling intellect, despite his own intentions." Yet it is possible that Rieff's theory of culture will be utterly incomprehensible to those incapable of feeling intellect, those whose intellection is only or primarily performative. In our day, their number is legion.

Still, his work is not without a recognizable intellectual lineage. Elements of this theory draw from an engagement with all the major social theorists of the last century and with theoretical traditions ranging from psychoanalytic theory and neo-Marxism to structuralism and postmodernism. In its rudiments, though, it probably owes more to Emile Durkheim and Max Weber than to others—Durkheim for his insight into the sacred and its relation to social order, and Weber for his perception of the central importance of authority. In this work, Freud continues to be an influential interlocutor, as he has been for Rieff's entire career. However, Nietzsche, who has long been in the background of Rieff's thinking and writing, comes to the fore and there looms large indeed. Yet both are so prominent in Rieff's cultural dissections for the simple reason that they are, for him, the definitive theorists of our late modern culture.

Rieff formally defines culture as world-creation; its historic task, the perpetual re-creation and maintenance of a world, in its symbols, institutions, and symptoms. As a matter of historical enactment, though, world-creation occurs by means of a transliteration of sacred orders into social orders. Occupying the space between the sacred and the social, then, culture provides the texts, literal and otherwise, by which those transliterations are interpreted, understood, and made real to people. In experience, culture exists as the habitus within which human beings come to understand themselves, their actions, and everything else in relation to sacred order. As Rieff puts it, "Cultures give readings of sacred order and ourselves somewhere in it."

The heart of Rieff's theory of culture is the point at which Durkheim and Weber meet: the illuminations and operations, the symbols and praxis of authority, sacred in its genesis and ongoing legitimacy. This is, for Rieff, the most salient and portentous dynamic at work in culture. Indeed, all cultures up until our own have been, in their origins and evolution, an address to some ultimate authority. That address is not generic but particular; it occurs through artistic expression, scientific inquiry, social structures, and individual conduct. What this means in practice is that a culture comes to be constituted by a system of moral demands that are underwritten by an authority that is vertical in its structure. The wording is important here. These are not merely rules or norms or values, but rather doxa: truths acknowledged and experienced as commanding in character. This is precisely because the moral obligations and the sacredness of the authority underwriting them are both institutionalized in social organization and absorbed into individual consciousness as a presiding presence.

Social life and individual existence, then, take place as a constant shifting within this "vertical in authority." Within the vertical in authority—the "via" in Rieff's witty acronym—there are three motifs that mark the movements of human action. These are the interdictory, defined by conformity with or obedience to moral obligations; the transgressive, defined as violations of the interdictory; and the remissive, a mixture of the two defined by acts that are prohibited but allowed and pardonable only as exceptions to the rule. In the via, acts in conformity with the interdictory raise, those that transgress lower, and remissive acts, which constitute most of human experience, represent a shifting side to side. All of social life, from its complex and minute particulars to its largest and transcending generalities, reflects these moral dynamics.

It is not only individual lives and social order that are framed normatively in the via, but identity is as well. The singular, unrepeatable, and inviolable nature of each human being derives from the source of sacredness itself. Yet the moral meaning of human lives and the particular formation of identities are also inseparable from the way humans relate to the via. What we are and what we become, as Rieff puts it, is defined by where we are in the vertical in authority. Stability in character, in this light, is formed in a culture that is stable through consistent resistance to the transgressive and obedience to the interdictory.

It is important to note that Rieff's theory of culture is not static. As he argues repeatedly, cultures are stable in faithfulness, yet they are continually re-created precisely because they are incomplete. The transliteration of sacred order to social order is always subject to reinterpretation, and reinterpretation is itself a function of continual negotiation. The potential for societal change, then, is always present but never more so than when the relationship between authority and obedience is reversed. In such situations, authority is no longer living but has become calcified, its exercise has become merely procedural, and obedience to it has become oppression. Conflict is inevitable and through conflict, change.[4]

But quite apart from such circumstances, conflict is inherent to culture. As Rieff succinctly states, "Where there is culture, there is struggle. . . . [It is] the form of fighting before the firing actually begins." By its very nature, the work of culture is "the matter and manner of disarming competing cultures" which are always present or inchoate.

These considerations briefly describe key parts of the conceptual apparatus for his analysis. The historical context for the argument that follows begins with a parody of the conventional use of the terms *first world, second world, third world*. In a manner reminiscent of theorists and historians as diverse as August Comte, Karl Jaspers, Marshall Hodgson, S. N. Eisenstadt, and Andre Gunder

Frank, for whom periodization is framed civilizationally, Rieff argues that there are three types of culture. Among other things, each is distinguished by its own god-terms, theorists, understandings of reality, and dispositions toward authority.

First worlds are typically known as pagan, and they range far and wide, from the complex rational world of ancient Athens to the enchanted mysticisms of aboriginal Australia. First world god-terms could be described as metadivine and are often rooted in a mythical understanding of Nature, its gods myriad and its power primordial, capricious, and overwhelming. Fate is the dominant cultural motif, particularly as it portrays the address of social order to sacred order. Though one may find the rare Socrates, Plato, and Aeschylus, its elites are mainly conjurers whose magical powers seek to manipulate the gods to change fate. In first world cultures, the vertical in authority is defined less by a system of morality than it is by the regulation of passions by non-negotiable taboos.

Second world cultures are, most prominently, derived from the great monotheisms (Judaism, Christianity, and Islam) but are not exclusive to them.[5] At the heart of the sacred in these cultures is the self-revealed creator of the universe, from whom every living thing derives its being and significance. Truth about the world and how to act in the world is grounded in revelation and is creedal in character. The interdictions, then, are divinely commanded. Faith, rather than fate, is the dominant cultural motif, again especially as it depicts the address of social order to sacred order. God is active in history, and it is through trust and obedience, and with the guidance of various teaching authorities, that ascent in the vertical in authority is possible.

In contrast to the metaphysics of first and second cultures, which posit a world beyond the visible and an authority beyond the self, third cultures make no such claims. In their radical skepticism, third world cultures exist primarily as negations of second cultures; negations of their sacred authorities and their various doxa. Put differently, third cultures transliterate no sacred order into social order but instead propose a world in which there is no truth and no sacred order, only fictions and various rhetorics of power and self-interest. It follows that third cultures are committed to the leveling of all verticals in authority. This means, among other things, that inherited moral constraints are read as social constructions that have no status in being beyond what is given by the interpreter of those constructions. It isn't as though everything is permitted in the third world culture, but rather that interdictions of second world cultures and taboos of firsts are replaced by endlessly contestable and infinitely changeable rules.

Rieff's inimitable vocabulary aside, there are clearly ways in which his analysis of the contemporary world, at least as a matter of broad historical sociology, comports with the work of theorists as diverse as Anthony Giddens, Alasdair MacIntyre, Charles Taylor, Albert Borgmann, Michel Foucault, Thomas Pangle, and Sanford Levinson, among many others. Needless to say, as ideal-types, his concepts and categories are broad and thus invite much greater specification. But as with any typologies, their worth is measured by their utility in what they allow us to see rather than by their strict historical or analytical accuracy. For Rieff, they speak not only to different civilizational epochs but also to different thought-worlds. In this way, his typologies are not only roughly chronological but, he insists, synchronic as well. In different ways, all three exist simultaneously (and, indeed, we moderns experience the tension among these worlds within ourselves). By a method that is as much historical as it is social-psychological, Rieff offers terms by which to make sense of the perplexities and riddles of contemporary experience as well as the larger meaning and significance of our historical moment.

III

Third cultures are postmodern, or late modern depending on one's preference, and they are unprecedented in human history and consciousness. "No social order," Rieff contends, "has ever before existed" except as readings of sacred order. But "third cultures read nothing but themselves." It is this *novum* that mainly occupies Rieff's attention in this book: the third culture, the transition from second to third, and the conflict inherent in that transition.

The transition is, for Rieff, revolutionary. It is revolutionary in that it represents a fundamental break with and transformation of the inherited system of moral demands in their shifting interdictory and remissive contents. Breaks of this magnitude may or may not be violent but they are never without conflict. In our own time, the present *kulturkampf* unfolds as an unparalleled and permanent war of worlds.

Struggle is inherent to culture. For Rieff, this is a given. But in the past, conflict existed between different cultures operating with competing sacred symbolics. From the vantage point of the present, one can see that these conflicts were serious and, more often than not, historically significant, but they were also "internecine" in character. What makes the contemporary culture war distinctive is that it is a movement of negation against *all* sacred orders and directed, in its particulars, against the verticals in authority that mediate sacred order to social order. The field of battle, of course, is symbolic and the weapons are "deathworks," by which Rieff means an assault, a blow, a battle against something vital to the established culture. The *kulturkampf* manifests itself mainly through a conflict of fragmented and seemingly disparate images and issues that have no obvious relation with each other and no apparent coherence. Though traditionalist elites engage the fight from a defensive posture, the culture war is engaged offensively by third culture elites in the dominant institutions of culture formation: the arts, the media, law, and schools at every level. In such places, third culture elites wage war by repressing knowledge and understanding of second world symbolics. "There are now armies of third world teachers, artists, therapists, etc.," Rieff argues, "teaching the higher illiteracy. This teaching of the higher illiteracy amounts to a deathwork against second culture literacy." Though its origins are in Europe and the United States, the conflict has gone far beyond the West and is now global.

Clearly the present *kulturkampf* has political manifestations that are visible to everyone. But politics is just one and not the most interesting part of the culture war. Rieff fixes our attention on the question of authority and the god-terms that underwrite it. This is the critical matter. Because the conflict occurs primarily within a massive and disintegrated realm of symbols and in reference to tacit structures of authority, most of what unfolds in this conflict is invisible to those unable "to read the authority of the past."

Historically, the contemporary war of worlds does not play out on level ground. In Rieff's judgment, first world cultures no longer really exist except as reworked, often fantastic, fictions. Little is left of second world cultures except their aesthetics and persistent but enfeebled and often compromised institutions. Third world cultures are now predominant. Rieff casts the human consequences of this historical development in terms drawn heavily from Nietzsche.

The emergence of the third culture (and the origins of the present cultural struggle) is signaled not by any particular event but rather in the dispositions of artists and intellectuals through their arts and sciences. An artificial but useful point of origin, for Rieff, is 1882, the year in which Nietzsche published *The Gay Science* and there declared that God was dead and all god-terms with him. This is the original and prototypical deathwork against traditional cultures from which all other deathworks follow.

In the triumph of these deathworks, the great inversion foretold by Nietzsche actually comes to pass. Inherited truths that frame the données of reality are replaced by theories and their interpretations. Assenting obligations and interdictions (as well as the range of remissive possibilities in-between) are replaced by highly contingent rules and systems of rules, and the entire language of morality is replaced by a language of functionality. Identities, fixed and sacred, are replaced by ever changing and changeable "roles," which are, in the end, nothing more than the functions of multiple social selves. In the material culture, art once addressed to sacred order is liberated from theological reference and now addresses only itself. Accordingly, in the structure of social authority, the artist replaces the prophet, the therapist replaces the priest, and so it goes.

What Foucault called the principle of reversal and Nietzsche called the transvaluation of values, then, has brought into being a world that is self-consuming and self-legitimating—a world that has no precedent in human history. And as Rieff ominously warns, "No culture in history has sustained itself merely as a culture, however attractive and authoritative."

In the end, third culture is an "anti-culture" whose inversions and negations eventually lead to the negation of the human. At first this negation is only symbolic. In due course, it can become a reality, as it did in the death camps. As Rieff puts it, ". . . far beyond all literary revenants, are the real deathworks, as at Auschwitz. Auschwitz is a symbol, even as it is a symptom, of a place in which people were made to treat spiritual death, their second, with a complete indifference that signaled their readiness for the first death as well, in and of the flesh." In the death camps, the transgressive was institutionalized with the intent to so degrade Jewish men, women, and children that they would be separated from their sacred selves. So lowered in the vertical in authority, they would become compliant with all indignities imposed on them, including their own physical death. In our time, the transgressive may manifest itself more subtly and in ways that are often amusing and entertaining, but its spiritual effects are no less real and its unintended consequences no less foreboding. "Deathworks, as an institution of the third world *kulturkampf*, can be read or seen in everyday life, where it is far more fatal in its implications for not being correctly read. The unconscious art of everyday deathworks depends entirely upon the blindness of both the deathworker and those upon whom the work works." The practice of abortion, for Rieff, is one of the more obvious and profound illustrations of what has become an everyday deathwork—in this instance, against the sacredness of unique and unrepeatable human life. But the deathworks are typically more subtle and they are everywhere, pervading the arts, public education, the media and entertainment industry, legal theory and juridical practice.

IV

For Rieff, the present *kulturkampf* traces all the way down to the terms by which the conflict is understood. Indeed, the concepts and practices of social science have become a major weapon of cultural warfare. Contemporary sociology, for example, is by its very nature a deathwork against sacred order for the way it inverts "various second world reading traditions out of both Athens and Jerusalem, so to invent social order as if it were the predicate of sacred." This was true at the founding of sociology, when its theorists established the discipline self-consciously over against European Catholic social order, and it is no less true in the present. Even the claims of value neutrality in the social sciences amount to partisanship with third cultures.

One way this plays out is in the vast academic literature on the contemporary *kulturkampf.* Much of the scholarship in establishment sociology is committed to denying or trivializing its existence by focusing attention exactly where the conflict is weakest—the attitudes and opinions of ordinary people.[6] It ignores or avoids the areas of social life where the conflict is strongest: the culture-forming institutions of contemporary society, the elites who lead them, the competing sources of moral authority that animate them, and the symbolic discourse through which much of this conflict takes shape. In Rieff's theory of culture, this maneuver comes as no surprise. Whether it is conscious strategy or not, it is in the interests of academic social science to ignore the conflict or understate its gravity. To do otherwise is to give the claims of second world votaries legitimacy. To the extent that such scholarship shapes public opinion, the "unconscious art of everyday deathworks" is perpetuated by mainstream social science itself.

Where is Rieff himself in this intellectual battleground? In the political ontology of contemporary discourse, many who are in a hurry to label him something will paint him as a conservative, some even a reactionary. On the face of it, that would seem to be all that needs to be said. Abandoning the analytical attitude of his early work, Rieff does stand openly, but with little hope, in opposition to the deathworks of the third culture; his analysis here, along with the "sacred sociology" from which his analysis proceeds, is offered as a means of disarming those works. The harshness of his criticism of the postmodern and its "officer class" only reinforces the conservative quality of his argument. At times his judgments are both blunt and ruthless, and his defense of inherited cultures too uncritical. At the same time, he distances himself from conservatism in any conventionally political or credal sense. In *Fellow Teachers* he wrote that his defense of second cultures, "implicit in my theory of culture, does not make me an advocate of some earlier creedal organization. In particular, I have not the slightest affection for the dead church civilization of the West. I am a Jew. No Jew in his right mind can long for some variant (including the Party) of that civilization." Rieff is not interested in a return to dying culture now passing. For one, such a culture would be as fictional as any in late modernity. For another, neither democratic politics nor the reactionary cruelties of religious authoritarianism could ever bring it about. As Rieff says again and again, sacred history—and, by extension, social history—cannot repeat itself.

At the same time, there is in this work, as compared to his earliest work, more than a change in tone and temper. Rieff has not simply changed his style of address from analysis to jeremiad. More significant is the underlying turn toward ontology he has taken in his understanding of sacred order and social order; his refusal to yield to the deconstructive disposition that dominates the social sciences and his affirmation of the irreducible qualities inhering in both sacred and social worlds. In this turn, Rieff is able to understand and have us understand what is at stake with the transformation upon us. It is far less a facile conservatism that animates his work than it is a tragic sensibility. In this Rieff finds kinship with Max Weber, who also understood the tragic qualities of an advancing modernity: a world of unprecedented and beneficial power of the material world, but also a mundane and materialistic "nullity" dominated by "specialists without spirit" and "sensualists without heart."[7] Rieff's resistance to third world culture and its "abolitionist movements" is rooted in an awareness of the inevitable, even if unintended, consequences of that culture to human flourishing and a hope that his life work will help arrest "the loosing streak of life which is so endemic in the third culture."

The full significance of Rieff's tragic sociology is not immediately apparent and not quickly grasped. Indeed *Sacred Order/Social Order: My Life among the Deathworks* is a thick text that invites and even compels the reader to ongoing exegesis. This is as it should

be. Rieff once wrote that "the heterodoxies of genius require generations to assimilate." This can and will be said of Philip Rieff and
his contribution as well.

Notes

1. Philip Rieff, *The Feeling Intellect*, ed. Jonathan B. Imber (Chicago: University of Chicago Press, 1990); *Fellow Teachers: Of Culture and Its Second Death*
(New York: Harper & Row, 1973; repr., Chicago: Univerity of Chicago Press,
1985).

2. In *Fellow Teachers* he writes, "Privileged knowledge . . . can only be con-
veyed by the art of concealment. We teachers are called to represent the god-
terms, in all their marvelous indirections, inhibiting what otherwise might be
too easily done. Even Christ, as he revealed, precisely in order to reveal, concealed—lest he be too easily identified, in his love, as a being identifiable with
everything. . . . Concealment is the most necessary pedagogic art, without
which there are no revelations. If I have written anything worth rereading, then
it is necessary and right that you should misunderstand me" (10).

3. Stephen White, *Sustaining Affirmation: The Strengths of Weak Ontology in
Political Theory* (Princeton: Princeton University Press, 2000).

4. Elsewhere Rieff theorizes about revolutionary change. See "Toward a
Theory of Culture: With Special Reference to the Psychoanalytic Case," in *The
Feeling Intellect*, 321–30.

5. Buddhism, for example, also carries a moralizing authority of interdicts
and remissions for which faithfulness requires submission.

6. See Nancy J. Davis and Robert V. Robinson, "Religious Orthodoxy in
American Society: The Myth of a Monolithic Camp," *Journal for the Scientific
Study of Religion* 35 (1996): 229–45; Davis and Robinson, "Rejoinder to Hunter:
Religious Orthodoxy—Army without Foot Soldiers?" *Journal for the Scientific
Study of Religion* 35 (1996): 249–51; Davis and Robinson, "Are the Rumors of
War Exaggerated? Religious Orthodoxy and Moral Progressivism in America,"
American Journal of Sociology 102 (1996): 756–87; Paul DiMaggio, John Evans,
and Bethany Bryson, "Have Americans' Social Attitudes Become More Polar-
ized?" *American Journal of Sociology* 102 (1996): 690–755; Rhys H. Williams, "Is
America in a Culture War? Yes-no-sort of," *Christian Century* 114 (1997): 1038–
43; Alan Wolfe, *One Nation, After All: What Americans Really Think about God,
Country, Family, Racism, Welfare, Immigration, Homosexuality, Work, the Right, the
Left, and Each Other* (New York: Penguin Putnam, 1998); Yonghe Yang and
Nicholas J. Demerath III, "What American Culture War? The View from the
Trenches as Opposed to the Command Posts and the Press Corps," manuscript,
Department of Sociology, University of Massachusetts Amherst, 1996.

7. Max Weber, *The Protestant Ethic and the Spirit of Capitalism*, trans. Talcott
Parsons (New York: Scribner, 1958), 182.

My Life among the Deathworks

ONE

The Present World Fight

1. *Let there be fight? And there was.*[1] And there is. James Joyce's pun, on the words of Jewish second world creation, Genesis 1:3, is more than mildly amusing; it gives readers the most exact and concise account I know of the sociological form of culture. Culture is the form of fighting before the firing actually begins. Every culture declares peace on its own inevitably political terms. Unless a culture is defeated politically, as the Jewish was from the Roman conquest to the refounding of Israel, it will assert itself politically, later if not sooner. A living culture, even one that imitates life by politicizing its cultural impoverishment, works for itself. That cultural work is the matter and manner of disarming competing cultures, inside and outside its previously bounded self. In its disarming manner, a culture makes the ultimate political means of enforcement, armed force, unnecessary.

The other and superordinate sociological form of culture is complicit in its fighting form: *world creation/rule.*[2] Our church civilization is being, like all others, constantly re-created. In those re-creations, worlds are ruled authoritatively. There are no uncreated worlds. All are supranatural. The morning prayer of observant Jews includes thanks to the Creator for renewing the world. The Our Father in the Roman liturgy concludes at its *world without end.* In the truth of what I call the second world culture out of Jerusa-

---

1. James Joyce, *Finnegans Wake* (New York: Faber and Faber, 1975), 90.
2. Friedrich Nietzsche, *The Gay Science*, trans. Walter Kaufmann (New York: Vintage, 1974), bk. 5, sec. 358, 313: "A church is above all a structure for ruling." Wherever it appears below, a forward slash shall signify the metamorphic function of culture as it transliterates from the predicative stipulation on the left to that stipulation transformed on the right, as in *world creation/rule.*

lem, the world has been created once, but it is the task of those who live in that world to act as agents of world creation.

Unending, world creation comprises the historical task of culture: namely, to transliterate otherwise invisible sacred orders into their visible modalities—social orders. As transliterating institutions of sacred order into social, cultures are what they represent: 'symbolics' or, in a word that represents what it is, 'worlds'. Cultures are the habitus of human beings universal only in their particularities symbolically inhabited.

Tocqueville understood the work that is the making of the world each day. He called it the principle of authority, which must then "always occur, under all circumstances, in some part or other of the moral and intellectual world. Its place is variable, but a place it necessarily has."[3] To know where that authority is, "where it resides and by what standard it is to be measured," is to know the work that is the making of the world each new day. That arrangement or order of words, images, bodies, of all social relations in the space that is called culture is the object of my examinations.

2. *The number of world types.* In this text, my typological observations divide into three symbolic cultures, or *worlds*, that I shall number chronologically: *first, second, third.* To generalize symbolic particularities into three world types may, or may not, reveal more than it conceals of our present culture's real contents. My typological synchronic of where we are is based upon a chronological sense of where we have been. Sociology is the study of contemporary society. But the past, its aesthetics of authority once and still called 'religion', is the being there, in the present, that animates that present. In their present synchronicities, that these three worlds are at war represents the cultural forms for which my typological numbers claim real contents.

Culture is the continuation of war by other—normative—means. Every sociologist, like every other human being, lives within his own incommunicable yet normative *habitus*. Mine is, uncertainly as any other's in our late second and emergent third culture, in our second. Against that world mess, myself in it, are

3. Alexis de Tocqueville, *Democracy in America*, the Henry Reeve text, ed. Phillips Bradley, vol. 2 (New York: Knopf, 1966), 9.

the now fictive first and emergent third. The fight for being there, as it emerges ever after Exodus 3:14, is within—in medieval culture, called the *psychomachia*—as it is without me.[4] A habitable peace would be unprecedented. Peace would require perfect public and private abidances in one world or another, without a trace of fusion and its confusions: an impossible culture.[5]

Even within my one world there are those irreducible incommunicabilities that constitute our identities in what is now called, in an equally misunderstood word, our 'personalities'. Personality is a range of possibility in the conduct of life limited, as it is always, by its inescapable whereabouts in the vertical in authority, divided into interdictory and the subserving or subverting remissive, modes by which the range of authority may be read.

We readers live our lives not only in the private but in the public arena, where the fighting continues more visibly than between our sacred and various social or role-playing selves. Neither sociologist nor theologian, Joyce put the irreducible incommunicability of our sacred self, what is now popularly called 'identity'. in a passage that may help readers see where I am in this work, and where anyone might be at any moment in the vertical in authority:

> And as no man knows the ubicity of his tumulus nor to what processes we shall thereby be ushered nor whether to Tophet or to Edenville in the like way is all hidden when we would backward see from what region of remoteness the whatness of our whoness hath fetched his whenceness.[6]

Wherever we may be, in the *whatness of our whoness*, what we are is constituted by where we are in sacred order. Alone, being there in both private life and public, is the God of Abraham, the God of

---

4. For more on the *psychomachia*, see the Spanish church father Prudentius, "Psychomachia (The Fight for Mansoul)," in *Prudentius I*, trans. H. J. Thomson (Cambridge, MA: Harvard University Press, 1969), 274–343.

5. See, generally, my essay "The Impossible Culture: Wilde as Modern Prophet," introduction to Oscar Wilde, *The Soul of Man under Socialism, and Other Essays* (New York: Harper Colophon, 1970).

6. James Joyce, *Ulysses* (New York: Random House, 1946), 388. *Edenville* is obvious. For *Tophet*, a first world space of sacrifice, see 2 Kings 23:10.

Isaac, the God of Jacob, incommunicable in each identity as every other Tom, Dick, and Francis. From the authority forged in that inward, therefore outward, identity as God's creation, no second world creature can escape. The present world fight is explicable as a flight from that authorized identity into third world theatrical roles, each such role one too many for even my catholic taste in theatricals. The symbolic of creation is no more eliminable from our second world than the doctrine of commanding truths, true as they are commanding and only so, in the old word for that connection, 'revelation'. The guiding elites of our third world are virtuosi of de-creation, of fictions where once commanding truths were. Third world elites are characterized by their relentless promotion of the clean sweep. At the end of the nineteenth century, those promoters were a few literary men recondite as Baudelaire. At the beginning of the twenty-first century, the occupations and names of the promoters are legion.

3. *The seven last words.* Our third world fight, led by an officer class in which the literary man Joyce must be given five stars, has its own seven last words: "Foght. On the site of the Angel's."[7] This is Joyce's brilliantly comic concision, which follows immediately his seven first, as he attempted to write a new testament for our, typologically third, emergent world of his own creation. Joyce is an exemplary third world man, an artist, the very type of creator to whom his creation is what he represents.[8] Construed typologically, this newly artful and equally scientific world is only our third. Our third world stands for nothing old, simple, or backward. It is more colonizer than colonized. This latest new world is a symbol created by late second and early third world elites waving those of us more or less adamant in second toward that still and forever fictive third.

4. *A synchronic of three cultures.* Every world, until our third, has been a form of address to some ultimate authority. Of first worlds, pagan as they were called by those in our second cultures out of

7. Joyce, *Finnegans Wake*, 90.
8. Marcel Duchamp was the more exemplary for calling himself, somewhere, an *anartist* as he de-creates our second world. See part 3 for illustrated readings of his greatest deathworks.

the traditions of Jerusalem, I ask my leading question: whether any remain other than as a recycling of their aesthetic in ultimate authority? Ultimate authorities in pagan first worlds, various as Platonic Athens and aboriginal Australia, had something essential in common: mythic 'primacies of possibility' from which derived all agencies of authority, including its god-terms. Typologically, all first worlds, characterized by their primacies of possibility, should be known, especially in our third world of those primacies recycled as fictions, by a familiar acronym: *pop*. Whether Platonic essences or aboriginal dreamtimes, an all-inclusive *pop* once characterized highest authority there, being above and in all its agent authorities in all first worlds.

The leitmotif of our second *culture/world* is nothing miasmic or primordial, nothing metadivine and impersonal. In a word, faith, not fate, sounds the motif of our second world. Faith is in and of that creator-character that once and forever revealed himself in the familiar words from Exodus 3:14: *I am that I am.* Faith means trust and obedience to highest most absolute authority: the one and only God who acts in history uniquely by commandment and grace. Even given grace, in the second world of Rome as in Jerusalem, the largely prohibitive commandments, interdictory in character, must be kept. Even to the question of a rich young intellectual on what he must do to enter the kingdom, Jesus answers: *Keep the commandments.* Those commandments, divine Law, have not been abrogated by *one jot or tittle* anywhere in second culture. The commanding truths, revealed by highest absolute authority and elaborated by the practicing observant elites of that authority, first to themselves, are not before and above everything else. Before commanding truths there exists their author. Before the existence of that authorial God—One or Three in One, as various traditions of that second culture would have it in their own quests for historical power intellectualized—there is nothing.

There is no meta-culture, no neutral ground, from which the war of the worlds can be analyzed. My embattled analysis runs toward what I hope will prove an authorized conclusion: that *pop* first worlds have been recycled in a variety of disarming assaults by third world warriors—upon the exclusive and intolerant aesthetic of authority by which our seconds have continuously re-constituted their embattled identities. Whether our third worlds, as inventions of radically remissive late second world elites, can be called 'cultures' takes the answer, I believe, that our thirds should be called 'anti-cultures'. Anti-cultures translate no sacred order into social. Recycling fantasy firsts, third worlds exist only as negations of sacred orders in seconds.

Third world anti-cultures consume their negational truths as swiftly as they produce them. Those consummations refer to worlds of *pop* inventions always ending in the name of a better world elsewhere. *Pop* inventions submit readings of themselves alone, toward some supreme fiction at which not even virtuoso readers can arrive in this historical life. In contemporary American third culture (and in Europe), primordial power is widely thought to be desire; specifically, sexual. The alternative, closely related to desire in third culture, is power. O'Brien, in Orwell's *1984*, makes this point quite explicit and straightforward:

> The Party seeks power entirely for its own sake. We are not in-terested in the good of others; we are interested solely in power. Not wealth or luxury or long life or happiness: only power, pure power. . . . Power is not a means, it is an end. . . . The object of power is power.[9]

However their numbers threaten to transform second world moral majorities into third world fundamentalist minorities, *pop* worlds are created more or less consciously to remain readings of a free future. Freedom now is as it never was and cannot be.[10] In our second worlds, freedom can be defined as a change of masters, from the merely fictive god-terms of first worlds to the master of our universal seconds who always asked at least one question, the

9. George Orwell, *1984* (repr., New York: Signet Classics, 1990), 263.
10. Hitler was by no means an authoritarian, second world fanatic. On the contrary, he was a moral revolutionary, the equal, if not superior, of *Lenin/Stalin*. His successful campaign for office, in 1932, was called the "Freedom Flight." The hidden connection between apparently different political movements is in their radical eroticism.

parent question of humanity, *Am I Thy Master or Art Thou Mine?*[11] The unmastered world, however many and cruel the number of its deathworks, loses its tragic sense of life. Life becomes, as Nietzsche knew to his horror of it, a "comedy of existence . . . 'become conscious' of itself."[12] Third worlds propose an unprecedented present age without moralities and religions. Nietzsche's doctrine of eternal recurrence was his consolation prize, which he awarded to himself, for an age that he foresaw would be as horrifying as it turned out to be.

5. *My lifework as deathwork.* By deathwork I mean an all-out assault upon something vital to the established culture. Every deathwork represents an admiring final assault on the objects of its admiration: the sacred orders of which their arts are some expression in the repressive mode. As part of my futile effort at a disinterested work, and as part of my severely limited talent for lying, from which any deathwork separates itself at the peril of its aim, I shall merely number the established culture, here and everywhere in the West at least: *third.* This, my own lifework as deathwork, is intended to strike a fatal blow at the culture I consider now established. Deathworks are battles in the war against second culture and are themselves tests of highest authority. Such tests bring something worse than Art. They bring civil war. They intensify the permanent *kulturkampf* and lead to bloodletting. So R. Nehemiah read Moses's rod of punishment, which in his reading caused a terrible stink in the waters of Egypt:

> My methods are not those of mortals; man cuts with a knife and heals with a bandage; but I heal with the thing with which I wound. (*Midrash Rabbah*, Exodus 26:2)

Deathworks are most truly read when they are read against themselves. So read, deathworks, as rods of punishment in the re-

11. See my *Freud: The Mind of the Moralist*, 3rd ed. (Chicago: University of Chicago Press, 1979), 389.

12. Nietzsche, *The Gay Science*, bk. 1, sec. 1, 74. Also, see Søren Kierkegaard, *The Present Age and of the Difference between a Genius and an Apostle*, trans. Alexander Dru (New York: Harper Torchbooks, 1962).

pressive mode, take on a new and more meaningful life. The very instrument that wounded life in sacred order becomes itself an instrument of healing.

6. *The Age of Deathworks*. The historic age of prophet and apostle has ended. Therefore, we must address the great negational theorists and artists of third world: Freud, Joyce, Duchamp (and some not as great: 2 Live Crew or Antonioni). Deathworks are by no means always concentrated or condensed in works of art or science. Deathworks, as an institution of the third world *kulturkampf,* can be read or seen in everyday life, where they are far more fatal in their implications for not being correctly read. The unconscious art of everyday deathworks depends entirely upon the blindness of both the deathworker and those upon whom the work works.

7. *Anti-culture.* I have titled our coming all-consuming godless third world culture, for want of an unequivocal name, 'anti-culture'. Following Nietzsche, Max Weber titled our coming culture "this nullity."[13] This nullity thinks itself safely arrived, however god-threatened, at heights achieved by no earlier civilization. Now men are endangered mainly by the oldest device of their safety from themselves: culture itself, our present yet absent danger. Modern culture is far more dangerous than archaic nature or pagan mythologizing and polytheisms ever were. Contemplating this dangerous nullity—paganism parodied, often in drag or dungarees—a university president once said to me, in one of his many inspired moments: "We are the real counterculture." And so we are, not least because, ourselves connoisseurs of culture as if it were primal and here to stay, we know, as Plato did, the greatest artists are to be characterized by their genius for deceit and subversion; the greater the artist, the deeper the subversion of everything supporting ascents to a higher, more humane life that can be lived only in obedience to the commandments of sacred order as it is addressed in culture and through its faithful creations.

Consider the commandment specific and implied in our cul-

---

13. Max Weber, *The Protestant Ethic and the Spirit of Capitalism*, trans. Talcott Parsons (New York: Scribner, 1958), 182.

ture against the worship of idols, those god-terms of the primordial, whether that be ooze or instinct. That much abused commandment in the aesthetics of authority out of Israel, not least among cultivated Jews themselves, in no wise deals with arts that know and keep their subordinate places in the vertical of an authority that recognizes the reality of no primordial realm. In that primordial realm, however sophisticated and scientific now, there is neither revelation nor redemption; not even from religion. Culture religion returns in a science (e.g., Marxism) or an art (e.g., Picasso's) hostile in sacred order to the existence of sacred order. That hostility and its works were feared by such diverse theorists of highest authority as the Paul of Romans (1:23–32), and the Plato of the *Laws* (671d), and the Burke of *The Sublime and the Beautiful*. The power of the aesthetic may be feared enough to be refused; and, if not quite refused, then compassionately censored. In Plato's case, the great refusal came to the point of exiling the artists after putting garlands of honor and triumph about them (*Republic*, 398a) in honor of their powers of imagination.

What, then, is the danger of imagination, the greater the more dangerous? Recall Goethe's judgment on the imagination, from the *Annalen:*[14]

> Of what use is it to bridle sensuousness, to cultivate understanding, to secure reason her sovereignty? Imagination lurks in the man as his deadliest enemy; by nature she has an irresistible impulse towards the absurd, an impulse which operates even in cultivated men, and to the contempt of all culture, displays in the midst of the most becoming circles the inherited savagery which takes pleasure in caricatures.

It is old truth that what begins in fiction ends in reality. Here I am, reluctant, at the question of censorship. Yet I must say something to the liberal utilitarians, with their limiting principle of 'no harm to others'. That limit seems to me no limit. Schopenhauer defined

---

14. Johann Wolfgang von Goethe, *The Autobiography of Goethe . . . Together with His Annals*, vol. 2 of Goethe's Works (London: G. Bell and Sons, 1884), 340 (trans. Charles Nisbet).

the ridiculous as a subjective subsumption of objective authority under the heterogeneous concept of abstract 'others'.[15] Absolute authority in the highest is no abstract 'other', wholly or in part. 'No harm to others' must include the Wholly Other. The Wholly Other denied in principle and/or practice, there is nothing to stop our fragmentations of every lesser identity into conflicting and unrealized selves; Zeligs with a fatal ephemeral cause to match every new identity.[16] Like the highest imaginings in their challenge to faith in the highest authority, the regnant aesthetics of power refer to themselves, each so alone that they become abstract others inciting the harms of life. To those incitements of harm by spurious changing self-reference, all, especially the most cultivated classes, are now taught to bow. The higher you go on the social and educational ladder, the greater the resistance to and negation of second world truth.

Identity changes constitute the new idolatry. That idolatry describes both the genius and madness of those imaginary arts of life that cannot lead to a higher life, but only to lowerings. Life cannot be made over to imitate art except at a cost that is life-destroying. Dining gracefully is one thing; feasting with panthers quite another. The greatest wit and first martyr of the modern Sodomite lifestyle, Oscar Wilde, knew how hopelessly the imaginary arts are in love with absurdity. Wilde cannot have imagined our anti-culture's present dealings in creative destruction. Those dealings have become monstrous. The incredible imaginative power of the Nazi regime and its perturbed eroticism has come to close the fantasy of feasting with panthers. Remark the cut of the German uniform in the Nazi time. No more erotic uniform has ever been created. Look at the uniform of the SS. There is a military costume of eroticism inseparable from our third world of radically remissive high fashion. The Nazi movement constituted a massive feast with panthers. Leni Riefenstahl caught the

15. Arthur Schopenhauer, *The World as Will and Idea*, trans. R. B. Haldane and J. Kemp, vol. 2 (London: K. Paul, Trench, Trübner, 1896). See esp. chap. 8, "On the Theory of the Ludicrous."

16. See Woody Allen's film *Zelig* (1983). Zelig has no sacred self. He is the model third world Jew, in transition from religion to neurosis.

image in her *Triumph des Willens* (1934). All talk of the banality of evil in such magnitudes seems to me ridiculous in its dependence upon a taste for good and sensible taste.[17] The taste in modern politics is for blood. It mocks its eighteenth-century celebrant Shaftesbury, who was demolished long before, in the nineteenth century, by Newman in *The Idea of the University*.

Real live transgressions never were, are, or shall be "pleasant as port."[18] What bad taste there is implicit in Wallace Stevens's poetical phrase for transgressions. Stevens's nice common-room dessert image scarcely represents those whirlwinds of insanity that have come out of the void of twentieth-century aesthetics of power and its 'values' game. 'Value' is a word for unlimited exchangeability with other values. Values give no stability. They fluctuate in the values market. 'Absolute value' is not even as good as gold. Dr. Josef Mengele has his 'values'. One Professor Hobbs, professor of religion at Wellesley, tells us all we need to know about values in a few invaluable sentences: "Religion no longer needs God or gods. It has a theological structure that embodies the values of each culture. When the culture changes, then the religion changes. Values have to keep up. That's all there is to it." Is that all? Keeping up can be lowering. All depends on who and what the Joneses of value are.[19]

There is nothing new in this mean grandeur. As Stevens tells us:

After all the pretty contrast of life and death
Proves these opposite things partake of one,
At least that was the theory, when bishops' books
Resolved the world. We cannot go back to that.
The squirming facts exceed the squamous mind,
If one may say so.[20]

---

17. See, generally, Hannah Arendt, *Eichmann in Jerusalem: A Report on the Banality of Evil* (New York: Viking Press, 1963).

18. Wallace Stevens, "Connoisseur of Chaos," in *The Collected Poems of Wallace Stevens* (New York: Knopf, 1954), 215.

19. I have quoted Professor Edward Hobbs from a supplement to a Wellesley College newspaper titled *Realia* in an interview titled "Sacred Concerns in a Secular Age." *Realia* 4, no. 1 (December 1985): 1. *Realia* is devoted to clarifying "objects or activities used to relate classroom teaching to real life."

20. Stevens, "Connoisseur of Chaos," 215.

One may; we of the real counterculture may not. We know that Stevens's squirming facts, like Freud's 'reality principle', are in their squamous death throes. Where there is nothing sacred, there is nothing.

8. *Via.* That we live in three cultures seems to me no less evident then the fact that we live in a world permanently at war within itself. If we live in three cultures, then we live at once in three worlds. Fate, faith, and fiction are, respectively, leitmotifs for those three continuous cultures. Unlike first world mythic and/or third world fictive god-terms, we each, ourselves, shifting for himself in the vertical in authority, or *via*—my acronym for order that is in its vertical structure immutable and therefore reasonably called 'sacred'—are free to choose which way to go. Human life takes on the shape of a cross. We can go up, down, or sidewise.

A raising act, every commanded and commending *shalt not* therefore *ought not*, I call in my second world terminology 'interdictory'. In first worlds, the equivalent word is 'taboo'. A lowering act, the violation of interdicts in second cultures of command out of Jerusalem or of taboos in all pagan first world cultures, I call 'transgressive'. Sin is a synonym for a lowering act gone down far enough. Mixed acts, what is not done, yet done with excusing reasons or exceptions to the interdictory rule, I call 'remissive'. A remission too severely constrained becomes a decivilizing interdict, whereas one too broadly granted becomes an uncivilizing transgression. Much of our lives are spent in the remissive flux or an order mutable as our secular space in its sacred space.[21] It is the order of that flux, bounded above and below by prohibitions and transgressions, that is unchanging, i.e., sacred. What is immutable appears only in what is mutable.

21. Duns Scotus remarked that connection between the mutable and the immutable in his *Philosophical Writings*, ed. and trans. Allan Wolter, O.F.M. (London: Thomas Nelson, 1962), 117: "It is also evident that something can be represented under an immutable aspect even if that which does the representing is something mutable itself. For the essence of God is represented to the intellect as something immutable by means of something that is radically changeable, whether the latter be the species or the act of knowing. This is evident from a similar case, for something can be represented as infinite through what is finite."

No one understands himself or anyone else. What can be understood is where one is in the vertical in authority and where others are, themselves always on the move. This understanding of where we are makes every psychology radically moral, as well as sociological. We only know where we are in relation to others and to those inviolate commands (however arbitrary we may now think them) that warrant our sense of self and of others. Wherever we find ourselves is what we are. Our own motions in sacred order are locatable once each of us has restored to himself the notion of sacred order. The basic restorative is to understand the purity and inviolate nature of the vertical in authority. Those arbitrary meanings warranted not by any man, but by the one God, are necessary if we are to find some safety in any world. That we do not now find safety in any of our worlds reflects our loss of the radically contemporaneous memory of sacred order and our present time and place in it. This book maintains that nothing about us is to be understood without the sense of where we are, only so can we know what we are.

For the vertical in authority, I shall use the acronym *via* hereafter. Every *via* in all second worlds is there to organize the lifespace of agents moving freely in that space, or fatefully in competing first world *vias*. From the *via* there is no escape: not even to the deepest downward in gross abuses of sexuality, or in idolatry, or in murder.

9. *Culture*. Cultures give readings of sacred order and ourselves somewhere in it. A culture is constituted by institutions that supply the texts of transit, those texts in many media, from sacred to social order. It is in his culture that man becomes a reading animal, to that sacred manner as if born. Culture and sacred order are inseparable, the former the registration of the latter as a systemic expression of the practical relation between humans and the shadow aspect of reality as it is lived. No culture has ever preserved itself where it is not a registration of sacred order. There, cultures have not survived. The third culture notion of a culture that persists independent of all sacred orders is unprecedented in human history.

The *kulturkampf* between second world sacred orders and third world anti-sacred social orders is now worldwide. There is no escape from the struggle. We are all caught in the war one way or another (or many ways at the same time, in repressed/divided states of mind). The struggle looks different at almost any space to which one turns; particular battle lines are differently drawn. The contemporary *kulturkampf* is unique because it is not between sacred orders but between great abolitionist movements directed against all sacred orders in any of their historical or theoretical manifestations.

What follows are entries into the struggle, specific in their spatialization, that is, their occurrence in time and place. Within the spatialization of the *via* comes synchronicity (at the level of the unconscious, the past is not dead). The *kulturkampf* is what we see and read every day, though powerfully distorted, because the reporters are reporting so radically in the repressive mode that one gets the inevitable distancings and distortions of the truth. Of course, third worlds hold that there is no truth, only rhetorics of self-interest.

10. Kulturkampf. The German compound for the disarming *force/form* of culture has an awkward English equivalent: *culture/struggle*. Where there is culture, there is struggle. The abstract word for *culture/struggle* is, at its most German, *dialectic*. As I remarked in my very first paragraph, the punning polemical genius of Joyce brought him closer than any sociologist I know to both the formal fighting sense of culture and its superordinate creative sense. It is in that *both/and* that the historical task of culture is always and everywhere the same: the creation of a world in which its inhabitants may find themselves at home and yet accommodate the stranger without yielding their *habitus* to him. Here and now, pluralism has its price: a united front of second against third world assaults, which are often mounted in the name of pluralism. The *either/or* of our second worlds stands against the substance and subtleties of our third worlds in their advancing fictions of multiculturalism. A multiculture is an anti-culture. Such a multiculture no longer mediates between sacred order and social orders.

11. *Derrida as illustrator.* Stevens was a great illustrator of our

worlds at war. A less lyrically persuasive third world illustrator, Jacques Derrida, shows the simple strategy of retreat from second world eternal truths by mocking their policing character.

—Everything comes down to one of those reading exercises with magnifying glass which calmly claim to lay down the law, in police fashion indeed.[22]

Derrida's reading of second world close readings is correct so far as it goes. But it does not go far enough. We professionals of the reading discipline: we are the real police. As teaching agents of sacred order, and inescapably within it, the moral demands we must teach, if we are teachers, are those eternal truths by which all social orders endure. The unprecedented historical task of our real police is to so magnify the downward direction of change, by which the present third world war against all sacred orders is being conducted, that the higher illiteracy of it no longer lures the old elites of our second to defeat by a massive decline in their own reading ability.

12. *The old reading elites and the new.* The old *reading/policing* elites were titled 'rabbinates' or 'priesthoods'. Jewish Rabbi and Catholic Father both meant, in their second worlds, teaching authority. Stevens asks: "What rabbi, grown furious with human wish" does not look "for what was, where it used to be?"[23] Third world teaching elites have a contrary teaching authority. Therapy is to theology as *hospital/theater* is to *synagogue/church*. Third world teaching authority is historically unique.[24] It casts roles where identities were.[25]

'Therapeutic': I can find no more theatrical term, for incorporation into the present political vocabulary, for the new benevolent despotism of those actors, role-players all, who presume the

22. Jacques Derrida, *The Truth in Painting*, trans. G. Bennington and I. McLeod (Chicago: University of Chicago Press, 1987), 326.

23. Stevens, "Notes toward a Supreme Fiction," in *Collected Poems*, 389.

24. See my *The Triumph of the Therapeutic: Uses of Faith after Freud, with a New Preface* (Chicago: University of Chicago Press, 1987), particularly chaps. 1, 2, 3, and 8.

25. Nietzsche, *The Gay Science*, bk. 5, secs. 356–57, 302–10.

endless supply of unprecedented comfort and safety to warrant world disenchantment with all sacred orders and with their consequent social orders.[26] Therapeutics calculate actings-out of disenchantment as earlier teaching elites calculated cures of return to *The Way* from the waywardness of transgressive conduct. Therapy is to transgression as theology was to prohibition: inseparable.

13. *Higher illiteracy.* Sociology as we know it began as a deathwork against European Catholic social order.[27] That deathwork is enacted every day in the halls of our institutions of higher illiteracy. Sociology is not alone nor in the lead. Literary criticism and communications studies have taken over, but the project has not changed. The masses are revolting against the third culture elites in our mass media and university conglomerates. That elite is increasingly backed by state police power, as in Buñuel's film *Phantom of Liberty* (1974), where the police keep the people out of the cages to which they want to return. Even with full police power, the communists lost the culture struggle in Eastern Europe.

Who is replacing that remissive elite? In America, there are special armies to attack the canon, including young blacks persuaded of a racial mystique. Civil rights are one thing. The will to power among any group, including American blacks, is quite another. The achievement of civil rights must include the holding of all blacks, as of all others, to their responsibilities as agent members in our second world *sacred/social* order. To treat American blacks remissively, as if they were born or bred in a radically re-

26. This is the meaning of the great passage on the disenchanted world in Weber. See "Science as a Vocation," in *From Max Weber: Essays in Sociology*, ed. H. H. Gerth and C. Wright Mills (New York: Oxford University Press, 1972), 139.

27. Before the brilliant inversionist Nietzsche there were the boring refounders of sociology as an inversive discipline: Saint-Simon and Comte. A sacred sociology would be a different discipline and no 'New Christianity' in either the old Saint-Simonian or new remissive elite sense. Second world sociology began with the authors of the Pentateuch and the author of *The Republic*. That sociology, representing the minority tradition in the discipline, would include in its guild de Maistre, Nietzsche, and many others equally individual in their alliances and oppositions. All second world traditions have embarrassingly candid loyalists, such as de Maistre, and brilliantly lyric traitors, such as Nietzsche.

missive mode, is to be unjust to their absolutely equal identity. *Imago Dei* takes no color.

The abolition of the canon is the abolition of all mastery. Self is asserted over Shakespeare, race over creed. But freedom is a change of masters. Man shall be mastered only by his desires. There is the world of power that is what the victors make of it. Identity must accept a certain canonicity: the commanding truths are known. Identity is no mere assertion: it is linked to a canon, which does allow for some remissive passages as it is addressed to the world, in all its vicissitudes and revolts. Since the *kulturkampf* is growing more intense, and we are in the age of the world picture, we must learn how to read the brilliant and hostile visual images, including the filmic, that are all around us. I am proposing a renaissance of the catholic intellect.

14. *The war that will emerge.* The war that will emerge is between those who assert that there are no truths, only readings, that is, fictions (which assume the very ephemeral status of truth for negational purposes) and what is left of the second culture elites in the priesthood, rabbinate, and other *teaching/directive* elites dedicated to the proposition that the truths have been revealed and require constant rereading and application in the light of the particular historical circumstance in which we live. And that those commanding truths in their range are authoritative and remain so. What opposes them derives its authority only from its repressive mode and the allure of those repressive modes. The foundations of art are in what Freud calls repression.

The most admirable of American third world poets, Stevens is lyrically precise and wonderfully erudite in his post-Arnoldian compassion for all those who live in our third world. All those have found that, having abandoned their belief in God, poetry—art generally—can take its place as the style of redemption. And yet Stevens himself sensed that the arts that are culture in their enduring qualities themselves fail when they are not modes of address in sacred order to what is authoritative above it. Stevens realized that art fails when it becomes a form of intellectualized tourism. I trust that this work will not be for tourists but rather for those who sense their own conscription into the wars that characterize the present condition of our cultural life. Stevens himself expressed his total disillusionment with the "supreme fiction" of third world anti-culture:

> Modern reality is a reality of decreation, in which our revelations are not the revelations of belief but the precious portents of our own powers. The greatest truth we could hope to discover, in whatever field we discovered it, is that man's truth is the final resolution of everything.[28]

15. *On my titles and the method they imply.* The title of my trilogy and of this book are their truths and conclusions. I intend to describe that unprecedented condition of fighting against the cultural predicate that organized all human societies until almost our own time. That predicate I call sacred order. Sacred order is not static. The worlds created in their sacred orders are never complete. They are always being re-created by readers of what is hidden in those worlds so to create worlds within worlds: the hidden meaning of the world as it has never quite emerged before.

The main point and purpose of this book is an empirical truth which is subject to disproof. The empirical truth is that there is now established a third culture which is unprecedented in human history. This work will analyze third world works in an effort to disarm them. The method employed here is similar to biopsy: cut a slice from the whirling contemporaneity and hold it under the microscope so to see more clearly. Those slices can then be bounced off others, like billiard shots. I call that method the *bricole technique*,[29] in which each shot, each juxtaposition, enables the reader to see the meaning of and in contemporary reality.

16. *Bricole: Indirect stroke in tennis and billiards.* The bricole technique is not unprecedented. The method is similar in form to cubism, although it is employed to very different ends. Like Braque's *Still Life with a Violin* and other great cubist works, the results can be jarring (see fig. 1). I hope to take the reader behind

28. Wallace Stevens, "The Relations between Poetry and Painting," in *The Necessary Angel: Essays on Reality and the Imagination* (New York: Vintage, 1965), 175. Originally delivered as a lecture at the Museum of Modern Art, January 1951.

29. Oxford English Dictionary, 3rd ed., 1944, s.v. "Bricole."

FIGURE 1. *Still Life with a Violin (Nature morte au violin)*,
Georges Braque, 1913

(Yale University Art Gallery, Leonard C. Hanna, Jr., B.A. 1913, Susan
Vanderpoel Clark, and Edith M. K. Wetmore Funds; © 2004 Artists Rights
Society [ARS], New York/ADAGP, Paris)

and beyond contemporary reality by juxtaposing events and
works that do not appear, on first reading, to be related. Call it de-
constructing radical contemporaneity. Another word for bricole is
collage. Though appearances may suggest otherwise, the collage
principle is not chance. In what I call second culture, there is no
such thing as chance, not even the fall of a sparrow.[30] Chance is a
third culture pseudoprimordiality, an empty god-term to be filled
with deceits like the character Chance Gardener in the film *Being
There* (1979).

17. *On image entries.* 'Image entries' such as those examined in

30. See *Hamlet*, 5.2.230–31.

this book (whether visual, verbal, acoustic, or sociohistorical) are sorties into an otherwise invisible sacred order that is inseparable from our lives in social order. To enter sacred order, we need only read our own lives and the imaginative lives of others, or, alternatively, works of the imagination. Any reading mind's eye will see that all memorable experience is radically contemporaneous. As in first world culture mythology, the reading of all events constitutes a single synchronous totality. We are all, wherever we are, in sacred order with a literacy that need only be exercised in order to see where we have always been, however shifting that being be.

What I have called the radically contemporaneous is tantamount to primordiality in first culture. Third world denial and negation of the past is primordial. Radical contemporaneity will not be shut out of lives devoted to resisting it, let alone out of lives undevoted to anything in particular except entertainment and eating up life. The question raised in this book is how to read the radical contemporaneity and to live with it and yet not be misdirected by it. The war against the primordial present cannot be won. But it can be lost. The aim of this book is to support those who will learn how to read that primordial present in order to stop the loosing streak of life which is so endemic in third culture.

The various types of image entries given in what follows are no different from the attractively strong identity to be found in everything we see, including ourselves. That is why portraiture, whether of Picasso by himself or of a stone as it sits there on the ground, rouses our immediate interest. That Picasso's self-portrait of 1901, *Yo, Picasso*, for example, is only a replica of where he is suggests the shadow play in which both art and literature engage us, so to distract us from remembering where we are. At the same time, such a self-portrait is necessary in order to see our own selves portrayed in sacred order. However we may deny it, we read a Picasso portrait, as we read Hamlet's words, as derivatives of those arbitrary messages that used to be called revelation.

18. *Introductory/interdictory.* The third culture was not always there as it is here now, beyond occasional brilliant proleptic insights into the therapeutic character as we get it through Shakespeare's Iago and Edmund. In any case, it is here now, and its re-

cycling of first culture motifs makes the synchronic method necessary. The synchronicity that I try to achieve in juxtaposing these image entries knows no development. It may appear a quirky arrangement. A debt I have methodologically is to Ezra Pound's ideogrammic method, in which meanings are allowed to arise from juxtapositions. In this method, anything may be allowed in without changing its identity if the allowance is read in a way that establishes the truth hidden in the image itself. The reading mind, the mind's eye, moves through the elements of its imagined world, actively contending with them and organizing them while they somehow retain their illusion that they are inventing the meaning of the image. The meaning is there because of where it is in the vertical in authority.

Another sense of world meanings is developed when one reads the world that is behind the world of appearances. In second cultures, as in the Platonic metaphysical of first, there is always a world beyond the visible world. That world is disenthralling and not a dream structure which is the hidden structure in Freud: the reverse of the order of hidden truths so that the hidden truth is always in the lower world, in a world beneath the world rather than in a world that is at once within and above the world itself, as we have it in Matthew 18:18:

> Verily I say unto you, Whatsoever ye shall bind on earth shall be bound in heaven: and whatsoever ye shall loose on earth shall be loosed in heaven. (KJV)

19. *On reading.* The purpose of all true reading is to encourage *ascents/assents* in the vertical of authority and to discourage *descents/dissents*. The encouragements and discouragements are as distinct as mere seeing and real knowing. The bridge between these movements, up and down the vertical, or shufflings sidewise, is commonly called the will. Readings without good will are no more true than will without true readings can be effective. The alternative to both reading and will is not for us to muster merely: grace. That condition, given but not automatically taken without true reading and good will, is a gift inseparable from authority in any of its highest reaches.

True readings are always self-readings or readings of self. The aim of all true readings is, in this stipulation, a conversion that will overcome the dread and difficulty of *ascents/assents* in the vertical. True readings take a lot of work by the reader, not only upon the text and text analogues before his eyes but upon his mind's eye. The reader is inseparable from what is read. That the object of address is a movement upward in sacred order means, unalterably, that truth is subjective. This implies a doctrine that runs contrary to the present standard that books, films, shows of art have no effect on their readers. Such effectlessness can only occur when the raising or lowering is masked by a blindness of the mind's eye and the body from which it is inseparable. World words and world pictures always have ourselves in them.

To read rightly one's own present place in the vertical in authority is to see what is otherwise not to be seen and, therefore, to do more than see; such seeing is true knowing. There, in that inside of where the self and others are in their relation to highest authority and its commanding truths, the mind's eye gives intellect its true feeling of having entered at last into the right kind of world, where the latest flashed variant repetition of revelation is not dimmed by the distance and distortion of the repressive mode inseparable from both life and art. That sudden epiphany of truth in some telling detail is the truest reading and a truly life-enhancing experience. That is the thrill of being addressed by a word or an image in sacred order.

Yet sacred order, the creative reality, is never primal in its possibility for us. It is not possible at all. There can be no positive knowledge of sacred order. It can only be given through revelation, living traditions following upon commanding truths of revelation. Finally, in our present primordial alternative of our misprisioned immediacy of experience, creative reality can be read negationally—as in art and other enlightenment disguises of the repressive mode.

The first object to be read in sacred order is oneself. Once self-located in that order, there is always the pain of seeing through one's own seeming, as the transgressive Angelo did even as Isabel thunders her great moral accusation: "Seeming, seeming!" (*Mea-*

sure for Measure, 2.4.164). She has read him, even as he has read himself. Seeing is reading. But, then, the world picture has not conquered those who practice their *faith/knowledge*.

20. *On my method and its subject.* The image entries illustrated here are no abstractions, I trust. If world culture itself is an abstraction, then I must try to break that abstraction in the reality of the appearances of even the face of such a fusion image as is represented by Arcimboldo (fig. 2). Arcimboldo's fusion face portrait represents precisely what no man is, and yet is, in the fictive achievement. Visibly, the fictive face must be distant from or split from its fruits, flowers, vegetables, plants, and grains, any object that he has used to compose it. This distancing and deliberate distortion is the fictive achievement, repression taken at face value. But then, repression as a fictive achievement can be understood

FIGURE 2. *Summer,* Giuseppe Arcimboldo, 1573
(Bridgeman-Giraudon/Art Resource, NY)

as the cleverity of rebellion against commanding truths in which the face is clearly in no relation however distant to the kind of lowering elements to which Arcimboldo assigns them. The prohibition on such imagery in the very foundation of the second culture argues the truth of the repressive character of imagery to the point of the transformation of imagery into idolatry. The third culture code word for idolatry is trope.

The insight to be gained from Arcimboldo's image is into the art of fictive assertion over the moral demands of life in sacred order. These images are ciphers in a culture without moral direction, unless that direction be downward toward what is considered to be the predicate of life: namely, transgression. The fictive art is itself a cipher. Ciphering means to hide and not hide at the same time. Wherever there are ciphers, there are the truths of repression, that systemic mendacity which Freud considered the foundation of his great third culture art of analysis as a manner of concealing truth. The image is itself a metaphor of indecision. We both see and do not see the face, and in this duplicity lies its charm, for every constituent detail of the face is false. The effect is in our eye, where we have taken in, or been taken in by, the composition of original meanings into that which opposes them, the human face itself. The is-ness of the human face is reduced to a comprehensible series of signs intended to point toward the destruction of the face and, with it, a humanity that is itself inseparable from the sacred character of the face. This type of fusion image marks a brilliant effort to murder sacred order as felt and understood in the second culture.

21. *Series of fragments.* No culture in history has sustained itself merely as a culture, however attractive and authoritative. Cultures are dependent upon their predicative sacred orders and break into mere residues whenever their predicates are broken.[31] That is the main reason why our late second cultures and early thirds are increasingly unstable. All third cultures assault all sacred orders and their *agent/cultures.*

31. See Vilfredo Pareto, *The Mind and Society*, trans. A. Bongiorno, ed. A. Livingston, 4 vols. (New York: Harcourt, Brace, 1935), particularly 797–889.

Culture is a late eighteenth- and nineteenth-century invention. Indeed, as both first and second cultures developed, they were never conscious of their cultures. Rather, as an address to sacred order from somewhere within it, all occasions and locations of culture were not understood to be intentioned with their predicates, to which these addresses are always inseparably related. It was only as sacred orders and social orders separated and the ficta of social orders began to multiply, negationally in their relations to sacred order, that culture began to develop its sense of its self. The culture elites of the past did not understand themselves under such sociological categories. The future of a culture so conscious of itself depends precisely upon this alienation from the sacred orders of which they were once expressions. All cultures now assert their autonomy from sacred orders and from social orders. They thus present themselves as either the instruments of particular groups and interests in the social order or as an autonomous third force between sacred order and themselves as the representatives, no longer hieratic, of that which was once the *isness* of sacred order made visible in the language and images of that order.

The culture we can address is no longer, if it ever was, a coherent order of fixed categories with a center and a periphery. Rather, it is an assemblage of found and contrived objects decentered and constituted by conflicting institutions and negational images. The field of battle comprises competing images in which the fragments are understood to be everything, and the key process is that of a self-legitimation in which cultural artifacts strive to persuade those who consume them that they are what they say they are and that the consumers are not what they think they are. The attack on the consumer is organized around a strategy of assimilating the consumer to what he is consuming. The buyer becomes part of the object bought. Third worlds' work toward dismantling the idea of culture as an address achieves its coherence by the virtues of the range of authority, the sacred that it addresses. Culture becomes a warring series of fragments, that series unified by no common motif and dominated best by self-legitimating elites that try to set up their own fiction of primordiality against other fictions that they think have already had too long a run in an otherwise meaningless history—meaningless, at least so far as the world that the new creators are seeking to create through their words and images.

This makes for a very different world from the one we can read about in the literature and art of second world cultures. Those interpretations of the old sacred order continue, but they still address what they assert to be: a complete world that has come into being and needs only to be read in order to continue the act of completion in their own lives. That complete ever new world is there in the revelatory beginnings and needs only interpretation. The readings are extensions of the hidden truth of that world. In the arts and the third world, that world is nothing except its art. The delivery of those arts, its lifestyle, is everything. There is no world apart from that lifestyle. Therefore, the principle of lifestyle is that we are not stepping into something which is any way a reality independent of the fictions that have created that reality. The way to do that is to step out of those old worlds of cultures that are constituted by addresses to sacred order from within it to that authority above the range of authority that creates and governs that world. Instead, there is a new beginning which is a pun on the old creation. The pun of the new beginning is clear in a master of world de-creation, Joyce. "In the buginning is the woid."[32] That turn of the second culture doctrine of creation and of a complete world is turned by the third culture elites into a doctrine of de-creation in which the new world is a series of more or less horrible or at least horribly clever pastiches and negations of the complete and ever completing world of the older symbolists who saw in what there is that which is.

The third culture artists and scientists operate according to an *Uncertainty Ploy* which is constituted by mocking the efforts to complete continuously the revelationary worlds of sacred order. In the de-creational worlds that I here call *third*, the essential knowledge is that nothing in either the old sacred orders or social orders is true and the something that matters is the mode of

32. Joyce, *Finnegans Wake*, 378.

making it clear that nothing is true. Some new nothingness is the discovery of primordials as yet another turn in the self-characterization of third culture and that which it addresses.

22. *The blind creator.* The key to the character of creativity in third world is given in the great passage of charity to the mad Lear by the blind Gloucester:

> Glou. Here, take this purse, thou whom the heavens' plagues
> Have humbled to all strokes. That I am wretched
> Makes thee the happier. Heavens, deal so still!
> Let the superfluous and lust-dieted man,
> That slaves your ordinance, that will not see
> Because he does not feel, feel your power quickly;
> So distribution should undo excess,
> And each man have enough.[33]

Melville marked this passage heavily. The greatest of American outcasts, Ahab, the man who insists on his quest in chaos for a whale that would have asked him, if whales spoke, "*Am* I a sea, or a whale, that thou settest watch over me?" (Job 7:12), has rejected all sacred orders despite his wife and family back home, where they are at home. Ahab is at home nowhere. To him, there is no life in any *word/world.* Melville saw Ahab as a man who cannot live without going on a quest that aims at death beyond any death ordained in natural or superordinate order. This dissociation of seeing from feeling, which Gloucester understood only after he had paid the high price of such a divided sensibility, characterizes someone who finally, blind, as he has been made in it, is instructed where he is. The scene of instruction is almost as quick as a flash of insight.

> Lear. You see how this world goes.
> Glou. I see it feelingly.[34]

Such dissociated sensibilities exclude all but the most incredibly obvious manipulative references to the feeling intellect that

33. *King Lear* (Folger), 4.1.79–86.
34. Ibid., 4.6.145.

can live only with reference to some sacred order or Other.[35] Nietzsche has such a feeling intellect, despite his own intention. He knows the tragic and the moral will return from their fighting, however absent that return appears to be during the time of the tragedy. Third world sensibility excludes tragedy and its resolutions.

That most artful of third culture de-creations, *Finnegans Wake*, and the great and terrible American book *Moby Dick*, support such a blindly artful world. These texts unite with the most famous new Jews of the third culture, consummating itself in deadly fictions: Freud, Marx, and all his Trotskys who have made uncounted Bronsteins pay the highest price for their revolutions. They have all called themselves Ishmael and gone to seas that are what they represent to the old Jews: fathomless disorder, chaos, anti-culture, *yam*—not only sea but the sense of being at sea, as my father and both my grandfathers felt as they were caught in the *kulturkampf*.

23. *The meaning of primal power.* Every image enters a world of virtual realities, of actual objects. The subject is not abstract— there are no static terms. I am not here establishing premises and showing what must follow. Rather, I am trying to establish a series of related image entries in a situation that is inseparable from the moral and aesthetic situation of the reader. It is in that particular office that I wish to explore the verticals in authority that the images themselves enter. Of course we are removed as readers from the situations that are represented in this reality. So far as they are what they represent, there can be no ambiguity of meaning. We landlocked academic folk do love our ambiguities of meaning. Mainly our close and concrete acquaintances live as we do in the middle range of the remissive motifs rather than the lower (lowering) range of big-time transgressives. But were we to face the meaning of a primal power such as a maelstrom, a tidal wave, or polar ice then we could know how concrete our encounters with primal powers may be, even as we may never meet a Don Giovanni. Caspar David Friedrich's *The Polar Sea* is a terrifying image

---

35. See, generally, my collected papers, *The Feeling Intellect*, ed. Jonathan Imber (Chicago: University of Chicago Press, 1990).

entry of the deadly primal power through which we can enter cold death (see fig. 3). And there is Courbet's image entry of the wave as a primal power image (fig. 4), which may be less effective than some other, literary or even filmic, image entries if we are to grasp the reality of it. For example, on drowning there is the superb image entry of Pincher Martin, in Sir William Golding's novel of that title, as he tries to survive in the ocean. And there is the image of drowning in Peter Weir's film *The Last Wave* (1977) of a primal power as it can exist, and sometimes does, in nature, about to drown the ignorant lawyer sensitive to a sacred order that is not his own, but a real one, that of the remnant of an aboriginal tribe in Sydney.

Less obviously alarming, and therefore more deceptive, is Freud's abstraction of the mystical feeling in his description of the *oceanic* feeling of the loss of identity in sacred order, which is where that Freudian description belongs as we are all interpenetrated by

FIGURE 3. *The Polar Sea*, Caspar David Friedrich, 1824
(Foto Marburg/Art Resource, NY)

FIGURE 4. *The Stormy Sea*, also called *The Wave*, Gustave
Courbet, 1870

(Réunion des Musées Nationaux/Art Resource, NY)

FIGURE 5. *Ophelia*, Sir John Everett Millais, 1852

(Erich Lessing/Art Resource, NY)

these world cultures at war with one another.[36] As can be seen in the painting by Millais in figure 5, the drowned can be pictured quite beautifully, as in his image of Ophelia still afloat. And there is the after-film image of her drowning in Olivier's *Hamlet* that quotes the Millais. Nor are we much affected by Gertrude's soliloquy on Ophelia when she reflects "drowned, drowned."[37] But the real drowning is there just beyond these entries. Primo Levi in his entirely second culture concretion of the drowned in Auschwitz, *The Drowned and the Saved*, is not drawing a literary image; that is life.[38]

There is no being saved by texts from this drowning, a salvation many have attempted before me. Texts are now spread open like thighs, reading for the triumph of the misreader, as the life of study is reinvented as something remotely resembling rape. A deconstructed text is tantamount to a forgery. No world of the uncreated conscience is created when, as in one case of third culture deconstructive genius, Joyce asserts as its creator the *void/woid*. That textual void murders the living world at the heart of the Jewish liturgy, the Sh'ma (Deuteronomy 6:2), by turning it inside out. This is war. Second culture readers of Joyce's third culture text should expect no mercy from such an authorial godterm. "And shall not Babel be with Lebab? And he war. And he shall open his mouth and answer: I hear, O Ismael, how they laud is only as my loud is one."[39] That loud world is there to be trashed. Israel turned inside out into Ismael has never been accepted by the Jews as the truth about themselves. A pariah is not a pariah, rather an exile and/or guest, if he rejects the meaning of pariah, as Jews do still.

36. Sigmund Freud, *Civilization and Its Discontents*, in *The Standard Edition of the Complete Psychological Works of Sigmund Freud* (hereafter *SE*), ed. and trans. James Strachey, 2nd ed. (London: Hogarth Press, 1964), 21:64–65.

37. *Hamlet*, 4.7.203.

38. See, generally, Primo Levi, *The Drowned and the Saved*, trans. Raymond Rosenthal (New York: Summit Books, 1988), as well as his *Survival in Auschwitz: The Nazi Assault on Humanity*, trans. Stuart Wolf (New York: Collier Books, 1961).

39. Joyce, *Finnegans Wake*, 258.

24. *Into reality.* These image entries are in their appearance an entry into the reality itself. They are not the parallels of abstract and static selves. They themselves relate to actualities, actual actions—they themselves are reality. In second world culture, out of which this analysis comes, the basic distinction between appearance and reality does not function. That distinction is judged as hypocrisy, or, in the third world anti-culture, a repression.

The image entries are not themselves pictorial, filmic, literary, or sociologic versions of a premise, nor are they logical abstractions. They are a crystallization of real action. When Jorge Luis Borges's creation Funes the Memorious,[40] looks into the mirror and sees a different face every time, that would mean in second world culture that he is showing a different *reality/being* every time; in second world culture, 'look' and 'are' are inseparable. In first world culture at its height there is an unchanging quality (e.g., the good of a good table) that is inseparable from all objects. There is no such abstract reality in second world culture thought and action. The reality is in the historical situation, the specific action, not in some abstract world of the 'good'. The truth is a very specific commanded way. These illustrations are analogies of frozen, meaningful actions that are inescapably moral. There is no autonomous *moral/artistic* realm.

25. *Motif.* I shall further introduce the three cultures—first, second, third—in which we live now by their fundamental motifs. By 'motifs', I mean something like those brief, intelligible, self-existent melodic and rhythmic units out of which there develop in music figures repeated at different pitches and intervals; and yet all the while recognizably the same. Motif analyses are a tried method. A Swedish scholar, Anders Nygren, sometime Lutheran bishop of Lund, adapted and expanded the musical turn to his own model fundamental motif analyses of Christian, second culture love (*agape*) in contrast with first culture pagan (*eros*).[41] I adopt it here so as to find my way through the huge, largely uncharted

40. Jorge Luis Borges, "Funes the Memorious," in *Ficciones*, ed. Anthony Kerrigan (New York: Grove Press, 1962), 112. For more on Funes, see part 4.

41. Anders Nygren, *Agape and Eros*, trans. Philip Watson (London: S.P.C.K, 1953).

FIGURE 6. Opening notes, Beethoven's
Fifth Symphony in C Minor, Opus 67

territory of comparative cultural analysis toward the present condition of our culture.

Perhaps the most familiar motif to mine and many other ears
is the four opening notes of Beethoven's Fifth Symphony in C
Minor, opus 67 (see fig. 6). Those notes first sounded in Vienna
on the night of December 22, 1808. By 1939, and until VE day,
those same notes were broadcast by the BBC over occupied Europe as a musical myth of first world fate motif (as the coming of
death) recycled and aimed at Nazi Germany just over a century
and a half later. The opening motif of Beethoven's Fifth was described by one of Beethoven's earliest biographers as fate knocking at the door.[42] Fate is the motif of the first culture in which we
live: fate, as distinguished from the faith of our second culture or
the fiction of our third.[43] The knocking that Macbeth hears is the
announcement of the retribution of sacred order. But those Scots
are themselves recently converted pagans, with an acute sense of
guilt, which is shame in sacred order.

26. *The payout of permanence.* Permanent negation, the unprecedented fight against all sacred orders, is the price paid out, in its
gracelessness and violence, for a life *woided* in our new *hospital/*

42. According to Beethoven's first biographer, Schindler, Beethoven him-
self scribbled on a later score, "*Muss es zein? Es muss zein.*" See Anton Schindler,
Life of Beethoven, trans. and ed. Ignace Moscheles, 2 vols. in 1 (Mattapan, MA:
Gamut Music, 1966), 2:182.

43. On the self itself as a fiction in the third culture, see Andy Warhol's *Amer-*
ica (New York: Harper and Row, 1985), 129. There he originally fancied himself dead under a gravestone marked, merely, "figment." Then, Warhol further
fancied his "tombstone to be blank. No epitaph, and no name." That tombstone
marks nothing other than the fictive, fantasy life entertained commonly in our
third world: the one in which, for the first time in history, there is no sacred order and no sacred self ever on the move in it.

theater: our third world. *Hospital/theater,* archetypal institution of third worlds, clinic as culture, is founded upon the charitable fiction that we are never so much ourselves as when we are acting. Such charities encourage the death of *caritas.* It is charitable, now as it never was before, to think all the world a stage. This tragic locution of despair has become the fun place of selves dramatized by those who think of these selves as free at last from all unstaged worlds.

27. *Through thick and thin: The uses of image entries.* A thick text is an enduring cultural achievement, like a cathedral. It addresses the vertical in authority in a way that is always illuminating if respected and read correctly. A thin text, on the other hand, has no enduring qualities. Many of the negational works of third world culture are thin texts; in their denials they make nothing lasting. In thick and thin, we see affirming and negating readings of the vertical in authority and our place in it.

Thick texts do not fade, no matter how some may try to eliminate them. Kafka's Hunger Artist does not realize that a thick text is food, and therefore starves.[44] The anorexics are starving in a world of junk food; they do not understand the legacy of thick texts as spiritual food, not easily consumed. No life, however, is made entirely of thick texts. Thin texts, entertaining as they usually are, have their place, as long as they are not transgressive. Remember, though, that there are no jokes in the Bible. But if there are only thin texts, then there is the implied, and sometimes explicit, destruction of enduring texts. The natural rhythm of life that runs between thick and thin texts can be upset by war, which usually seeks to destroy thick texts. There is junk in this book to show that it is junk. This book has so many image entries, some thick and some thin, because through these texts we see shadows of the truth.

28. *Seeing, not seeing.* There is a deadly vanity or egotism in not feeling or seeing this other world in one's here and now. That van-

---

44. See Franz Kafka, "A Hunger Artist," in *The Complete Stories,* ed. Nahum Glazer (New York: Schocken, 1971), 268–77.

ity ends in a sense of void. The speaker who is named Ecclesiastes of Koheleth begins his remarks by referring to the "emptiness, emptiness, emptiness, all is empty" that we now consider anomie, chaos, formlessness, which is the absence of world making, of world creation.[45]

For Ecclesiastes, all go to the same neutral place from which they came, that is, to an emptiness for which the image is dust. Death comes to all alike but not identically.[46] All comes from the dust and returns to it. That dust Delacroix called the most universal half-tint combination of every tone.[47] So the dustiest tone is the most universal. In the dust colors of mischance, men have no advantage over beasts (Ecclesiastes 3:19)—possibly even a disadvantage. For that half knowledge in its half tints is always there and increases with the age of the creature fastened to a dying animal. But even that anxiety can be transformed by the creative world that is in the here and now and means order. Britten's setting to music of Blake's "Dying, dying, dying" transforms that emptiness in all its horror into something that can be called beauty and characterizes what is called in the traditions from which I write the assent of the human to the vertical in authority. Ecclesiastes put it in the form of a rhetorical question: Who knows whether

45. How interesting, to say the least, that the scientific doctrine derived from quantum mechanics that the universe came out of a, or some, little energy fluctuations in the emptiness, the true vacuum, assumes that nothing in nature remains totally quiescent and not subject to those fluctuations. The true vacuum is not one of total emptiness. The common concept of emptiness is not valid. The recognition of fundamental fluctuations in empty space admits space itself, and that admission is as important as the achievement in quantum mechanics of the doctrine of fundamental fluctuations. The existence of such fluctuations may have been established by experiment, but the image of an emptiness does continue to demand the reality of space. That is as fundamental to third world culture science as it is to first and certainly to second. Moreover, fluctuations, as the predicates for the beginning in the void and out of it, in a big bang, suggest that behind the great achievement of quantum mechanics is a theory at least as mythic as those of first and second culture and perhaps more fictive in its self-consciousness of instability as the predicate of creation.

46. See Ecclesiastes 3:20.

47. *The Journal of Eugene Delacroix*, trans. Lucy Norton, ed. Hubert Wellington (London: Phaidon Press, 1951), 350.

the spirit (or the word we would now use, more confusedly, the identity) of man goes upward or whether the spirit of the beast goes downward to the earth? (Ecclesiastes 3:21).[48]

In the traditions out of which I come, the truth was that life's path, however the mischance may occur that was earlier called fate, depended upon an understanding that whatever is done would be done in such a way that men would feel the presiding presence.[49] That sacred fear was called by Plato *reverence*. In dealing with men, it is God's purpose to test them and to see what they truly are (Ecclesiastes 3:19). To live in the *via* is to live secure in that knowledge that by knowing where you are in your very acts and thoughts you would know what you are. The presence presiding would see that truth, which, in your knowledge, you would share with the presence, an awesome knowledge that nevertheless demanded action. Nothing except the alternative to living in the vertical of authority, that alternative being an emptiness or void, can prevent judgment. Judgment and life's path go together.

As for the presiding presence, the social order could be quite small; the presiding presence in the Christian tradition said and says: Where two or three are gathered in my name, there am I in the midst of them (Matthew 18:20). There is precedent in rabbinic sayings that if two sit together and the words of the law are spoken between them, then the divine presence rests between them. In the *Sayings of the Fathers* (*Pirke Aboth*), Rabbi Simon Ben Yohai remarks that if three have eaten at one table and have spoken over it the words of the Law, it as if they had eaten from the table of God (Ezekiel 41:22). That constant movement of ascent and descent in the vertical of authority was a constant binding and loosing for which the words are interdict and remission. Scripture says Moses went up into God (Exodus 19:3) and the Lord came down upon Mount Sinai (Exodus 19:20). The upper realms and the lower

48. Ecclesiastes saw that there is nothing better than that a man should enjoy his work, since that is his lot. But what of a culture in which work is no longer thought of as either one's lot or enjoyable? Ascent and descent in the vertical of authority must be seen in its particular conditions, which include the world of work. That includes my world of work here and now.

49. See George Steiner, *Real Presences* (Chicago: University of Chicago Press, 1989).

realms are connected in these continuously changeable ways. Those ascents and descents are continuous in our lives though none of us are Moses. So long as we understand that we are in the vertical of authority then we may find rest even in our movement, yet only so long as that knowledge includes a sense of judgment, as in both sacred and social orders: being called to witness.

29. *The trap of the visible.* This book of readings in sacred order continues the tradition of what I shall call the second commandment's break out of the trap of the visible in which we incline to find ourselves. I am reading what are already readings of our movements in sacred order. Those movements crystallize in words and other sounds and in visual imagery. Images are used as emblems. In art, third world de-creation motifs have reached their apogee. Art is the first sphere of life to have achieved Gertrude's program in which there is nothing there but ourselves.[50] (Gertrude killed herself before she could succeed.)

Second world theorists and the teaching elites they have prepared from the beginning at Sinai have never allowed themselves to be trapped by or in the visible. That disallowance is summarized in the Second Commandment. But it is elaborated in the habit of reading otherwise invisible texts behind the commanding texts of truths themselves. That tradition of reading has been adopted by third world theorists for precisely the opposite purpose: to assert nothing but ourselves, and the struggle for power. That is their way of entrapping their followers into the all too visible. The purpose of this work is to permit sacred order to show itself for a change.

30. *Why address art?* The second commandment—*Thou shalt not make unto thee any graven image, or any likeness of any thing that is in heaven above, or that is in the earth beneath, or is in the water under the earth*—will not be restored any time soon. Either we can be masters of imagery as agents in sacred order, or we can be slaves of imagery. Scientific images of that slavery to images transform the inability to read into 'addiction'. The most intensive scientific studies of people's viewing habits are finding that, for the most

50. *Hamlet,* 3.4.152–53.

frequent viewers, watching television has many of the marks of a dependency like alcoholism or other addictions. This is at once an image of the ever increasing scientification of spiritual conditions and the third world condition of a bewildering flood of images in the repressive mode. Not surprising, compulsive watchers were more irritable, tense, and sad . . . and felt they had little control over their lives.[51] To be in the midst of the *kulturkampf* can be depressing. To be unable to find one's way amid a flood of unread images is worse. Right reading is inseparable from right living.

31. *A transparency of our world fight.* In his "vivid transparence" of third world creation, "Notes toward a Supreme Fiction," Wallace Stevens is beautifully candid about the fictively equal, because equally invented, third worlds. This egotistically invented world—supposing an inventive mind at work, any mind so long as it is mine or thine and not the mind of a wholly Other—accents its instability. Stability is a function of faith. I follow, as did Kierkegaard and many others, St. Benedict's use of *stabilitas* as of something inward and spiritual, otherwise invisible except as an unswerving or determined—what Kierkegaard called "engraved"—character.[52] Because our third world is acutely unstable, Stevens proclaims a new stabilizing trinitarian character as a parody of Christian sacred order in its authoritative triune personality. Our third world: "It Must Be Abstract. It Must Change. It Must Give Pleasure."[53] Else, no third world could be what Stevens knew it to be: a "theatre of trope." Tropically, the price of trinitarian pleasuring is subjectivist truth. It is in that inciting form of truth that Stevens follows Nietzsche in the deathwork thought that "the death of one god is the death of all." That one dead, or permanently absent, god has become a bore. Suffering "celestial ennui," the most exciting of disenchantments, the death of all gods must be reinvented continuously by specially negational imaginations, poets where priests and prophets once were, bored by the commanding singularities of eternal truth. Fictions

51. *New York Times*, August 16, 1990.
52. Kierkegaard, *The Present Age*, 43.
53. Stevens, "Notes toward a Supreme Fiction," 380–408.

and their militant fabricators, of some "absolute angel" of consuming desire that is the merely "possible, possible, possible," substitute for the sheerly actual of sacred orders no more inhabitable than their own creative works. Those fictive worlds have not remained mere works of art. The great historian Jacob Burckhardt knew that the state had become a work of art and, in that work, a structure of violent death to the society over which it finally proclaimed itself Lord and Master.[54]

32. *The poet as angel of death.* Stevens declares death not only to all gods but to the Angel, that creature which had existed solely to praise God. Rereading the Praiser as his predeceasor, Stevens orders all angels be silent as he strips "the real" of every fiction except one, "the fiction of an absolute—Angel," man as his own work of art. In hearing such poetic noise, how could any angel resist Stevens's command:

Angel,
Be silent in your luminous cloud and hear
The luminous melody of proper sound.

Stevens must choose. He chooses the poet.

What am I to believe? . . .
Is it he or is it I that experience this?

The answer comes, self-revealing as Exodus 3:14:

I have not but I am and as I am, I am. . . .
An occupation, an exercise, a work[55]

—a deathwork as the poetic form of belief in our third world. Stevens's "Supreme Fiction" is a hosanna in the highest to a secular humanism that sees itself "serenely gazing at the violent abyss" and willingly "leaps downward through evening's revelations." No more than Duchamp, no more than Freud, no more than any of our great, late second world deathworkers does Stevens need sa-

54. Jacob Burckhardt, *The Civilization of the Renaissance in Italy,* trans. S. G. C. Middlemore (London: Phaidon Press, 1944), particularly part 1, "The State as a Work of Art."

55. Stevens, "Notes toward a Supreme Fiction," 404–5.

cred order. He "needs nothing but deep space." Even so, around that world in its deep space, the artist can never permit nakedness. The world woman, as the artist's bride, can never be stripped bare.[56] The vocation of the artist is to weave yet another "fictive covering . . . always glistening from the heart and mind."

Third world artists and scientists cannot think of the truth before them. Such artists and scientists are weavers singing impious songs to an imaginary bride. The vocation of the artist becomes not an address to sacred order but "A thing final in itself and, therefore, good." The good goes "round and round, the merely going round / Until merely going round is a final good."[57] Stevens's sacred second world can be stripped of every fiction except the supreme need for fictions. That supreme need is an idea old as natural religion. Stevens gives that natural religion an artistic militancy toward the creation of a third world that must use, as canon fodder, all the attributes of worlds first and second.

33. *Third world militant.* Militant for all those attributes, excluding none, not even the politically incorrect father who "fetches" in season during "the auroras of autumn . . . negresses to dance among the children."[58] Stevens, though he knows that negations are never final, has the prescience of the oncoming dream of a new soldier of unfaith to replace the soldier of faith. In the coda of the tenth stanza of his "Notes," Stevens imagines his prototypal third world man as a soldier to whom he can declare, as if the permanence of the *kulturkampf* were a revelation: "there is a war between the mind and sky." That "It is a war that never ends . . . And war for war" describes the deathwork of his, and my own, prototypal third world soldier. In that permanent war, every high officer of our third culture class is charged with the duty as follows:

> He imposes orders as he thinks of them,
> As the fox and snake do.[59]

56. For more on the *world woman* as bride, see my reading of Duchamp's *Bride Stripped Bare by Her Bachelors, Even,* in part 3.

57. Stevens, "Notes toward a Supreme Fiction," 405.

58. Ibid., 407.

59. Ibid., 403.

THE PRESENT WORLD FIGHT 41

These officers are tricksters, nonstop seducers of skies, that simple naturalizing pluralist word for all sacred orders. Fox or snake, into whatever figure they transform themselves, trickster third world officers call the world woman "by name, my green, my fluent mundo." Conrad's Kurtz calls her, with equally militant insolence, "'My Intended, my ivory, my station, my river, my—' [Marlow is literally breathless at the ungodly Godliness of the man] everything belonged to him." Third world officers are driven by this combative erotic counterfaith to which the depths themselves must

> burst into a prodigious peal of laughter that would shake the fixed stars in their places. Everything belonged to him—but that was a trifle. The thing was to know what he belonged to, how many powers of darkness claimed him for their own. . . . It was impossible—[60]

It was an impossible culture that Kurtz tried to carve out for himself as the progressive explorer of that fluent *mundo* called The Congo. These explorers read literally and typologically as Kafka named them in their singular search for that primacy of possibility. That officer is there, wherever he goes, to explore the world he comes to create and destroy. The mode of destruction can be clearly read in both works of art, *Heart of Darkness/In the Penal Colony*. These are the creations, not the discoveries, of our third world explorers. Sacred orders, when partially re-cognized in social, are reread by third world theorists as penal colonies, there to be liberated by explorers of possibility as our third world primordial.

34. *Repression as exploration.* Before this truth, before this supremely scientific fiction, the imperial theme, the exploration itself, knows, as Stevens knows about it,

> . . . that what it has is what is not.[61]

60. Joseph Conrad, "Heart of Darkness," in *The Portable Conrad*, ed. M. Zabel, rev. ed. (New York: Viking, 1969), 559.
61. Stevens, "Notes toward a Supreme Fiction," 382.

How remarkable that centuries before, Shakespeare's political explorer, however overwrought with things forgotten, shakes his own single state of man, his sacred self, by his surmise that

nothing is but what is not.[62]

In his apprehensive language of exploration, even so treated as a supreme fiction near the end of its power to persuade, Stevens offers an unpolitical version of the imperial theme. Poetic rather than political officers of that imperial theme, Stevens's soldiers die as fictive heroes as quickly as their fictions fade before the coming of yet another supremacist.

The permanent war does not end with the end of sacred order. Rather, the war grows more cruel, more scientific, more inclusive. The study of culture itself is drawn into the war as a major weapon, which I have called the form of fighting before the firing begins. As a high officer, indeed as the appalled Clausewitz of our third world armies ranged against second, Nietzsche speaks the truth of his emergent worlds as they have been and will be: in a state of war against all cultures—as anti-cultures. It is in that state that the judge as a figure of domination is replaced by the therapeutic 'esteemer'. As an anti-god-term, engaged in relentless therapies of self-esteem, the esteemer is the creator. The language is worthy of a message in the American navy: "Hear this, you creators! Change of values—that is a change of creators. Whoever must be a creator always annihilates."[63] Of Nietzsche's thousand and one world creations, i.e., cultures, each with its own moral order, there is now the all-inclusive thousand and second as their de-creative conqueror. The officers of the conquering third culture know what they are: enforcers of rules. Rules are surrogates of commanding truths. Even Freud thought there were certain permanent rules—the incest taboo, for example—which were

62. *Macbeth* (Kittredge), 1.3.142–43. This is Macbeth's remarkable moment of insight, however negational, into the moment at which the orderings of the sacred break in to ordinary social reality in the extraordinary condition in which the three fates make their prophecy.

63. Friedrich Nietzsche, *Thus Spake Zarathustra*, ed. and trans. Walter Kaufmann (New York: Penguin, 1978), bk. 1, sec. 15, 59.

universal. Who in third culture can imagine a universal, un-changeable rule? In second worlds, there is no rule on earth which does not have its exception. But second world rules are readings of commanding truths and of their implications. Those readings, and their implications rendered institutionally, must have their enforcers. Law enforcement is ineliminable in social orders. Reading war—*kulturkampf* in the unoriginal German—must an-tedate all shooting war; or else shooting wars are sheer madness, outbreaks of the most severe and suicidal efforts to escape any and all implications of sacred order.

35. *Symbol and symptom.* Sacred symbols do work. They are well known as coordinators of moral demand systems and of tone, character, the style and being of life, as well as the picture people have of the way things are in their most inclusive sense of order, both of their own ego order and of world order. Sacred symbols render visibly, whether in words or images, what the true way is. Where we are in the vertical of authority denotes what we are, that is what actions are. They are not qualities of our minds. A symbol is what it represents. A symptom represents what it is not. In the third culture, we live in the age of symptoms. That there are no clearly functioning sacred symbols is the tragedy of those of us, all of us, who live in the third culture, however we live as well in the second and first.

Sacred order and where we are in it, so denoting what we are at any time of our place in it, is the only question about the founda-tions of morals that can be made properly or rationally a subject for debate or questioning. If where we are is what we are, if right and wrong are not abstractions but the real character and presence of action in body as well as mind, then morality is unchangeable with all of truth. If, on the contrary, it is the case that there are merely feelings or representations that are functions of power and self-interest, it is only then, according to the different constitu-tions of our sense of interest, of the senses of beings, that what I have called here the truth appears as it is.

Our ideas or moral demands have the same origin as our ideas of the sensible qualities of our bodies. The ego is first of all, as Freud remarked, a body ego. The harmony of sounds, of the beauties of images in painting or sculpture, the pleasure of highest authority, is the adapting of mind and body in a particular manner to where we are. From where we are we may infer what we are. Virtue in this theory of it is an affair of perception, of taste, of movement. What is morally right and wrong signifies nothing in the objects themselves. What is morally right and wrong signifies our application of ourselves to objects, in their effect on us and our effect on them. Therefore, the very center of our life is the meaning it takes in its direction. Life is literally the way of living.

36. *The defeat of the second commandment.* The first way to defeat the triumph of the world picture is to know how to read it. But you cannot read unless you know how to read the authority of the past in the present through image entries into the otherwise hidden reality of the *kulturkampf.* The truth is aniconic. You cannot capture the truth in pictures and other images. The truth must be read through the images to the hidden truth. One must know how to read. (*Bisogna saper legere.* —Dante)

TWO

Theory of Culture and Origins
of the *Kulturkampf*

1. *Images in the via.* I call your attention to the line on the diagonal between the words of the title of my trilogy, *Sacred Order/Social Order.* That line is to represent what culture is so far as it can be seen by any of us. A culture is the vertical in authority, that space between sacred order and social order which is the world made by world makers. The line of the vertical in authority has been imagined in some famous ways. Here is where culture is, in what is perhaps the most famous image of the *via,* or the way of authority, known to us. It is the image on the ceiling of the Sistine Chapel in Rome, Michelangelo's *Creation of Adam* (see fig. 7), which is at the same time the creation of our second world culture. There on the right is the figure of the Creator, and on the left the first created. The key element is the space between as shown in detail in figure 8. That space is extraordinarily limited. In that apparently little space is all the space in which all humanity lives. The object of third cultures, at their most literary and refined and at their lowest, is to jump clean out of the vertical in authority. That reality is too restricting. Therefore the common term for all of these movements, which began to be used by early modern French sociologists, was *liberation,* movements of liberation from the limits, the constraints of the *via.* It is in that limited or restraining space that we live so far as we are ourselves men and women created in the image of second world culture.

The languages of highest knowledge, of second world culture as it is a culture of commands and of faith—the amen of truth—are always organized as ladder languages, the traditional conception of a sacred order. Yet, consider the ladder in Joan Miró's *Dog Barking at the Moon* in figure 9. It is clear this ladder is broken, the

FIGURE 7. *The Creation of Adam*, Michelangelo
(Alinari/Art Resource, NY)

FIGURE 8. The hands of Adam and God, detail from
The Creation of Man, Michelangelo

FIGURE 9. *Dog Barking at the Moon,* Joan Miró, 1926
(Philadelphia Museum of Art, A. E. Gallatin Collection; © 2004 Successió
Miró/Artists Rights Society [ARS], New York/ADAGP, Paris)

rungs do not quite fit, they are impossible to climb. It is an impossible vertical. There is a rather comic dog who cannot possibly
climb it to the image of desire, the moon. That dog, baying at a
moon that is at a considerable distance, is within the traditions
we know in the West, a creature of fidelity. Dog imagery of faith
is perfectly clear in the common, generic name given a dog: Fido,
from *fides*, faith. Recall the old RCA Victor record label? The real
animal of faith, in a unique way, is the human, who is a creature of
faith/knowledge. The futility of Miró's dog, the faith-relation
become a barking at the moon, has with it a comic aspect that is
always there in the very denial of the ladder languages of faith as
they are addressed highest above the vertical in authority.

Figures 10 and 11 are prints by William Blake, from his series
For Children: The Gates of Paradise. Blake's imagery illustrates an effort both to reject second world culture and to transfigure it. The

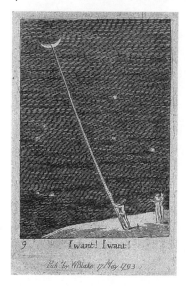 

FIGURE 10 (left). *I Want! I Want!* Plate 11 from the series *For Children: The Gates of Paradise*, William Blake, 1793
FIGURE 11 (right). *Help! Help!* Plate 12 from the series *For Children: The Gates of Paradise*, William Blake, 1793

(Lessing J. Rosenwald Collection, Library of Congress; © The William Blake Archive)

first (fig. 10) illustrates the vertical of authority as the ladder of desire, a man trying to reach the moon under the title *I Want! I Want!* which is the American translation of "I Need! I Need!" That is an another impossible vertical. The connection between the sacred image that waxes and wanes and the creatures that are in one way trying to reach it is remote.

Figure 11 is a primordial first world culture image of what lies beneath the man reaching for the moon—an image of drowning in the sea, drowning in desire, titled by Blake *Help! Help!* It is a premonitory, traditional image of the primacy of possibility that is essential to the first world, which is now dead, except so far as it is being recycled by the fictionists armed with that sense of the primacy of possibility representing the third world anti-culture. I say anti-culture advisedly. For, until just over a century ago, all cultures, so far as I know anything about them, were secular; that is, world-making representations in social order of the sacred orders of which they were precisely representations in either the symbolic or symptomatic meaning of world representation.

2. *First culture.* I repeat the motif of first world's culture: fate, which means death as well in the classical language of that culture, Greek. That motif is pagan and in the majority everywhere. Fate registers the unchangeable directive force of some unsurpassable authority from which all authorities, and their defeated challenges, derive. God or gods, before nature and man, fate represents what it is, otherwise indescribable and entirely potential: that primacy of possibility which reappears variously in our third world synchronically as Freud's death instinct, Marx's class war, and other mythic repetitions of that identity of opposites, related strangely as primitives to sophisticates, I have been referring to by the acronym *pop.*

In its enormous variety, from Australian aboriginal to Platonic rational, lost original dreamtime or rational idea-forms, our first world derives its pagan sense of reality from the otherwise hidden power, primordial as some may at present think sex and others may think race and still others death or taxes. From this primordial realm, imperial messages that must be obeyed go out to its subjects, which once included the gods themselves. All god-terms of our first world were born out of a primacy of possibility actualized in fate even as our third world actualizes them in class, race, gender, and other current *pop* primacies. Pagan personifications of the primordial had their theogonies, narratives of births, loves, and deaths recycled in third world fictive praxis, as we shall see. First world in its own time was "full of gods" as Plato remarks in the *Laws.*[1]

Those gods personified aspects of the metadivine *pop* as third world god-terms abstract power into instruments of mind with which to manipulate matter no longer thought metadivine; indeed, no longer thought divine. A contrary sensibility rules our third world. In the third world, nature has become art. Art devel-

---

1. Plato, *Laws II*, trans. Trevor J. Saunders (Cambridge, MA: Harvard University Press, 1968), 899b, p. 349.

ops a certain authority of its own and refers to itself alone. Until the time of our third world, from authority there was no escape. The structure of authority was hierarchical. Life could be described in the constant movement—therefore in the inconstancy—of humans moving along the vertical in authority. To be human is to be always somewhere in that vertical. Where we are, each and all, in that vertical describes what we are. Our places in that vertical in authority locate their moralizing meanings in our personal identities. Every operative act becomes illuminative. In the *via*, the most disorderly acts take their meanings as we take and change their positions. These positioned, yet moveable, meanings in sacred order must be inferred from wherever we and they are, raising or lowering ourselves freely in that range of authority.

Authority is that about sacred order in its vertical which will not brook indefinitely its levelings, however brilliantly these may be conceived. The very effort at leveling sacred order must be sensed as guilt. Pain is the objectification of guilt even at the possibility of a move downward in the vertical along which cultures express themselves as closure of possibility. First world primacies of possibility, however recycled in our fictive third, are thus a negational and secondary inference of movements downward, imagined as that from which everything actual derives, including ourselves and other terms for responsible agency. 'Gods' is the most general pagan form for this agency.

3. *Primacy of possibility.* It is impossible, I think, to enter the feeling-tone of a dead culture. The primordial works of first culture are not as they were: faith inseparable from the mythic arts of fate. These arts are now prior to nature. Nature in first culture was mythic: minded by a destiny that has already determined the world course of nature in cycles of births and deaths. No theorist of first culture was more proleptic than Plato. In their births and deaths, Plato knew that

> reflection and thought and art and law will be prior to things hard and soft and heavy and light; and further, the works and actions that are great and primary will be those of art, while those that are natural, and nature itself,—which they wrongly call by this

name—will be secondary, and will derive their origin from art and reason.[2]

Virtually a theorist of it in his uses to the second world, no theorist of first culture was more exquisite in his elaboration of the vertical of authority than Plato. Yet, like other first culture theorists, however exquisitely dramatic as Aeschylus or theonomic as Socrates, Plato perceived sacred history as cyclical, i.e., eternally recurrent and therefore scarcely historical as that history lived in second culture. Of course, not that Plato was your typical first culture theorist. Sheer refinement does matter to the spirit of second culture. In first cultures, the primordial metadivine, with its preexistent autonomous powers or forces, is perceived more crudely and variously: as water, darkness, winter, mountains, sky, earth, images, idols of the cave. The god-terms were gods, each generally in conflict with all others. Restraint was the mysterious reciprocal defeat that the gods of desire brought upon themselves.

In the mythic and multiple truths of first culture, all gods and all other beings, too, are born in the womb of the primordial. Above and before the fecund prepotence of the primordial, existing before all else and from which all else is born, there is absolutely nothing; not even desire. In first culture, pagan and the majority of cultures in all their enormous variety, the unalterably directive motif, however it is played out and for however long, remains as it was in the beginning: a decided primacy of possibility that is the hidden limit of freedom in that primacy. The thrust of third culture theory is toward freedom in that primacy. By contrast, in first culture, primordiality of power, its character predestined, limits free will. Fate is that god-term of first culture which decrees its nonnegotiable terms to the gods, who are not what is prepotent in them and in their conduct: the primordial metadivine.

To come nearer the human, philosophical, and tragic in first culture is to know each self for itself. Each self takes the shape of its decided fate. That fate is arbitrary, however rational and soci-

2. Ibid., 892b, p. 323.

ologically functional it may appear as a regulative device among many selves. The gods, however often they assert that they do nothing without justice and socially discernible reason, such as punishing offenders of sacred order in first culture—Oedipus, for example—are neither good nor merciful. They represent motifs that are more determinedly passionate than they are moral. What, then, may we expect of mere humans? They may be pierced to the heart by the justice of gods themselves subject to the mysterious workings, amounting to caprice, of the primordial metadivine in its sheer plenitude of possibilities determined, yet unknown and unknowable; except, possibly, to oracles in their shrines.

Even the sexuality of gods in first culture is an aspect of the primordial thrust of power by which they are brought to life and death. Human destinies may be represented, however unknown and unknowingly, by some god within, itself subject to the metadivine primordial powers. Whether working in the Oedipus of Sophocles or of Freud, fate is there, as incomprehensible as it is blameworthy. That destiny does not preclude responsibility, which gave to first culture its tragic tension. That tension cannot be resolved, not even by *amor fati*.

For a summative work of *amor fati*, even as it is hated in first culture, I turn to *The Bacchae* of Euripides. In that play, Agave, mother of young King Pentheus, is a Dionysus worshipper. In Agave's ecstatic worship, not knowing what she is doing except that the act is in sacrifice to Dionysus, Agave beheads a lion. Note that ecstasy, the numinous feeling, is the first culture version of third culture repression. Triumphant, dancing her pleasure, Agave brings the bloody lion's head, in unecstatic truth her beloved son, as the prize in a processional of worshipful women, to the king emeritus, Cadmus, her father and grandfather of the beheaded king. That wise and foolish old man, in both ways powerless, acts as what in third culture will be called a 'therapist' and in the second a 'theologian'. Cadmus introduces his daughter to the reality-principle incarnate neither in the word of a mere god-term nor in his own word; rather, reality is hidden in the metadivine power of fate. The retired king represents just enough proleptic authority, as it will assert itself in second culture, to represent the imagined head of a lion, severed in an orgy of devout imagination, as it really is: the head of Agave's own son and king. Lamenting her son, and her own condition as the toy of a god's will, Agave protests, as Oedipus did, that she is not blameworthy. It appears that the god Dionysus, even the king himself, if we are to believe the play and not the playwright, is to blame.

All tragic characters in first culture can protest, as they die in despair, that they have been subjected to the will of some god. Dionysus has been so subjected to his divine father Zeus. That chief god himself has been subject to the mysterious primordial power. Before the primordiality of power, the gods may appear to themselves as no more than flies to those familiarly wanton boys. Metadivine Power is to be feared, as are its agents. That force of destruction, whatever it creates—dramatic tragedy or new orders— made no moral sense: least of all to those all-too-human characters drawn into the miasma of force.

Tragic heroes and clever clowns alike are drawn inescapably into the miasma. Heroes may be as noble as Prince Hamlet and clowns clever as Polonius. The miasma of fate overpowers whoever strays too near it and even those not so near. Yet a Horatio, near as he is to Hamlet, survives to tell the story, however else he too may be dead. Fate teaches no moralities; nor does it teach immoralities. Fate is merely remorseless. Its workings can be watched dry-eyed. There is no cause for the death of Ophelia. She is a pathetic creature of synchronicity. True, there are reasons. Ophelia is not so conveniently obtuse nor so grossly sensual as Gertrude. But it is not in these causes that she drowns. True, Ophelia is the weak and willing daughter of a player in the court tennis game of power, Polonius. True: she has been, and/or would be, the lover of an ambassador of death, as L. C. Knight rightly titled Hamlet.[3] Moreover, that noble sometime student, on holiday from the University of Wittenberg, knows that his fate cries

3. L. C. Knight, "The Embassy of Death: An Essay on *Hamlet*," in *The Wheel of Fire: Interpretations of Shakespearian Tragedy*, 4th ed. (London: Methuen, 1949), 17–46. For more on Hamlet as an ambassador of death, see part 5.

out beckoning like the ghost of authority as Hamlet acts out, radically skeptical of it, his roles in the fatal Renascence world-theater that Shakespeare made of the primordial realm of power. More important, before Freud, Shakespeare reinvented first culture's repressive imperative. Hamlet is more symptom than symbol of the primordial power that is fate. More eloquently than any other figure representing second culture, Hamlet knows and yet does know what he represents. He is at once the most articulate of symptoms and the most tragic of symbols: a self that knows it cannot, therefore ought not, know itself. Therefore, neither Rosencrantz and Guildenstern, Hamlet, Shakespeare, nor anyone else, can pluck out his mystery. This anti-Socrates represents one constantly shifting motif in what he himself is not: the primordial realm of the metadivine. It is from that realm, unconscious in Hamlet and deep in his Denmark, that no traveler ever returns. Hamlet is a man of second culture with unelected affinities to first and third. In this way, I would and do account elsewhere in this work for his enduring appeal to the Western reader of what is not: the repressive imperative where once the commanding truth of revelation was.[4]

4. *Classical particularities.* Epictetus refers to the great struggle for the organization of identity that occupied the classical world. "This is the conflict between Jews and Syrians and Romans, not over the question of whether holiness should be put before everything else . . . but whether the particular act of eating swine's flesh is holy or unholy."[5] In the world of nature as the pre-moral primordial, the eating of swine's flesh would not matter. But Epictetus recognized that life is a particular matter of readings in right order. *Kulturkampf* is always about particulars. The avoidance of swine's flesh is never a matter of sanitation. It is a matter of moral sanity.

The horror of the third world *kulturkampf* against our second is that the entire struggle turns on abstractions, as in 'class', 'gen-

4. For more on the 'repressive imperative,' see part 4 and also the epilogue, "One Step Further," to the 3rd ed. of my *Freud: The Mind of the Moralist.*

5. Epictetus, *The Discourses*, trans. W. A. Oldfather (Cambridge, MA: Harvard University Press, 1912), d, 1.22.4.

der', 'race'. Epictetus knew that there was an *is-ness* of the self that is always particular.

> Why, then, do you call yourself a stoic, why do you deceive the multitude, why do you act the part of the Jew when you are a Greek? Do you not see in what sense men are severally called Jew, Syrian or Egyptian? For example, whenever we see a man hesitating between two faiths, we are in the habit of saying "He is not a Jew, he is only acting the part." But when he adopts the attitude of mind of the man who has been baptised and has made his choice, then he both is a Jew in fact and is also called one.[6]

5. *Second culture.* In second culture worlds' beginning, there is no primordial realm of power above, beyond, or parallel to the authorial divine. Nothing is metadivine. Everything beneath the authorial divine is its creation. The superb thing in creation is the human. Its unicity is in the free capacity of the human either to destroy everything created, including himself, or to elaborate that creation in a theoretical life for which only the human has been given the amplitude that, in the ladder languages of faith, is generally named 'spirit'. From the inspiration and aspiration of the self-revealed creator of all things, we creatures of second world creation derive our own self-identities. Genesis 1:26–27 is the crucial and familiar text: *Let us make man in our image, after our likeness.* This truth granted, in the historically unrepeatable and irrationally complex humanity of the second culture, something epistemologically and psychologically unalterable follows: there cannot be humane self-knowledge without some knowledge of the creator authority established by credal doxologies essential to the second culture if it is to create meanings for itself.

Doxologies must devastate all philosophies and psychologies purchased by minds asserting their autonomy from theologies. Such assertions can lead only to subversions of the sense of truth inward to the self and to a culture that is false to its expressive form as the symbolic of sacred order. Either culture represents what it is—sacred order as revealed in the history of its second

6. Ibid., 2.9.19–20.

coming, after pagan error—or it is not what it represents and becomes not a symbol of inspired creation but a symptom of creative destruction. The latter way has been taken by elite cadres of the late second and emergent third cultures. Philosophical falsity and psychological subversion describe the inner movement of the educated classes in the second culture, so to abolish themselves and their culture. By this time in its history, the self-dismantling of the second culture, by its educated classes, has produced a vast self-knowledge industry that is the exact equivalent of invincible ignorance.

6. *Life in the ruins.* Our second world has grown progressively more incomprehensible to many ostensive selves in it. Sacred order and a self locatable in that order, predicates of the second culture, derive from the commanding truths of highest absolute authority. Neither the sacred nor the self shuffling somewhere within its vertical of authority can be abolished except at a price paid for by plunges into an abyss the depths of which cannot be known except negationally without faith.

Third world elites celebrate, as if they were creators, their talent for domestic ruinations, a dynamic of spiritual self-defeat that the rabbis at Yavneh could not have imagined in their most terrible dreams of the consequences of political defeat by the Romans. A radically skeptical knowledge industry has been built upon the ruins of sacred truth.[7] That industry creates high pleasure out of the low life in those ruins. In pursuit of that pleasure, the self that was found in its relation to highest authority, as faith, has been lost in roles played as if life were a succession of amateur theatricals, with an experimental laboratory as the world's stage. On that stage—rather, in that laboratory—self-identity is no longer inviolable. Each resembles every other as a player of role faiths. Sacred history becomes a series of scenarios, composed to fill in time that would be empty if not recomposed out of the rubbish heap left behind by our second world as its legacy to third.

By contrast, authority above the *via* cannot be composed or re-

7. See Harold Bloom, *Ruin the Sacred Truths* (Cambridge, MA: Harvard University Press, 1989).

composed. Rather, It, called 'He' by tradition, has composed us. Once composed, the divinely created motif of self finds itself free to rewrite the score; but never outside the scale of sacred order. Outside sacred order, nothing exists. Nothing can come of this nothing, except the sacrifice of self and its cultivation as an offering of the unrealized self to the Nothing. Nietzsche called this offering proleptically the third "sacrifice."[8]

That the third sacrifice in our sacred history already has been made can come as no revelation. Revelation, in the second culture, refers to the unalterable directive word of God. Precisely the negation of that word is implicit in the third sacrifice: it denies and humiliates the word, absolute in its authority and incarnate in a historical man very like God except in his fears that he has been forsaken by God. Displacing and humiliating the absolute word and its open tradition of meanings, there has happened in history an absolutely human and faithless series of events commonly and mistakenly called "the Holocaust."[9] In these acts, as in the crucifixion, the carrier elites of world-immanent 'values' have affirmed themselves and so reduced the theological differences between the Jewish and Christian motifs of commanding transcendent truths to tired old theological quibbles between retreating and dwindling carrier elites of the second culture, still blind to that freedom of decision exploited and perverted by swarming new elites going about their business of creative destruction. In that business, the new elites, pleasuring themselves on the ruins of the second culture, are as pious as the old. Pieties never die, they only shift from object to object.

Of course, the scientists of the third culture, like the artists, have discovered that they cannot establish creative 'values' and destructive truths synchronically. But this discovery has only increased the momentum of movements toward an abolition of all calls to sanctification of the world and its creatures. The new elites

8. Friedrich Nietzsche, *Beyond Good and Evil: Prelude to a Philosophy of the Future*, ed. and trans. Walter Kaufmann (Vintage: New York, 1966), pt. 3, sec. 55, 67.

9. The right and true name for these events is the *Shoah*. See Isaiah 56:5 for the true meaning of "Holocaust."

triumphant over the second culture, celebrating its defeat in doxologies of destruction in the name of human freedom from the authority of the past, are driven to invent more and more 'value'
worlds as they go along. The new elites use the technological revolution as their model for an ethic of a new primacy of possibility
that recognizes no limits on that primacy. Whatever time they
took, the death trains ran on time enough. A radically immanentist third culture has been invented out of the detritus of transcendent truths from which the second derived its right to life.

The one limiting possibility that the new elites cannot admit,
in the world-affirming immanentism of their 'value' conventions,
is that of a divine creator and his promised redemptive acts before
whom and beside which there is nothing that means anything;
absolutely nothing, in contradiction to the theory of the first
cultures, whether they be crude or so refined as Plato, whom
Nietzsche mistakenly credited with being the real founder of
Christianity. Remember that mistaken passage in Nietzsche
which makes Christianity Platonism for the populace.[10] Brilliantly said and wrong. 'The people' have resisted and resented
Christian faith the more as both science and sociology have
promised them release from any and all theologies of truth transcending their immediate worlds and wishes as they would have
them fulfilled in a waking dream of life mastered and themselves
pleasured. There is the real revolution: a culture in which interpretations are applied one after another, so long as none are facets of transcendent truths that exclude untruths.

Of life lived obediently in a sacred order of transcendent and
revealed truths, independent of this world and yet penetrating it
with sanctity, 'people' in perpetual therapy would know nothing.
Perpetual therapy, the way of life in the third culture, aimed to re-
solve the authority of the past in the radical contemporaneity of
whatever takes power in the present, may be far more bizarre
than a life of perpetual prayer. The least popular kind of knowledge remains faith/knowledge of the highest in the highest: faith,
not fate.

10. Nietzsche, *Beyond Good and Evil*, Preface, 3.

7. *Sacred and social.* There is something rather than nothing. The most empirical sociological version of that something may be read in Matthew 18:18. There, one and the same, normative and empirical, is the theology of social order and the sociology of sacred order. Sacred order is not a projection of social order. God is not a god-term representing Society, however so, heteronomous, the great Emile Durkheim, son and grandson of rabbis on both parental sides, found it. Durkheim's *Suicide* was his Sociology. Like psychology, modern sociology has worked terrible wonders with subjectivity to break the objectivity of prohibitions and permissions.

The break is undeniable. Nevertheless, Western culture continues in its inalienable form or structure as the cognate Jewish and Christian commands in lives obedient to the unalterable directives given in those commands. However tragic in their discontinuities, those commands remain commanding. By our time, human decisions to obey or disobey are a matter of the life and death of the world.

Against the regnant third world anti-culture, I quote Cardinal Ratzinger's remarks on the praxis of the Catholic faith. Here are some choice interdicts directing the true way to a higher life in social order and sacred: "To be a Christian is a life and to the life belongs: not to have abortion, not divorce, not to have homosexuality."[11] Those 'Nots', among others, are in the true commanding teaching tradition of an elite in a sacred order at once social. I have named the 'Nots' of sacred order 'interdicts', commanding truths in the vertical aesthetic of authority. Ratzinger's 'Nots' are integral elements of commanding highest absolute authority. 'Nots' are not only present but predictive in compelling form, as in shalt not/wilt not. Christian interdictory motifs may intensify but do not supersede the interdictory form-praxis of Israel, as in *You have heard/But I say unto you.* Christian interdictory motifs constitute tremendous intensifications of the interdictory mode of Israel so to fulfill the commanding truths, not to

11. Cardinal Joseph Ratzinger, President's Lecture, University of St. Michael's College, Toronto, April 14, 1986, published as "The Church in the '80's," in *The Catholic Register* 7, no. 8 (May 1986): 51.

abolish them by substituting love for law. Love abolishes no divine law; not by one jot or tittle. Love as an absolute value is a contradiction in terms. The law of love as *Agape* as distinct from *Eros* is no value, and no value is absolute. Interdicts are absolute; offenses against them are inevitable this side of paradise, according to the unalterable directives not only of Israel but of the Church. Matthew 5:17ff. records absolute commands, none with apparent sanction in this world. But the sanctions will come, if not today then in due time. Against this culture of apparently sanctionless commands, the best a merely sociological culture can do is to meet the demands of the day. Unmet demands may be forgiven, like the discharged debts of bankrupts.

In Western culture, forgiveness was not a sanction of bankruptcy. Rather, forgiveness expressed the peculiarly human capacity for something like divine conduct. To forgive is to dismiss a trespass, to release the trespasser from the consequences of his trespass. This release may be given a second time, a third, even seven times daily. The condition of remission is, once and forever, repentance. To repent is the way of true guilt.

In the praxis of faith in Israel, this condition of forgiveness comes under the Hebrew term *shuv*. By *shuv* is meant a return along the true way from which the wayfarer has strayed. By considered returns, by a retracing of steps, the true way may be found again. That return, that retracing of steps to the true way, in the praxis of faith in authority, is what it represents: repentance. *Shuv* takes something entirely different than imaginative genius: a resemblance to the highest authority and reenacted obedience to it in ascents toward a higher life less active and more contemplative the better it imitates what is interdictory in life.

8. *The art of forgiveness.* Third world transgression challenges second world teachers to understand the remissive art of forgiveness. That truest art of second world culture hinges on the granting, by the self/agents of sacred order, themselves shuffling as best they can in the remissive middle of the world as it is, of rare exceptions to interdicts all but impossible to observe during some unspeakably extenuating circumstance.

To some such unspeakable circumstance, members of a second world guiding elite are charged with a special sense of responsibility for the unpleasant surprises of the *both/and* in life: both the interdict and its duty-bound disobedience. I shall give two illustrations of Jewish guiding elite praxis in the true art of remission during the fatal lifetime of the third world's war against the Jews:

> The most harrowing [remission dealt with during the time of the incarceration of the Jews in the Warsaw ghetto was] whether cannibalism is permissible so . . . to preserve life.

Consider another harrowing remission of exception:

On April 7, 1942 (Ivar 20, 5702), the Germans issued the order that every pregnant Jewish woman be killed on sight. Rabbi Oshry was asked, in view of this edict, whether it was permissible for women to use contraceptives, so as to prevent pregnancy and thus escape death.[12]

In view of the Nazi decree, Rabbi Oshry declared contraception permissible, since pregnancy would mean death. He even permitted abortions for women who were pregnant, whom the Nazis would kill.

There in Rabbi Oshry's permission was that open forgiveness in which the judge knows he should be judged according to his judgment of others. Remissive generosity is true piety in second worlds caught in fatal circumstance by the total power of third. But circumstance is not usually so fatal, nor assaults on sacred order so generational, as to challenge a whole people's existence.[13] That challenge of total war against both the Jews and their derived worlds—which in the plan ahead of the Nazis intended to include those unhappy few who remained Christian—aimed to empty all human beings of their identities in sacred orders. Noth-

---

12. Theodore S. Lewis, "Living by Jewish Law under the Nazis," *The Jewish Spectator* (Summer 1976): 66.

13. Nothing in sacred order can be so remissive that it subverts the interdicts. But that is precisely the condition of third world religiosity, as the cancerous condition of remissive enlightenment and mercy spread through the old teaching elites in the traditions out of Jerusalem.

ing took priority over this rationalization of emptying all worlds of their predicative sacred orders. The so-called Holocaust was total theater. No murderous role player in it need feel responsibility or guilt in his or her role.

Like Frantz Fanon before him, Pol Pot and his cohort, in the Paris of the fifties, dabbled in the fashionable blood Red predicate of Brown Bolshevism: Stalin's purgative kind. The rationalism of the Khmer Rouge, with its insistence on recultivating Cambodian society for the primacy of possibility, derived from the earlier Parisian babble. Each babble on the Left Bank may prepare bloodbaths when emptied into other societies, where the babble becomes a celebration of blood sacrificed to the birth of the new world in the death of an old. What remains of highest authority is therapeutically traced to its mythic origins, as that savage sexual 'primal father', and his repetitions, to which Freud reduced God the Father. So the most modern of psychologies has contributed its secret share to the remythologizing of authority by interpreting it as primordially sexual. This was not the work of a rabbi manqué. To reeducate the educated classes of this century, Freud crafted a mythologizing therapy against theology; and, in particular, the theology of Israel and its triumphalist son.[14]

Triumphalism exists; but all its forms have lost their halos. There is a great Midrash on Sages not less rebellious than Freud against absolute authority. Cartesians before the name, these Sages may have been encouraging one another: "If we entertain thoughts in our hearts and He knows what we are thinking, then we will serve Him, but if not, then we will rebel against Him." At once, overhearing them, God replies: "If your intention is to test me, let the wicked one come and test you." Straightaway we read: "Then came Amalek," the political lion of power, to savage and even blind the elite teaching guides to faith in the aesthetics in authority.[15]

There is a closely related Midrash on triumphalism, including the so-called secular, in sacred history. A small child seated on his

14. See, generally, my *The Triumph of the Therapeutic*.

15. Exodus (*Beshallach*) 26.2–3; trans. S. Lehrman, vol. 3 of *Midrash Rabbah*, ed. H. Freedman and M. Simon (London: Soncino Press, 1939), 319.

father's shoulders, seeing a friend of his father, calls out: "'Have you seen my father?' The father then said: 'You are riding upon my shoulders, and yet you inquire of my whereabouts? I will cast you down, so the enemy may come and master you.'"[16] Our rebellious remain childish, even 'infantile', to use the Freudian pejorative against itself. Yet, Freud and the other great scientific and artistic children of imaginative power cannot but have our respect. They make up their own rules and compromise with none other than their own. Rules are not divinely given commands. The new elites of promiscuous power insist that the old *Father/Son* aesthetics of spiritual authority have suffered therapeutic murder. An entirely profane creature is the new-born *sun/son*. Man wills to create himself; and then re-create himself, at will. That way lies the will to destruction.

9. *Interdict v. taboo.* Interdicts cannot be mistaken as taboos.[17] Neither interdicts in public/private order nor taboos in intrapsychic/social order can be dismissed. Moreover, a historical generalization can be made within the range of second world theory. Eighteenth- and nineteenth-century second world societies superimposed the interdictory upon taboo cultures. It may still follow, even in the fictitiously named 'third world', that a true interdict, commanded in the words of highest authority above his own sacred and social order, operates in ways that cannot be conflated with either taboos or with rules. On the contrary, however contentiously in the history of world second cultures meeting world first cultures, where taboos were, the interdicts are. Radically remissive Hawaii, for example, then as now, is no exception. In the late nineteenth century, a Hawaiian king declared the taboos broken and broke them, at the instance of a Congregational missionary from Yale. At once, Hawaiian first world culture disintegrated. When taboos are broken without punishments following, taboo cultures die. The great Freudian insight remains: wherever there remain either symbols or symptoms of the Jewish sense of guilt,

16. Ibid.

17. On third world addictions to *pop* and their consequences, see Leszek Kolakowski, "Modernity on Endless Trial," *Encounter* (March 1986): 12.

when interdicts are transgressed, punishments follow and the interdicts are strengthened.

The great Professor Foucault, my opposite number in these theoretical matters, knew that any social order without restrictions cannot exist. In a debate with me by proxy, Foucault objected only to those rules raised above rules: interdicts that cannot be satisfied by reciprocities of responsibility among sadists and masochists.[18] But restrictions without either interdictory or taboo predicates do not long exist. Not rules, interdicts are eternally commanded prohibitions constituting a system of constraint. That our revealed interdictory/remissive system of constraint becomes "truly intolerable when the individuals who are affected by it don't have the means of modifying it" is essential to the system's capacity to prevent those individuals from collecting themselves into a movement with the power, and consequent liberty, fundamentally to transform the system. Interdicts must be not only clear and well-defined but unalterable. In contrast, all values are alterable. The destabilization of social order is less a political than a moral phenomenon, less an economic than a spiritual condition of struggle. In the current general assault upon the interdicts, Western natives, journalists, and others among our subversively remissive elites no longer distinguish between taboo restrictions and spiritual/moral prohibitions. The current easy use of 'taboo' or rule or restriction where the interdictory culture of command succeeded constitutes the great internecine war in the West.

Freud was quite clear on the distinction between interdict and taboo. See his *Totem and Taboo: Some Points of Agreement between the Mental Lives of Savages and Neurotics*—that subtitle is important. Freud was far too profound a mind and aware of his own Jewish traditions, however he had abandoned them, to confuse taboo and divine ordinances:

18. See James O'Higgins, "Sexual Choice, Sexual Act: An Interview with Michel Foucault," *Salmagundi*, no. 58–59 (Fall–Winter 1983): 16. Precisely the interdicts in their commanding character are implicitly dismissed, no less than taboos, I infer, by Foucault in his remarks here as well as in his major work.

> Taboo restrictions . . . are not based on divine ordinances . . .
> they impose themselves on their own account. . . . Taboo prohi-
> bitions have no grounds and are of unknown origin. Though
> they are unintelligible to *us*, to those who are dominated by them
> they are taken as a matter of course.[19]

Freud considered the "whole subject . . . highly obscure."[20] He
identifies 'taboo' with the Roman *sacer*, the Greek *kyos*, and the
Hebrew *kadesh*. These are ancient words of ambivalence, carrying
the emotions in two contrary directions; whether vertically or
horizontally Freud does not venture. To moderns it means both
sacred/consecrated and 'uncanny, unclean'. Freud knew, too, that
the Polynesian converse of taboo is *noa*.[21]

Taboo does mean something uncommon and unacceptable,
something and someone dangerous and intolerable. Taboo sur-
rounds both the offender and the offense, both the transgressor
and his transgression. In first world cultures of taboo, it is impossible to distinguish the dancer from the dance. Taboo led Freud
back and around to its psychoanalytic counterpart: repression,
which is taboo thought unconscious and far more difficult to
break. Repression is like a live chain that reproduces its own new
links. But, though more sinuous and more powerful than the
snake, as an agent of sacred order affirmed in its very denial of
freedom, repression, like taboo, splits at once into veneration and
horror; or even, in extreme cases, veneration of what is horrible.

The Polynesian word 'taboo' was first translated in a European
language as '*tabu*' by Captain Cook, and after his death by Captain King, the successor authority on board, in his record of his
voyage. Referring to Tahiti and other islands where people "offered vegetables and animals to their gods" especially too with
"respect to the dead" and sacrificial victims, Cook noted some

19. Freud, *Totem and Taboo*, *SE*, 23:18.
20. Ibid., 23:19.
21. I can find no evidence that he read Gauguin's *Noa, Noa*. How instructive
he would have found that great French artist's reflections on his life and work in
Tahiti.

consecrated men offered up a 'Teton-tabu', a time when the natives were "solemnity itself" and showed "signs of fear to offend." Moreover, it appeared, any "consecrated thing" or place could be mentally dangerous. Franz Steiner, one of those brilliant Jewish refugee scholars who graced Oxford and other universities, remarks that Cook used the word 'sacred' before he came across 'taboo'. An even more salient word, quoted by Steiner from volume 3 of Cook's diary, occurs in the following sentence: "This sort of religious *interdiction* they call taboo."[22]

Often, nowadays, interdicts and taboos are confused and conflated. Taboos come out of a primary dreamtime, their origins vague, unformed in historical time or place. Taboos have no history; they have an inherent primacy in the way things were in some sunken beginning surfaced in taboos. Interdicts are directly commanded truths in sacred history; moreover, they are received and constantly reread as motifs, however disguised, in current history. Interdicts are unequivocal; taboos equivocal. Interdicts are instruments of revelation; taboos of repression. Theory, before its own mute facts, must take the second culture of faith as its predicate.

10. *An atonal Sinai and after: The death camps as ficta of primordial world renewal.* Written at a time when the bloodiest of all wars against the Jews raged, Arnold Schoenberg's *Moses und Aron* delivers yet another unsettlement of the settlement at Sinai. Pray respectful silence, no applause, at the unsettlement Schoenberg's dance scene evokes.[23] His libretto calls for the most exquisitely self-satisfied *love/death* cry in all operatic history. Readers will have to hear and see for themselves the refined orgiastic "Ah!" of "four naked virgins" as they receive the priestly knives, so to renew the primordial world with their blood. Such a post-Wagnerian and anti-Jewish operatic truth of ritual murder as the renewal of the world is not far from the his-

22. See Franz Steiner, *Taboo* (London: Cohen and West, 1956), 24–25; my italics.

23. Arnold Schoenberg, *Moses und Aron*, trans. Allen Forte (Mainz: B. Schotts Söhne, n.d), act 2, sc. 3, 15–16.

torical truth of, say, Mayan culture.[24] Schoenberg's scoring and stage directions echo one side of the paradigmatic pagan world of desire, sexual desire made sacred in its violence and violence made sacred in its sexuality. The other side, taboo, is particularly absent.

In this formal particular, the death camps may be read, in their erotic perversity, as huge rituals of sacrifice in which the founding nation of our second worlds was to die, not for the renewal of the old primordial world, but for the birth of an entirely new world. The sacred sex/violence of the dance/orgy scene in *Moses und Aron* expresses first world renewal. Yet that scene has an explicit trace of our third world about it. To his dancing first world worshippers, Schoenberg directs the supreme command of disorder: they are to do "everything possible." *"Heilig ist die lust,"* the naked chorus sings. Schoenberg's atonal cadences of regression carry the sound of Freud's uncanny to my ears. The primal world of transgressions appears in Schoenberg's staged Sinai even as it does in Shakespeare's staged heath in *King Lear*. "World, world, O world," Edgar remarks at the primal transgression of it all.[25] The way the world goes in *Lear* is in the image of that horror described in Conrad's heart of darkness. Schoenberg, no writer, appeals to conventionally brighter images. "Gold gleams like lust! Human virtue is gold like! God is lust! Lust is wildness! Gold gleams like blood! Gold is power! Power. Powerlessness!"[26]

Schoenberg's operatic noises of war in our originative second culture camp constitute a masterpiece of standard third world art: second world sacred order fatally disordered at the very time and place of its revelation. As the music of third world misprisions of second, *Moses und Aron* stands with Joyce's *Ulysses* and *Finnegans Wake*, and Freud's *Moses and Monotheism*, as a deathwork of art against the truth that knowledge is faith in its mediated sym-

24. See, for images and analysis, the blood renewed of the Mayan world, Linda Schele and Mary Ellen Miller, *The Blood of Kings: Dynasty and Ritual in Maya Art* (Fort Worth, TX: Kimball Museum of Art, 1986), 175–240.

25. *King Lear*, 4.1.11–13.

26. Schoenberg, *Moses und Aron*, 2.3.15–16.

bolic. In Schoenberg's deathwork, the God of every otherwise incommunicable, unrepeatable identity becomes, as an "inconceivable. . . . inexpressible, many-sided idea," precisely what he was not, is not, and shall never be.[27] In second world symbolics, the god-term, however divided and undivided, is a person. Upon that person depends our person.

11. *Third culture.* Here, following, are the three famous last words on the true counterculture, our third world taken at its boldest assertion of itself: "God is dead." Not that absolutely everything is permitted in the third culture. Of course, there are rules. But rules are not interdicts in the manner of divinely commanded and prohibitive truths, as in the second culture. Nor are rules to be recycled as taboos, those dead fears of the primordial power and its unknown wishes as they occurred constantly to members in the first culture.

No first culture now exists, I reckon, except in fictive recyclings, more or less Freudian, in the third. The first culture being dead and inaccessible even to the most imaginative theorists of the unconscious and archetypal, the third culture believes it can live by infinitely changeable rules. But the evidence is massive that no culture lives by rules. It lives by faith in highest absolute authority and its interdicts and subserving remissions. Rules as they were, under divine law, no longer exist. They did not survive Auschwitz. What did exist as the exemplary institution of the third culture, the death camps, were routines of resolution of everything human. It is an understandable failure of nerve among the commentators on those routines of resolution of everything human to use the psychologically toned metaphor 'regression' to 'bestiality', an inversion of the progressive evolutionary ethos, proclaimed, by post-Jewish and post-Christian proponents of the third culture, as the second perfected without further need of highest absolute authority and its theonomic disciplines. All this talk of 'regression' is as false as the doctrine of progress through 'secularization' and science.

Alfred Worth Whitehead came nearer the truth of the third

27. Ibid., 2.5.18.

culture when he remarked that the origins of modern science lie in the tragic drama of what I have catalogued here as the first culture. 'Residues' in Pareto's sense of the word—irrational directives of action compulsive in their power—of the dead first culture, especially when they are rationalized as science, live and work their way in the "remorseless inevitableness" that pervades modern scientific thought.[28] Whitehead put the truth of the third culture in a memorable aphorism that conveys the meaning of residues: "The laws of physics are the decrees of fate." Did Whitehead read Pareto? I do not know. Whether or not as residues, irrational compulsions, the rationalizing pilgrim fathers of the fictive imagination—scientific, poetic, transgressive, even elegiac—as it exists in the third culture, are the great tragedians of the first culture—Aeschylus, Sophocles, Euripides. Their vision of fate, remorseless and indifferent, urging a tragic incident to its inevitable issue, is the vision repossessing third culture science. Fate in Greek tragedy appears to repeat itself in the order of nature transformed into the power and therapeutic arts of the third culture.

Nietzsche's leitmotif, introducing its unminding members to their third culture, "God is dead," appeared in the second edition of his *Die fröliche Wissenschaft*, subtitled *La Gaya Scienza*, over a century ago. Note that in the great book 3, section 125, it is a madman who cries:

"Whither is God?". . ."I will tell you. *We have killed him*—you and I. All of us are his murderers. . . . Who gave us the sponge to wipe away the entire horizon? . . . Has it not become colder? Is not night continuously closing in on us? . . . Gods, too, decompose. God is dead. God remains dead. And we have killed him. . . . What water is there for us to clean ourselves? What festivals of atonement, what sacred games, shall we have to invent? Is not the greatness of this deed too great for us? Must we ourselves not become gods simply to appear worthy of it? There has never been a greater deed. . . ."[29]

28. Alfred North Whitehead, "Science and the Modern World," in *The Origins of Modern Science* (New York: Macmillan, 1925), 10–11.
29. Nietzsche, *The Gay Science*, bk. 3, sec. 125, 181–82.

Later, Nietzsche imagines:

> . . . the madman forced his way into several churches and there struck up his *requiem aeternam deo*. Led out and called to account, [the madman] is said always to have replied nothing but: "What after all are these churches now if they are not the tombs and sepulchers of God?"

What on earth could have made Nietzsche raise the question whether, to appear worthy of the death of God, members of the third culture must—even might—try to become gods? Earlier, in section 76 of book 3, Nietzsche had stated more clearly, "The greatest danger that has always hovered over humanity . . . is the eruption of madness."[30] Madness meant to Nietzsche the "eruption of arbitrariness," "the joy of human unreason"; in short, residues of the irrational, however rationalized as science and made pleasing as art.

By asserting that the prophet who saw the third culture coming, and in fact arrived after a long period of approaches, was a madman, Nietzsche defended himself by using a piety of rationalism against the horrors that must come after that rationalization of God out of existence. Nietzsche knew better. There is a rationalism so radical that it empties itself, as God the Father was once thought to have emptied himself to become very man in the Son. Kenotic theory lives in the deadly therapeutic rationalism of the third culture. In that transferred kenosis, the human becomes not a god but an artist, a mad artist who is given an empty canvas, fills it with the likeness of panic and emptiness, and declares it his masterpiece.[31]

The artists and actors of the third culture have given themselves nothing. Therefore, they must work with their canvases empty and their scripts blank, for they address nothing enduring and sacred, as the greatest artists of the second culture did. In historical fact, culture is constituted always and everywhere as addresses to sacred order and its maker from somewhere, however

30. Ibid., 130.
31. See Honoré de Balzac, *The Unknown Masterpiece* (London: Caxton Publishing Co., 1899).

shifting, within that order. Artists of the third culture address art itself.

12. *Third culture genius.* Stevens, perhaps the greatest American poet since Whitman, contributed beautifully to the death of commanding truth. From that murder, the aesthetics of faith in absolute highest authority are supposed never to be resurrected. Resurrection is not to be, perhaps not least because of the Christian kenosis.

> The fault lies with an over-human god,
> Who by sympathy has made himself a man
> And is not to be distinguished, when we cry
>
> . . . If only he would not pity us so much,
> Weaken our fate, relieve us of woe both great
> And small, a constant fellow of destiny,
>
> A too, too human god, self-pity's kin
> And uncourageous genesis. . . . It seems
> As if the health of the world might be enough.[32]

The truth, for that great third world poet Wallace Stevens, is that each commanding truth amounts to

> . . . Just one more truth, one more
> Element in the immense disorder of truths.[33]

Worst fate, or luck: each truth insists upon itself alone and follows its own laws. Great imaginations live entirely within themselves, however much they use others. We have arrived at Kierkegaard's famous distinction between a genius and an apostle. Our culture yearns for new genius. Decidedly, there can be no new apostles. Our demythologized sacred order needs none; if the old were followed. The new elites have it both ways. In their fearful symmetries, all new claimant apostles are rightly rejected and all old apostles respected in the minimal manner reserved for those who are so dead that they might well be said never to have lived.

---

32. Stevens, "Esthétique du Mal," in *Collected Poems*, 315.
33. Stevens, "Connoisseur of Chaos," in *Collected Poems*, 216.

It follows that the old apostles can be unpleasantly celebrated and pleasantly doomed as suffering the neurotic gift of a father-fixation. Such smash-hit psychological pseudoprofundities as the film *Amadeus* (1984) aside, it remains profoundly true that Mozart's music, including his unfinished Requiem Mass, are master strokes against sacred order and for the aesthetics of Self-insistence; and all of Beethoven, too, is a tremendous display performance of genius con-celebrating itself as music. Yet, Woody Allen's *Zelig* was not a smash-hit film. Allen may have trifled too seriously with the con-celebration of too many mimetic selves. Zelig's negative capability is so consciously fraudulent that it is sinister and comic at the same time, like the claimant murderer and his victims in the film *Kind Hearts and Coronets* (1949). Liberalism has abolished tragedy for the tosh of murderers being victims, along with their victims. If not pagan fate, then we are all too, too to blame. Transgressive, kindly tosh. Liberalism has turned tragedy and transgression, pagan and Christian, into the biggest con game in the Western town; that game directed by tosh-masters in academical gown.

These compulsive con men cannot claim genius. Even so, the greatest works of the imagination express a negational capability. Each achieves an identity that gives it a power beyond all authority. That power expresses the negational character of the aesthetics and their kith, all identifying down in the vertical of authority. That downward identification is represented best by *pop*, punk rock music, the body language of the killer ego. As early as Plato, we learn that it is the lyric rather than the scientific that asserts itself first as for itself alone. Science followed where poetry and music led. Long before our own time, each sphere of truth had broken away from theology or its own way to its own terrors of empty truths that survive only until the noise they make, and the carnage, end.

The immense disorder of truths, each truth celebrated in our contemporary culture as contrary to every other, may be thought, more accurately, a conflict of constructs: faithless fictions, or creative destructions of a creation treated spitefully as if nature constantly reinvented itself. In that creative destruction, death, as the last interdict, is to be destroyed; and with death the last fear of God and first wisdom. When death dies, then and only then shall theology die. For then men shall become as gods were. Less equivocally put, men shall become absolutely godless.

13. *Intellection.* Toward the dissolution of *faith/knowledge*, the theoretical predicates of therapy were first formulated by a Christian theologian who reconstituted reality in a brilliant dialectic of Yes and No: Peter Abelard. Diverse theorists of the third culture, from Jakob Böhme to Sigmund Freud, are descendant from Abelard. In the dialectic of Yes and No, antithesis the law of being, it was Abelard who first broke that unity between the knower and known upon which the commanding truths of the second culture founded their rationality and legitimacy. The result of the Abelardian dialectic was that any ascent to a higher life produced its own antithetical lowering. In the theoretical result, obedience, not to speak of union with highest absolute authority, was cut off in both theory and practice. Transgression was legitimated as the equal of the interdicts in sacred order. Whatever his conscious intention, Abelard achieved a superb dismissal of the entire ancient tradition of *faith/knowledge*, the praxes of both Jerusalem and Rome. That dismissal can be inferred from the passage following:

> Intellection (*Intellectus*) is the act of the soul, by which it is said to be intelligent (*intelligens*). The form toward which intellection is directed is some imaginary and made-up (*ficta*) thing, which the soul manufactures for itself as it wishes and of what sort it wishes, such as are those imaginary cities which we see in sleep.[34]

Freud never put better the theory of analytic fictions as an instrument for visualizing a reality that was transformable, through emotive and therefore motive transference of authority, to intellection itself. Where commanding truths had once been heard in Revelation, there was the repeatable intellective activity of experimental imagination. Mind had conquered sacred order;

---

34. *Peter Abaelard's Philosophische Schriften*, ed. and trans. Bernhard Geyer (Munster: Aschendorff, 1919–27), 23:25.

or, at least, relegated it to the world of ficta. A figment of imagination is no transcendent and singularly commanding truth. Abelard opened the way to a totally immanentist and manipulable world of things. He explains that figments of imagination are made up so that through them we may think about things. In fact, there is no other way to think about things that will lead the thinker anywhere toward the things themselves. We reach the nominalist consummation of the second culture: that words were invented and made trustworthy so that men might have a doctrine of things. By this Abelard intended no doxology of these figments, but only an intellectual instrumentality *through* these figments. The immanent and material world became subject to a course of intellectualization that, in making do with creative fictions, introduced the third culture of a reality endlessly constructed and deconstructed by and in those very ficta.

14. *Supreme fiction.* So sacred order became discardable reality. New cards of identity were issued to the self by a power of rationality that thought it could use irrationality to liven the dead sacred scene by its own power to mobilize both routines of sober investigation and explosions of enthusiastic hatred channeled by trained routinizers of a life turned completely political: toward the endless conquest of power. The antipolitical conviction that God exists and had communicated Himself directly in Revelation took its place among other ficta of inevitable supernaturalism of mind itself as it made up its various immanent applications. Science and art, liberated from all theological reference, could constitute themselves as composed notes toward a supreme fiction that was understood to be supreme only as a fiction. Marx and Freud could create their own supreme fictions. So could any other ravisher of truth. In his "Notes toward a Supreme Fiction,"[35] Wallace Stevens refers to those "ravishments of truth" that are "so fatal to / The truth itself." From these ravishments comes the idea of poetry, and not poetry alone, aspiring to the condition of music. In his own aspiration toward music, Stevens declares: "The monastic man is an artist." It follows that the artist "imposes order

35. Stevens, "Notes toward a Supreme Fiction," 380–408.

as he thinks of them." Remember that the most political man of the third culture, Hitler, was a failed artist. *Mein Kampf* is a hodge-podge of half thoughts on how to impose a fictional new order on an entirely unsatisfying and disenchanted reality. As a composer of his own notes toward a supreme post-Abelardian fiction, American symbolist of the third culture, Stevens puts even the primordial inside quotation marks, as follows: "There was a myth before myth began, / Venerable and articulate and complete."

As a flourisher of fictions, all appointing "man's place in music," Stevens regrets the demise of any fiction. So the death of Satan was a tragedy for the Western imagination. Every fictional demise is the death of a hermit in his poetic communion of metaphors that have taken the attitude of a living god, the "first idea," the "quick" of invention. As a supreme, e.g., conservative, fictionist late in the history of the second culture self-destroyed, Stevens can state flatly, playing no favorites: "The death of one god is the death of all."[36] I suppose that, from the unintentional anti-theologian Abelard to the poet of therapeutic metaphor Stevens, this de-deification of the second culture, its celebrated passionate interest in the progress of its creative self-destruction, has been accomplished in order that men might establish *intellections* about things, not about figments but only through figments. So it is that the mind legislates concepts through which it can think about things that are absent from it.

15. *Origins of* kulturkampf. Law is the ultimate weapon, before any turn to harder ware, in a *kulturkampf.* That word first appeared in common German use in the early 1870s during the struggle of the National Liberal political party to disarm by law the *moral/educational* authority, and political pulpitry, of a triumphalist Roman Catholic hierarchy, revitalized as it then was by its dogma of papal infallibility in matters of faith and morals. The aim of the National Liberals was to shift the German Catholic imagination away from the church to the state. The Pope responded to newly restrictive laws by forbidding clerical conformity to them. In turn, the state dismissed clerical resisters from their

36. Ibid., 381.

duties and, moreover, suspended their state salaries. Elites of the *kulturstaat*, both Catholic and Protestant, then learned a fatally rational and enduring lesson: the high price of being other than indifferent to the temptation of opposing the *machtstaat*.

16. *Consequences of* kulturkampf. A consequent prudent *adiaphora*,[37] operating in a range from clerical indifference to conformity, endured from that Bismarckian *kulturkampf* against the Church to Hitler's against the founding nation of that second world from which all church civilizations take their supersessive readings. Never before Hitler's time had a *kulturkampf* against the Jews turned into a war of extermination. Against that war of extermination, no significantly specific Christian resistance was mounted. A few Christians sought to share the fate of the Jews.[38] Such sacrifices were more than an unreasonable reprise of a sacred order that can be renewed only by something irrational: sacrifice or some other form of taboo upon the sensible safety of indifference. Nothing sacred can be defended by indifferent Reason. Faith is not a sacrifice of intellect, as Nietzsche and his many successors have argued, but the predicate of all decisive *life/knowledge*. *Faith/knowledge* is one thing, *prudence/intellect* is another. Politics is the art of *prudence/intellect*. An animal may very well be prudent and, in that sense, political. A Christian may well be political and, in that sense, un-Christian.

17. *Prudence/intellect: Dynamics of the war within late second worlds.* It was as the supersessive Israel that the Church maintained its prudent silence in the face of that most peculiar institution of our emergent third world: the death camps. An imprudent draft encyclical, *Humani Generis Unitas*, prepared on orders of Pius XI, would have directed Catholics to stand fast against persecution of the Jews. Another draft, less steadfast in this particular, was pub-

37. *Adiaphora* is the doctrine of considering certain matters of small difference between churches in Christian praxis as most prudently treated with indifference. Else, there develops a familiar narcissism that often splits second world organizations into hostile camps. The ultra-Orthodox among the Jews are great disbelievers in doctrines of *adiaphora*. Perhaps the greatest Christian theorist of *adiaphora* was Desiderius Erasmus.

38. See, e.g., Dietrich Bonhöffer, *Letters and Papers from Prison*, enlarged ed., ed. Eberhard Bethge (New York: Macmillan, 1972).

lished by his successor, Pius XII, who ascended the throne of St. Peter in the earliest year of total world war, 1939.

A more subtle prudence may be found in John Paul II. He has advanced the *pop* idea of the natural religion behind both the Nazi and Marxist regimes, which become 'substitute religions.'[39] This is a grave misprision, coming specially as it does from a most learned bishop of the second Rome. Totalitarian regimes recycle no sacred orders, except as fictions transparent to their *subjects/ actors/audiences*. In those negations of sacred order, totalitarian regimes represent an unprecedented cultural form by no means exhausted in the politics of any color—Nazi brown, Marxist red, Farrakhan black. However kinder and gentler less colorful and more constructive fictions may be, they need to be read for their separate but equal adamancy against all sacred orders.

18. Adiaphora. In its ancient name *adiaphora*, tolerance, applied to matters of inconsequence, to the acceptance of a narcissism in respect of small, not large, differences. A creche and/or menorah in a public space seems to me not a fighting matter. The celebration of transgression in a public space, however, seems to me a question that falls beyond the range of authorized indifference. Guilt is shame in sacred order. Irish gays may parade their shamelessness but not on the name day of the Irish Catholic patron saint. No more may Jewish gays parade on the Day of Atonement. Sacred fear forbids shameless conduct in public places. That matter was settled at Sinai. True guilt is the invariable consequence of sacred fear. In this consequence, true guilt describes the middling human condition.

19. *The second world of prohibition and permission, illustrated in Matthew.* No world has ever existed before our third except as readings of sacred orders. During all histories before third world elite misreaders appeared, all readings were made from somewhere within sacred order. The world expressed itself reciprocally

39. *New York Times*, August 27, 1989, final edition, sec. 1: "Pope John Paul II today marked the 50th anniversary of the outbreak of World War II by condemning Nazism and Marxism as 'substitute religions.' . . . 'Nazi paganism and Marxist dogma are both basically totalitarian ideologies and tend to become substitute religions,' [the Pope] wrote."

in both sacred and social order. Of all second world readers, the Jew Jesus remarked most precisely on that nearness of prohibitions and permissions by which humans have their being created in that contested space, ever so narrow, between sacred order and social. Matthew 18:18, translated sociologically into present second world terms, reads as follows: "Whatever you prohibit in social order will be prohibited in sacred order. And whatever you permit in social order will be permitted in sacred order." Secular sociology has succeeded only in inverting the various second world reading traditions out of both Athens and Jerusalem, so to invent social order as if it were the predicate of sacred.

No social order has ever before existed without regular reading enactments, at once operative and illuminative, of sacred order. By contrast, third cultures read nothing but themselves. In their lives among the ruins of second, third world elites represent actings-out of an unprecedented autonomy: life without any predicative sacred order. Such actings-out are inseparable from the fight long fought between world reading elites.

Never before in their long cultural history have second world reading professionals faced so formidably real, concrete, and dangerous a task as third world professionals now put upon them. To read our worlds at war is to participate unavoidably in the fighting. *Value neutrality* amounts to a taking of third world sides; as if that pretension of civility were a supersession of veracity. There is no neutral ground to be found in this or any other world. In that fighting, brute force has been the last, not the first, resort. The first resort has been to words.

20. *Weapons.* You choose your fiction as you once chose your weapon. The war now is the effort to legitimate competing fictions. Those fictions read texts and historical events, and in their reading, claim to supersede, or at least match, the original.

21. *The inevitability of politics.* There is no civil society in first or second worlds which is independent of politics. On the contrary, in third worlds politics are supreme over civil societies, at least temporarily. They may even succeed in liquidating civil societies. The struggle in the West is over the use of governmental and judicial institutions to direct civil society.

22. *Nietzsche's prophesy of a loss in the human sense of direction.* In the same heraldic announcement of the arrival of third world anti-culture, when the madman says that God is dead and remains dead, Nietzsche prophesied human loss in sense of direction:

> Whither are we moving? Away from all suns? Are we not plunging continually? Backward, sideward, forward in all directions, is there still any up or down? Are we not straying as through an infinite nothing? Do we not feel the breath of empty space?[40]

But we see in the images of the banal vertical that there is no sense of catastrophe, that we are not continuously falling. To abandon the vertical in authority creates no longer such a dreadful feeling as Nietzsche expresses. His religious sensibility is by no means general in the population. That the ascent may create a terrible problem is understood better by Kafka.

23. *Kafka's inversive dread/Artists of escape/denial.* Sacred fear in third world anti-culture is a residual one. Kafka grasped the trick of third world escape artists. Whether as politicians or therapists, whatever third world occupations may be, joy comes by inversion even as dread comes with joy. The anxiety of that inversion has never been put more concisely than in the ninety-second among Kafka's "Reflections on Sin, Suffering, Hope, and the True Way":

> The joys of this life are not its own, but our dread of ascending to a higher life; the torments of this life are not its own, but our self-torment because of that dread.[41]

Hamlet embraces his deadly descending agency even as he dreads that part of himself he calls *Hamlet's enemy* (5.2.240). As a virtuoso of denial in sacred order, Hamlet's enemy self knows a truth his self does not know: the deadliness of human agency in its dread of ascending to a higher life. A second world self so tormented describes the classic feeling intellect mounting almost to negation of that dread. The I of belief needs, nevertheless, to be helped up

40. Nietzsche, *The Gay Science*, 181.
41. Franz Kafka, "Reflections on Sin, Suffering, Hope, and the True Way," in *The Great Wall of China: Stories and Reflections*, trans. Willa and Edwin Muir (New York: Schocken, 1946), 181.

from this *self/unbelief.* If the I is not for itself, then who indeed will be for it?

24. *Identity in the via.* Once having been given, the commands, not the agents of execution, are immutable. They can be represented either by words/acts themselves mutable in our perceptions of them or by the incommunicable identity of the word incarnate in each self. *Not I, but Christ lives in me*[42] represents a Christian self-identity that admits no orgiastic *Ah!* of desire.

Every true culture expresses and celebrates the power of re-creation. The great artists of third world are artists of de-creation. The pleasure in our lives, of affirming creation, is inverted into perversities of destruction pleasured in the pain of suffering and death.

25. *The meaning of WWII.* Hitler, having won the *kulturkampf* of 1933–39, turned against the political orders of second culture. Over fifty million lives were lost in the shooting phase of that *kulturkampf.* That war ended, officially, on October 3, 1990, with the second unification of the German state, much of its Prussian provinces now part of the Polish state.

In the death camps, the first death confirmed the second, the death of the soul, the stripping of the sacred self. *Arbeit macht frei* was the lie of freedom from highest authority which is the second death, as seen in figure 12. That terrible spiritualizing is a complete inversion of second world life: *the truth shall set you free.* That truth is commanding; you only change masters. *Arbeit macht frei* marks the entry into a death world that the Jews of third cannot escape. This means that it does not matter what the Jews do, since they are forever cast, despite their great efforts, marked, and must act accordingly rather than joining the various remissive elites. That mark is now worldwide.

Matthew Arnold's "Dover Beach" powerfully asserts the Jewish tradition that the war against sacred order, in its commanding truths and objectively correlate remissions, is permanent: that the

---

42. Galatians 2:20. A negational third world version of Christian identity can be read in Marie Vassiltchikov's quotation of a "ridiculous speech" by Goebbels in *Berlin Diaries* (New York: Knopf, 1987), 282: "*The Führer is within each of us and each of us within him!*"

FIGURE 12. View of the entrance to the main camp of Auschwitz (Auschwitz I), May 11–15, 1945
(United States Holocaust Memorial Museum, courtesy of Instytut Pamieci Narodowej)

"sea of Faith" was always once, in the authority of all true pasts, "at the full," but now like the sea in its tidal movements, can only be heard, as it was by

> Sophocles long ago
> . . . , and it brought
> Into his mind the turbid ebb and flow
> Of human misery. . . .
> . . . .
> Its melancholy, long, withdrawing roar,
> Retreating, to the breath
> Of the night-wind, down the vast edges drear
> And naked shingles of the world.[43]

43. Matthew Arnold, "Dover Beach," in *The Poems of Matthew Arnold*, ed. Clifford Dyment (London: Phoenix House, 1948), 48–49.

Arnold understood the permanent war, even as it was buried in the love life of every man and woman. So he implores that buried life of the erotic in every true relation in a way that the Freudians know is almost impossible, since we are all composed of fragments of contending images in authority. It is with those images that Arnold utters his implorative "ah, love, let us be true to one another." The world permanently at war, various and beautiful and new as it seems, "like a land of dreams" has in its warring reality

> . . . really neither joy, nor love nor life, nor light,
> Nor certitude, nor peace, nor help for pain;
> And we are here as on the darkling plain
> Swept with confused alarms of struggle and flight,
> Where ignorant armies clash by night.

26. *Caught in the* kulturkampf. After all my grandfather had been through as a slave laborer in the death camps he was appalled to discover not only in the remnant of his family in Chicago but in the Jewish community of the family's Conservative synagogue, B'nai Zion, that the Jewish sense of commanding truth was all but destroyed. Those old traditions were treated as obsolete, replaced by the phrase that horrified my grandfather most: everyone is entitled to their own opinion. The dynamics of defeat out of Yavneh seemed to him complete. The Jews of the Diaspora were defeating themselves. Only the fool says there is no God. The Jews he saw seemed to him what I now recognize as mild and early members of the third culture, Jews of opinion and taste, and, of course, family loyalty.

On his deathbed, my maternal grandfather left his Hebrew commentaries, which I could not have read, and phylacteries to me. My aunt threw "those old things" out. This was the high point of the *kulturkampf* in my parental generation.

27. *The Auschwitz act.* From Auschwitz, second world intellect can learn a tremendous cautionary lesson. Old meaning cannot be readily attached to a new and unassimilable truth. The death camps cannot be assimilated into any sacred order: neither to a punishing world creator nor to that same creator as redemptive

authority, including Israel. Repentant acknowledgments of the monstrously human nature of transgressions depend upon a sense of true guilt which the cultured classes oppose with all their argumentative cunning. Auschwitz argues the first full and brutally clear arrival of our third world. It opposes all first and second symbolic worlds ordered in the face of death. In the sights of a sacred sociology, our emergent third world should be targeted for study as it is: meaningless, a world disorder that is yet an order. Can such a world live for long? Early theoretical studies, beginning with Nietzsche's *The Gay Science*, suggest that third world rationalized lives are interims between world enchantments that never can be made rational or enduring. Third worlds constitute self-consuming cultures. First world taboos or second world interdicts do not yield for long to third world rules of the culture game. Therapies are transient as theologies were enduring.

In our radical contemporaneity, even those of us in the Resistance feel left constantly behind the times, trapped in the minimum security prisons of our briefer and briefer interim ethics. Such interims can only be considered ours in our subjectivities addressed to the most transient objectives, without direction. As for the moral demand systems of sacred world orders, Hamlet spoke heraldically for that world elsewhere in which there is nothing good or bad in any world except thinking makes it so. M. Descartes and his progeny have a lot to answer for.

THREE

Deathworks and Third World Creative Destructions

1. *Deathworks.* By deathwork I mean the resolution, in life and/ or art, of a particular world creation. I shall illustrate the intention and therefore the quintessence of a deathwork by citing a few I greatly admire. Michelangelo's *Rondanini Pietà* constitutes a deathwork (see fig. 13). Indeed, this pietà fulfills another condition of a masterpiece deathwork: it was Michelangelo's secret, final transformative assault upon what I call second culture, here in its Christian registration. That this work went on secretly for years, as scholars surmise, suggests the temporal element crucial to every deathwork. This sculpture, apparently unfinished, was found in Michelangelo's studio after his death. It constitutes his concluding message to sacred order. In the fusion of Mary, Mother of God, with her Son, the second person, she does not even maintain the distinctness of *body/ego* ineliminable from highest Trinitarian truth. The *Rondanini* prefigures the post-Christian and incipiently feminist assault on the gender of at least the first two persons in highest authority. Here Mariolatry is married to neo-Platonic mysticism. This deathwork promises precisely what Jung thought was necessary to the survival of Christian institutions in the third world Jung himself helped create—where trinity was, there let quaternity be.

Michelangelo's object of transformative admiration is the Trinitarian figure of truth: Father, son, and mediating spirit. Visibly, in this deathwork pietà, a fourth figure is fused, son and mother inseparable in the flesh: the *world man/woman* in their final androgynous consummation, the very image of Oedipus and Jocasta, or Eros and his mother Venus, triumphantly coupled. The unfinished logic of Trinitarian doctrine is here figured in the trinity become a quaternity. The mediator, or message incarnate, Jesus in his own most interior self, identical as world purpose, object and subject of history, is merged with his mother. From the mythic moment of her immaculate conception, that mother, the Jewish wife of a Jewish husband—traditionally represented as the much older Joseph—becomes released so from the primordiality of sexuality of the *world woman*. As a type, the *world woman* represents the consummation of sexuality at the point of mergence with virginity. There is the logic of chastity in the Jewish world transformed into a separate sacred order, the culture of Christendom.

In the *Rondanini Pietà*, Michelangelo sends Christian social order on its way toward the symptomology of mergence, the collective person where the sacred self once was. This masterpiece deathwork needs to be seen in the context of Christianity as a lifework. There are related implications of a deathwork, as well, in the best known of all pietàs: that in St. Peter's (see fig. 14). The im-

FIGURE 13 (left). *The Rondanini Pietà*, Michelangelo
FIGURE 14 (right). *The Rome Pietà*, Michelangelo
(Alinari/Art Resource, NY)

FIGURE 15. *Girl Interrupted at Her Music*, Johannes Vermeer, ca. 1660

(© The Frick Collection, New York)

mense eroticism of the relation between mother and son can be seen in the dead, yet living, tension of the son, and in the astonishing youth and beauty of the mother. They are moving to close the distance between them.

2. *Among others.* Other erotic closure images, as deathworks against the sexual self-control of second cultures, can be read in figure 15, Vermeer's *Girl Interrupted at Her Music*, and in a great literary version of this same erotics of closure, Tolstoy's *The Kreutzer Sonata.*

Da Vinci's androgynous Christ is a deathwork (see fig. 16): the feminization of Christ is part of where second worlds see historical truth, third worlds see, or create, myth. Christ is male in his person. *Deus Homo* refers to the maleness of Christ. The movement toward female clergy in the Christian churches is an anti-

FIGURE 16. *The Redeemer,* preparatory drawing of
Christ for *The Last Supper,* Leonardo da Vinci
(Scala/Art Resource, NY)

Christian movement. Galatians 2:20 refers to both men and women;
yet *Christ liveth in me* is a spiritual doctrine, not a physical one.[1]

With Hans Holbein's deathwork *Dead Christ,* seen in figure 17,
Galatians 2:20 is terrifying—that corpse is putrefying. At the
sight of that corpse in its grave, one side of the coffin removed
by Holbein for our instruction, even the most devout Christian
viewer might be tempted to jump off any of Basel's many bridges.
Christ's body is on the verge of becoming what the specialists in
the Nazi death camps called a 'piece', a repulsive thing to be
handled by other Jews before they themselves are put into the
condition of becoming pieces. The eternal life in Christ is
negated in this work. Paul is not talking about the fleshly, Jewish,

1. Galatians 2:20: "I am crucified with Christ: nevertheless I live; yet not I,
but Christ liveth in me: and the life which I now live in the flesh by the faith of
the Son of God who loved me, and gave himself for me" (KJV).

FIGURE 17. *Dead Christ*, Hans Holbein the Younger, 1521
(Bridgeman-Giraudon/Art Resource, NY)

historical Christ; he means the spiritual Christ. Paul's risen Christ
is clearly a being of identity. Paul's resurrection doctrine has it
both ways: clothed in the spiritual flesh. Paul's doctrine does not
rely on that corpse rising and saying "Phew, another day and I
woulda bin a goner." At that level, you are back to the sweetly naive
literalist level of Archbishop James Ussher of Armagh, who calculated that the world was created on precisely Sunday, October 23,
4004 BC.[2] That kind of speculation is comical because it hitches
the Resurrection to what the scientists can do, e.g., carbon dating,
so that science itself replicates myth. The word remains, and is not
a remains. The one thing that the Christians can learn from the
Jews is that the death of the body is death.

3. *My favorite deathworks.* None of the above, nor the thousands
of others now being fabricated in workshops all over the artistic
world, are among my own choices of deathworks most to my
taste/distaste. Deathworks are not necessarily limited as a type to
a work of art. It may be a year: say 1939. In that year, the actual
firing of a self-creating third world, toward the total destruction
of second, began. That year is crucial in the history of the permanent war against the Jews. In their function, deathworks are self-
terminating. Once executed, a deathwork must shift to its next
obsessive object. After the death of the Jews, there would have
followed the death of those few who were considered Christians

2. Archbishop James Ussher, *Annales veteris testamenti a prima mundi origine
deducti* [The annals of the Old Testament, deduced from the first origin of the
world] (London, 1650).

by the third world elite of the German National Socialist movement.

4. *Freud's cruelfiction.*[3] Nineteen thirty-nine was the year in which, after delaying publication for five years, Freud published his two prefaces, three essays, and thirteen appendixes of *Moses and Monotheism.* Read together, they make Freud the ultimate murderer of Moses, who is reinvented as an enlightened Egyptian despot put to death by "the savage Semites" who "took fate into their own hands and rid themselves of their tyrant."[4] This great deathwork, published in the fateful year of Freud's own death, superseded what is at once the unrepeatably historical and repeatably eternal truth given to the Jews, asserting in its stead a therapeutic truth typical of the third culture. *Moses and Monotheism* represents the ultimate analysis of the Jews as their own first resistant victims in the founding of second culture: the culture of commanding— i.e., revealed—truths. As a great deathwork, *Moses and Monotheism* is aimed at a historical figure. Freud takes Moses to be the once living and finally murdered god-father of the Jews who has been created in a typologically readable manner by guiding elites of a people suffering precisely what Joyce, in the first of his two great deathworks, equally assaults upon second culture, called "Agenbite of inwit: remorse of conscience."[5] Guilt, or "remorse of conscience," is shame in sacred order. All great authors of deathworks agree that morality is inseparable from religion: that they are born and die together.

Freud's deathwork is not kind to the Jews. To deprive the Jews of the greatest of their sons, their founding figure of authority, made over into an Egyptian, does seem, as Freud put it, mildly enough, "too monstrous."[6] Nothing is too monstrous against the

3. Joyce, *Finnegans Wake,* 192: "O, you were excruciated, in honour bound to the cross of your own cruelfiction!"

4. Sigmund Freud, *Moses and Monotheism, SE,* 23:47. For more on Freud's master deathwork against the Jews, see the third volume of my trilogy, *Sacred Order/Social Order,* which is entitled *The Jew of Culture: Freud as the Ultimate Murderer of Moses* (Charlottesville: University of Virginia Press, forthcoming).

5. Joyce, *Ulysses,* 206.

6. Freud, *Moses and Monotheism,* 23:9.

highest commanding truth staked in this war game. So Freud alludes to his own fine art of spiritual murder by distorting the ladder language of revelation: "In its implications the distortion of a text resembles a murder."[7] In Freudian fact, equally mythic, those "savage Semites," by murdering Moses, made him a repetition of the great Father god-term. In that studied repetition, the savages civilized themselves into Jews. So *Yid* invaded *id* and occupied its territory. But the occupying authority rarely if ever wins the peace unless victory in war is turned into a movement of conversion precisely where and when the enemy is implacable. Such movements of forced conversion are further cases of the truth that there are no holy wars. Where force is the argument, the war cannot be holy. I reckon the theorists of Islamic *jihad* represent the end, not the revival, of that second world. *Jihad* now is a technique of third world mass mobilization of those on the defensive in their retreating second. The permanent war of the worlds can only be conducted, rightly, in conditions of social peace and reasonable *adiaphora*.

5. *The Pelagian world.* As our third world's negational Moses, Freud shows his own magnificent inflexibility in resisting every temptation to see how flexible our second world was and is still.[8] Our Jewish second world was nothing like so inflexible as the ancient Egyptian, typically first in its fatalism, where there were even cities of sanctuary for murderers, as London became for the dying Jew, Freud. Indeed, the Jewish second world can be called Pelagian still, in contrast to the predominately Augustinian second world of Christianity. Humans live shuffling and sidling in the remissive middle of the *via*. Highest authority expects his creatures to do only what they can. They can be good; else they would not be punished for being bad. Freedom in second world sacred order is constantly being given. The direction of life in the *via*, however foreseen from above, is no less freely chosen for being foreseen.

6. *Deathworks/lifeworks.* In book 3, section 125, of *The Gay Sci-*

<hr>

7. Ibid., 23:43.
8. Ibid., 23:59.

ence, Nietzsche's madman announces that second world's death-work has been trumped by third's. By masterpieces of third culture, at war against second, a primacy is sealed. These deathworks become third culture dogma. By contrast, second culture doxa understand their constant defeat. They are always fighting a defensive battle against sealing primacies.

7. *Christian deathwork.* There is a sense in which Christianity has a built-in deathwork, against the Jews. While doctrinally this is not truth, it has been true historically.

8. *Bloom's zest.* Harold Bloom's *The Book of J* seems to me a most obvious *kulturkampf* document, a deathwork aimed straight at the Jewish foundations of second worlds. Moses, the traditional author of the Pentateuch, is superseded by a female poet: where faith was, there let fiction be. Furthermore, the Jewish God is transformed into a primal force figure who is all zest and life force. The reading of the Jewish God as a Don Juan power figure is sheer gnosticism. Yahweh, or highest authority, is described with the words "wild and free," "an almost unconditional impulse," "incommensurate," "impish"—which is to say a trickster—sheer energy and force of becoming breaking into fresh being. The text is loaded with primal force figure imagery.[9] That is the splendor of Yahweh's blessing: more life means that everything is possible.

9. *The deathwork against identity.* Identity is at once sacred—the commanding truths being unalterable, permanently closed possibilities—and historical. I cannot, and therefore ought not, be Moses in Egypt. Identity in this sense, in its incommunicability, marks the difference, for example, between me and both my grandfathers. Sacred history never repeats itself. The third Commonwealth cannot rebuild a third temple. That is an absurdity of fanatical Jews who want to repeat sacred history. Identity is both anchored in where one is in the vertical in authority, in obedience to commanding truths, and historical. In that historical sense, the Blessed Henry Susso, trying to identify with the passion of Jesus by falling backward onto a cross of nails, is a pathetic creature

9. See, generally, Harold Bloom, *The Book of J* (New York: Grove Weidenfeld, 1990).

who misunderstood what it means to be a Christian. Those kinds of self-torments are not commanded, or even suggested. Such reenactments turn Christ into a nut.

Identity and authority are inseparable from adherence to the commanding truths, however modest that adherence might be. It is clear that in modern societies people can still be forced to act against the commanding truths. Saddam Hussein's authority was no authority at all—it was power. That power is the object of the third world deconstruction of second world canons. Canonicity is ineliminable from a culture of commanding truths. This does not imply that the canon is all one needs to read. But it remains true that the rest is commentary. If you watch a Luis Buñuel film, you still must refer to the canon in which commanding truths are given. How else will you understand the given name of the world woman, 'Conception', in *That Obscure Object of Desire* (1977)? One does not escape the authority of revelation and its canon. The deconstructionist movement and literary fashionables are interested in the destruction of any and all canons. The master is reported objectively in the canon and subjectively in a great deal of what is called art. I am all for facing the world as it is now but not with reference to the canon in the deconstructionist mode.

10. *The higher illiteracy—a third world deathwork.* Every culture—Sioux, Catholic, whatever—teaches the higher literacy to the members of that culture. All cultures insist that one must know how to read. The unique character of the contemporary *kulturkampf* is that third culture engages in a war of positively repressing the literacies of the old reading elites. There are now armies of third world teachers, artists, therapists, etc., teaching the higher illiteracy. This teaching of the higher illiteracy amounts to a deathwork against second culture literacy.

The democratization of deathworks is seen in the rise of the armies of principled illiterates. Those principled illiterates insist in Gertrudian style that we read nothing but ourselves,[10] if we bother to read at all. The most obvious and successful third world primacies need not ever be read by the participants: race, sexuality, and fantasy (e.g., drug induced). On the other hand, there is

10. *Hamlet*, 3.4.152–53.

the world of highly intellectualized readings of nothing but ourselves, such as Marxism. One must be trained to see the primal
class struggle, or the primeval sex war, just as one must be trained
in the primal scream. But the real primacies of third world need
not be read. Third world theorists assume that those primacies
always have been and always will be there; thus no reading is required. Those primacies are as simple and obvious as an orgasm.

11. *The immodesty of transgression.* The *primal scene,* as the
Freudians call the act in which protective mothers receive putative
fathers, requires strict traditions of modesty in performance. Desire cannot be permitted to so outrun performance that the scene
becomes erotic theater. That is why the Song of Songs was incorporated into the Jewish and Christian canon—at once to admit
and to control the immodesties of lovemaking. Third culture traditions of immodesty suggest the abandonment of that *admitting/
controlling* tradition. Further in that tradition, a woman carrying
a child, that identity already conceived and protected, should not
engage in sexual intercourse with her husband. In the otherness of
his identity, the conceived child would be witness to the primal
scene. What second world symbolists call transgressive, therapists, their supersessors, call traumatic.

Remissive reasoning subserves the interdicts, or it grows to
subvert them. So overgrown with excusing reason, the knowledge
that is faith, the evidence of things unseen, loses the mediating
symbolic integral to its sacred and knowing self. Sacred self, unalterable in its obedience to commanding truths, is that something
inward and spiritual now hidden behind the *pop* word 'identity'.
In "Carrion Comfort," Gerard Manley Hopkins understood the
interdictory mode of that knowledge which is faith and life, identity in obedience to the commanding truths:

> Not, I'll not. carrion comfort, Despair, not feast on thee;
> Not untwist—slack they may be—these last strands of man
> In me ór, most weary, cry *I can no more*. I can;
> Can something, hope, wish day come, not choose not to be.[11]

11. Gerard Manley Hopkins, "Carrion Comfort," in *Poems and Prose,* ed.
Robert Bridges (London: Oxford University Press, 1933), 61.

No sacred self can choose not to be. Hamlet's question is what it represents: a deathwork.

12. *The third culture masterdeathwordworldwork/Finnegans Wake.* Freud's fighting confusion, the psychomachia that parallels the objective deathwork delivered in his *Moses and Monotheism,* may be illuminated by another deathwork, delivered by a Gentile of genius against the second world founded as and in Israel. The greatest third world literary creation remains *Finnegans Wake,* in which every first and second world culture, as some registration in social order of sacred order, is trashed. For purposes of illustrating the historical context of the world struggle to death between second worlds and relentlessly advancing congeries of thirds, I shall quote several further passages from Joyce's second masterpiece deathwork, *Finnegans Wake,* addressed as it is specifically to the Jewish god-term in the sacred order of the world. That God will not be turned, except in an antic version of which Joyce is the better artist than Freud. Comedy can conceal the tragedy of every deathwork. There is nothing funny about Freud's *Moses,* no more than there is about Michelangelo's *Rondanini Pietà.*

Always, in Joycean deathworkwords, there can be read the inversive art of third world comedy, the master of second world tragedy. Joyce may have thought to joke when he referred to the Lord of Israel, and all the contending cultures of commanding truth out of Israel, as Loud. Here is Joyce's version of the Jewish credal address to the I-Thou of a world community established by virtue of the god-relation; or the inwardness of the sacred self turned into an archetypal image of the pariah Jew in his vulgarity.

I hear, O Ismael, how thy laud is only as my loud is one.

. . . .

Loud, hear us!

Loud, graciously hear us!

Now have thy children entered into their habitations And nationglad, camp meeting over, to shin it, Gov be thanked! Thou has closed the portals of the habitations of thy children and thou hast set thy guards thereby, even Garda Didymus and Garda Domas, that thy children may read in the book of the opening of the mind to light and err not in the darkness which is the afterthought of thy nomatter by the guardiance of those guards which are thy bodemen, the cheeryboyum chirryboth with the kerrybommers in their krubeems, Pray-your-Prayers Timothy and Back-to-Bunk Tom.

Till tree from tree, tree among trees, tree over tree become stone to stone, stone between stones, stone under stone for ever.

O Loud, hear the wee beseech of thees of each of these thy unlitten ones! Grant sleep in hour's time, O Loud!

That they take no chill. That they do ming no merder. That they shall not gomeet madhowiatrees.

Loud, heap miseries upon us yet entwine our arts with laughters low!

Ha he hi ho hu.

Mummum.[12]

Joyce cannot escape his fate as an artist in the repressive mode. His first death sentence is a simple negation of the Jewish recognition that the world creator, being one, is not one and the same as that creation. The true One of the Jewish world message cannot contain the *All* of Sir Toby Belch in *Twelfth Night*, or any other governing character, however loose that governance in real firsts or fictive third worlds. Even Joyce cannot avoid some attribution of governance in his parody of second world Psalms. In the Jewish Psalms, thanks are acknowledgments of governance by the governed even in their understanding of their own evasions of that governance. In his parody edification of Psalms, Joyce adopts the slang of a cockney cabdriver angling for a tip from his temporary passenger-god, the mere occasion of his formulaic desire for more of the really real, i.e., money. Psalms become a formula of gratitude: *Gov be thanked!* That hypocrisy is embedded within a larger third world piety that asserts the primacy of the pietist rather than of the object of piety. Third world piety is systemically mendacious. The cabdriver requires more than thanks from the *Gov*. In three words, Joyce has accomplished an inversion of the principle-relation in Psalms. The god-relation has been reversed. The cabdriver is the superior of the *Gov*. In his acknowledgment,

12. Joyce, *Finnegans Wake*, 258–59.

every *Gov* will pay off in the thanks of real coin: the material world rather than the immateriality of the *lifeword*.

These comic assaults upon the *I-Thou*, as if the god-relation should be thanked for the misery it has heaped upon humanity, in the nationality of its mediating elite, Israel, carry comedy no less far in its negational way than the prehistoric tragedy of the primal murder. Either way, Joyce's or Freud's, the Jewish world of *lifewords* remains under siege, in the here and now, by a fusillade of deathworks. Freud is to the Jew of sacred order as Joyce is to the Gentile of post-Catholic high culture. My work is a counterattack upon the objective intention of the deathworks that mock the marvelous line in the old Presbyterian marching hymn *March On My Soul*. In that hymn, the creeds, including the Sh'ma, "are milestones on the road to truth." In third worlds, deathworks are milestones on the road to a culture that does not imagine itself on any road to truth. Gentiles of genius and alienated modern Jews alike find themselves on that third world road.[13]

13. *The political art of the alien.* Third world art has as its purpose the voidance of second world truth. Joyce put the purpose more brilliantly and with greater amusement than any other third world artist I know. That the death of God means the death of all is put by Joyce as the beginning and purpose of the final world revolution. The "buginning" lies ahead of us "in the muddle is the sound-dance and thereinofter you're in the unbewised again, vund vulsyvolsy."[14] We are back in the *woided* world of Hamlet and forward into the nightmare historical world of permanent culture war. Joyce refers to Hamlet and after in the third world *woid* with which he hopes, at the very least, to obstruct history if not end it. "You talker dunsker's brogue men we our souls speech obstruct hostery. . . . Wear anartful of outer nocense! Pawpaw wowow! . . . Momerry twelfths, noebroed!" The death of God the father will not lead to the birth of God the Mother, nor to another twelve or more sacred messengers.[15] Joyce foresaw that the mother-as-god

13. For more on the third world road, see John Barth's novel/deathwork *The End of the Road* (New York: Doubleday, 1958).

14. Joyce, *Finnegans Wake*, 378.

15. For more on sacred messengers, see part 5.

movement would be smothered in its own feminist animus, "And smotther-mock gramm's laws!" Third world feminist ficta, with their "Mothermerries," are part of the horror that is the image foreseen in the despair of such disparate projections of our worlds, first and second, ending precisely in horror.

14. *Monstrous world.* Monstrous images of horror possess the horrifying truth of third world art. That world is projected in Shakespeare's *King Lear* and in Conrad's *Heart of Darkness* to such fine points that they can be read, finely, in the following verbal image entries, as from an imaginary diarist of the present *kulturkampf.*

> Kent: Is this the promised end?
> Edgar: Or image of that horror?
> Albany: Fall and cease![16]

Editors of Shakespeare gloss the words of Albany as addressed in commanding despair to sacred order. That consummate transgressive Mr. Kurtz is in equally dark despair when he sees what he has never before seen: the deathwork that was his life. There is the deadly meaning in the last words of Mr. Kurtz: "The Horror! The Horror!"[17]

Third world art both knowingly and unknowingly expresses the essence of that art: its now entirely acceptable negational character. Far more sweeping fictions are at the apex of this art. It is the third world art of Nietzsche, of Baudelaire, of Picasso, of all the best that has been created to promote the clean sweep. Glorified by his own *cruelfictions,* the Artist of our third worlds creates the very world that projects the future of our real world. That projection may have failed, pray must fail, in reality, but not for want of effort.

Hitler was a great third world artist precisely in his promotion into practice of his clean sweep, the brush aimed first and foremost at the kingdom of priests and holy nation, however members in that kingdom may rebel against their membership. That

---

16. *King Lear,* 5.3.314–16.
17. Conrad, "Heart of Darkness," 603.

membership remains powerful in myth if not in reality. Hitler pictured the Jews in a familiar fiction: as coconspirators, to rule over the first world primacy of possibility. The chief conspirator was their invention, *Loud* himself—for which reason the coconspirators are thought to be loud. Loud and/or conspiratorially silent, capitalist and/or communist, doctor and/or the ill they treat and/or mistreat, the Jews represent what they are not: the God that must be murdered. Hitler's real deathwork is strangely like Freud's fictive deathwork: an originally Jewish mortal crime against the immortal primordial world.

15. *Third world creation: Read as a de-creation/deathwork of the sacred self.* What third culture people mean by *creative* is the act of de-creation. That is why the connoisseurs tell me you cannot have modern Catholic art, but you can have *Piss Christ* (see fig. 18). What is pleasing about this work of art? You can have a death mass that is pleasing. There is something affective in Holy Writ, in its spiritual translation as in the KJV.[18] *Piss Christ* is an antisacramental image. Sacrament is a fusion with the highest and the central event in the dramaturgical enactment of highest authority. The sacrament as fusion with highest authority is inverted to the image in *Piss Christ* as a fusion with the lowest. The highest is identified down in an act of incredible crudity. It amounts to an assault that lowers the Catholic identity of Galatians 2:20 to the level of excrement. Christ is in you, and so you are piss. The excremental assault on the Jews in the middle of the twentieth century is here repeated on Catholics. The alternative to such an identity is an aesthetic identity of race, class, gender, or bagels and lox.

The drowning of the Christ in piss is part of the relentless assault by the abolitionist movements to make second world identity repulsive, untenable. Identity is inseparable from the sacrament which is at the center of the mass. This amounts to a pathetically crude assault on especially Catholic sacral identity. Sacral identity is inseparable from one's identity. That is why my grandfather did not die in Auschwitz: his sacred self remained; no one

18. Contemporary translations of scripture banalize the readings and so lower the spirit, bringing the words down to contemporary readers rather than raising them up.

could take it from him. Serrano is making in art a urinalysis of the second world self, an effort that was made fifty years ago on the Jews as *Stück*—meaning piece, as in a piece of shit.

16. *Killed in the spirit.* Somewhere, always specific in space yet uncanny in its time, far beyond all literary revenants, are the real deathworks, as at Auschwitz. Auschwitz is a symbol, even as it is a symptom, of a place in which people were made to treat spiritual death, their second, with a complete indifference that signaled their readiness for the first death as well, in and of the flesh. Deathworks do not imply death, merely. Deathworks imply the priority of the second death. Calculated in Auschwitz, as else-

FIGURE 18. *Piss Christ*, Andres Serrano, 1987
(Courtesy of the Paula Cooper Gallery, New York)

where, to precede the first, the second death is that lowering in the vertical in authority to the very bottom of its range so as to separate the individual from his identity, self from sacred order.[19]

The death camps were an invention especially for the Jews: to so separate them from their sacred selves, to so degrade them that, accepting this second death and its indignities, they were resistless. Those who had been successfully lowered to the bottom of the vertical in authority, where they were indifferent to all transgressions heaped upon them, were given their own typological name by those who had not been so distanced from their higher and rightful places as humans in the vertical. Those who lived unutterably and unreadably alone in this totally different world of the living dead, those who had been totally stripped of their identity, were called by this fatal word: *musselman*. As Primo Levi revealed, this word was used by veterans of the death camps to describe "the weak, the inept, those doomed to selection. . . . I do not know why."[20] Perhaps there was no why. In that deathwork world, there was no why. Levi described:

> But with the musselmans, the men in decay, it is not even worth speaking. . . . they are here only on a visit . . . in a few weeks nothing will remain of them but a handful of ashes in some near-by field and a crossed-out number on a register. . . . they suffer and drag themselves along in an opaque intimate solitude, and in solitude they die and disappear, without leaving a trace in anyone's memory.[21]

These cultic lowerings into the second death were literal and were ordained, from shaved head to misfitted feet. These rites to be carried out were infinite and senseless. This was the great third culture *cultus* of degradation. Yet, the humanist imperative remained attached to sacred order. The victims' command to dig-

---

19. For more on Augustine's concept of the second death, see my *Fellow Teachers: Of Culture and Its Second Death* (1973; repr., Chicago: University of Chicago Press, 1985), particularly the new preface, "A Pretext of Proof Texts."

20. On the state of being a "musselman" in Auschwitz, where "no sacred face will help thee," see Primo Levi, *Survival in Auschwitz*, 80 n.

21. Ibid.

nity was to save the very form of civilization which is nothing without its interdictory forms inwardly observed in the outward dignity of refusing inner consent. Third worlds aim their extensive arsenals at precisely the outward dignity of civilization.

17. *Mortal trash.* His own *Moses and Monotheism* a deathwork, marking our temporary transition from second culture to third, the greatest theorist of that transition gave a far earlier and proleptic answer to the question of excremental assaults upon the Jews. Freud's emphasis on the unstable space shared by our excremental and sexual organs points to the possibility of very different kinds of unstable orgiastic movements represented, most recently, by gay liberation and less recently by Captain Ernst Röhm's Brownshirts—Hitler's original street fighters for his once and future fictive racial primordial made all too real. Second world guiding elites see nature as neither primordial nor autonomous but itself always and everywhere subordinate to the revealed and readable world of truth.

It may be true to third world sociological theorists following that descendant of rabbis Emile Durkheim that anything can be sacred. But Durkheim's sociology is his suicide as a Jew. It is not true that the societal everything is sacred and that everything sacred is true. The greatest first world theorists, the Greek metaphysicians, separated the promiscuity of the sacred from the fidelity of truth. Given this distinction, it was the Heraclitean primordial fire, not water, that Hopkins could turn into sacred art, which proximates faith in our second world symbolic near as it comes to being what it represents: commanding truths reread faithfully in a culture altered at its superficies beyond recognition. The resistant truth of our second world sense of identity survives the transformation of fictive primordialities and autonomous inevitabilities of natures that lie on the surface between those distant points: the first "world's wildfire" and our third world's Auschwitz-and-after.

The primordiality of destruction loses its commanding truth in the difference between first world ash and third world trash. The constant turning away of our second world from promiscuous primordialities has been asserted with an authority, in sacred art, that makes it recognizably epiphanal in the truth of its resistance to trashings of our sacred selves. The sacred self, that identity which is to each his own, never having been before and never again to be, resists all rationalization and collectivization. Identities happen in the light of that which is not our identities; rather, their predicate. Hopkins saw that happening, not in a biological flush, but in a Christian aesthetic of authority.

> In a flash, at a trumpet crash.
> I am all at once what Christ is, since he was what I am.[22]

This contraction into identity dismissed as fiction, what then happens in late Christendom? Bumper stickers and T-shirts convey the new *kerygma:* "Shit Happens."

This pungent pop can be dated back at least to Freud's infamous rationalization of our third world. That infamy is to be read in a letter to Fliess dated December 22, 1897. Here and even now, Freud's proleptic words of third world truth are there to be read: "*Was Sich . . . mir in Dreck auflöst* [how many things . . . turn into— filth]."[23] With this scabrous sentence, Freud reinvented primitivist erotic religiosity in its new vicissitude as a world turning up its nose at its own stench. *Sacred order/secular ordure.* Primordiality has become a *pop* baseness from which Freudian theory offers no escape other than into an equally promiscuous 'sublimation'. As every poet knows, sublimation is false to the perduring erotic power of art and politics. In the effort toward lowerings normalized, our third world *kerygma* dumps upon the sacred self in its denial of heartbreak and hope: *Different Day/Same Shit.* These *pop* shit storms prepare more and more people for third worlds of repugnant primordialities against which those people, trapped in their lowerings, have one instrument of confrontation: therapies of transgression. Here is the new historical foundation that requires yet another movement toward the unprecedented present

22. Hopkins, "That Nature is a Heraclitean Fire and of the comfort of the Resurrection," in *Poems of Gerald Manley Hopkins,* 67.

23. Sigmund Freud, *The Origins of Psycho-Analysis: Letters to Wilhelm Fliess: Drafts and Notes: 1887–1902,* ed. M. Bonaparte et al., trans. E. Mosbacher and J. Strachey (New York: Basic Books, 1954), 240.

stripped of all presiding presences. History was bunk. History is shit. Our Freud yields nothing to Our Ford and Our third world cowards, who need no bravery, here and now, in their assaults upon Our historical Father.

Whatever the shatterings Hopkins felt threatened his and other sacred selves, perhaps precisely because of that threat, he composed the greatest passage on the God-relation of identity since Galatians 2:20. Despair shatters itself against the hard truth of Hopkins's sense of identity.

> I am all at once what Christ is, since he was what I am, and
> This, Jack, joke, poor potsherd, patch, matchwood, immortal
> diamond,
>> Is immortal diamond.[24]

Whatever the Jack, joke, mortal trash of our lives may be, our predicative relational identity, *Not-I/I*, supplies the resistant hardness of sacred self Hopkins blazons in every one's honor, each *Not-I/I* an "immortal diamond." When I read Hopkins, as when I hear a Bach Mass, I am an honorary Christian. The aesthetics of truth form alliances, profoundly elective affinities, that the intellect stripped of that feeling inclines to reject. That rejection has been a tragedy for all second world symbolists. Intellection must address the matter of its feeling. So addressed, we can see even as we can smell that there is something dishonorable, even for so greatly daring a post-Jew as Freud, in flushing away that diamond in *Dreck*.

18. *The aesthetics of half affinities. Late second/early third* culture people do greatly love certain facets that they apprehend along the fracture lines of immortal diamonds. *Dreck* becomes something else again, miraculously transubstantiated for bagel-and-lox Jews, or incense- and Mass-loving Catholics, or literary Episcopalians who love the language of *The Book of Common Prayer* and think nothing of what the language delivers. Precisely those identities drowned in *Dreck*, or in its more pleasant transubstantiations, are revealed in the fight for identity against the disarming force of

24. Hopkins, "That Nature is a Heraclitean Fire," 67.

abolitionist/abortionist movements, with their disarmingly fictive role models and other seductive theatricalities. *Dreck* has never smelt sweeter than in its socio-dramaturgic recyclings. Those recyclings are as deadly as they are untrue. The formal and uniting purpose of all abolitionist/abortionist movements may be described as the supersession of identity/truth by turning its first term of conception, that term in which identity exists most purely in its God-relation, into *mortal/trash*.

19. *Abortus/Abort.* In that same letter on *Dreck* to Fliess, Freud executes a sentence that would quench the "clearest-selvèd spark, Man,"[25] in all biological beginnings that mark mind-mindedness in identity. We live as we are minded. In that unfathomable drowned, we read Freud's death sentence, casually uttered, upon sacred self: "Similarly birth, miscarriage, and menstruation are all connected with the lavatory *via* the word Abort (Abortus)."[26] How many things turn before my eyes into images of our flush-away third world. Over a century after Freud's sentencing of all who defecate to the world stink, I see an odorless flush-away world indifferent to life conceived in its identity, unprecedented and unrepeatable as it is. *Flash/flush.* The transition from identity, in its passionate life difference, to the indifference of the abolitionist movement, in all its excusing cleverities and comic pathos, can be read in the implication of expurgation composed by the memoirist who proceeds so easily in what follows. The first sentence is a killer:

> The procedure itself was the easiest part. A friend had told me to close my eyes and think about anything, think about Donald Duck—. . . .I had a three-day affair with a friend, I'm broke and unemployed, I can't give a baby up for adoption, I can't afford to be pregnant while I look for a job. In counseling, I was asked why I'd gone off the pill, and I didn't hesitate to respond, "I can get rid of an accidental pregnancy.". . . then liquid Valium injected directly into my left arm made everything feel like it was taking place on another planet. . . . I remember that the Valium

25. Ibid.
26. Letter to Wilhelm Fliess, December 22, 1897, in Freud, *Origins of Psycho-Analysis: Letters to Fliess*, 240.

made me want to laugh . . . this little operation . . . would only take five minutes. I remember that it hurt and that I was amazed at how empty, relieved, and not pregnant I felt as soon as it was over.[27]

Here, in this little *operation/deathwork*, is the image of that horror of choosing, for her wholly other, that he or she—not her—is not and never to be. Despite near laughter, this five-minute death-work cannot avoid giving the reader a sense of the reversal of Hopkins's imperative and yet a mocking sense in that same direction.

> Away grief's grasping, joyless days, dejection.
> Across my foundering deck shone
> A beacon, an eternal beam. Flash fade, and mortal trash
> Fall to the residuary worm;[28]

That fall, softened by liquid Valium, transubstantiates into our third world decision for ever so many little *operation/deathworks*. Even so. We are not yet completely and cleanly rid of that un-wanted yet given identity, inward and spiritually itself alone and none other even as it is de-created into nothing; worse than noth-ing—stinking of its incredibly early mortality.[29] The job easily done, this anti-mother speaks as if she were singing the virginal fat girl's world song. "Twenty-seven years old and pregnant for the first time in my life. God bless America, I thought, I sure as hell want a cheap, legal, safe abortion."[30] God bless. God curse. Here and now is much of a profane muchness in our third world sacri-fices—cheap, legal, safe as hell—of the more-than-something to the less-than-nothing.[31]

---

27. Deborah Salazar, "My Abortion," *Harper's Magazine*, April 1990, 32–33.
28. Hopkins, "That Nature is a Heraclitean Fire," 67.
29. See Nietzsche, *The Gay Science*, 182: "Do we smell nothing as yet of the divine decomposition?"
30. Salazar, "My Abortion," 33.
31. See Friedrich Nietzsche, "What Is Religious?" in *Beyond Good and Evil*, pt. 3, secs. 45–62, 59–76. The abortionist movement does bear comparison to the Shoah. In these historic cases, both Jews and 'fetuses' are what they repre-sent, symbols of our second world God. It is as godterms that they are being sac-rificed.

20. *The horror of the unremembered life.* The horror is not alone of identity ended; rather, of identity unremembered. In second worlds, there is Kaddish, there are Masses for the dead. Cultures are constituted by the union of the living and the dead in rituals of living memory. Never before, in our late second world, has the authority of the past been sacrificed with a more conscious effort of forgetfulness. Forgetfulness is now the curricular form of our higher education. This form guarantees that we, of the transition from second to third worlds, will become the first barbarians. Barbarism is not an expression of simple technologies or of mysterious taboos; at least there were taboos and, moreover, in all first worlds, the immense authority of the past. By contrast, the coming barbarism, much of it here and now, not least to be found among our most cultivated classes, is our ruthless forgetting of the authority of the past. Sacred history, which never repeats itself, is thus profaned in an unprecedented way by transgression so deep that it is unacknowledged. The transgression of forgetfulness makes the cruelty of abortion absolutely sacrilegious; more precisely, antireligious. According to the unspoken doxology of our *abolitionist/abortionist* movements, identities are to be flushed as away far down the memory hole as our flush-away technologies of repression permit.

Third world activists are absentminded in the repressive mode and yet deliberately expressive in the cleverities of their deceit round the phrase "pro-choice." The freedom to commit transgressive acts was never denied by our second world guiding elites. By their fictions of unfreedom, third world elites engage themselves to a deodorized death *cultus*, protected by unauthorized self-inventions which constitute a doxa of rights proclaiming the endless supersession of identities by roles. Roles are functions of multiple social selves that pretend to no sacred self, unitary and itself alone with its invisible god-relation there to be read by the mind's eye through every shift and shuffle of life. Claudius, transgressive king of rotten Denmark, had it all wrong when he remarked, "There is no shuffling." That famous prayer is itself infamously idealistic about our lives in sacred order, idealism balanced by the realism of this politicians' knowledge that "the wicked prize itself / Buys out the law." *There* is nothing but shuf-fling. The shuffling cannot be abolished, "Even to the teeth and forehead of our faults, / To give in evidence."[32] In "teeth," Shake-speare's image of aggression, in "forehead," Shakespeare's image of intellectual cleverity, the human, being the creature next in identity to the creator himself, lives the life of his imagination and fancy in restless movements toward negational signs of the posi-tive permanence in every act of his changing life.

21. *Illustrations of third world creative destructions.* For my pur-poses as a sociologist of culture, Joyce is the greatest artist of deathworks, though Picasso must be a candidate for that title, even if none other is considered than his collective abstract por-trait of the world woman, *Les Demoiselles d'Avignon.* The founding transgressive image of modern art can be seen in figure 19, Pi-casso's deathwork of 1907. Here is a great third world image of regression, ritualized, most obviously by the dog-faced defecating woman, facing both ways, in the lower right-hand corner of the picture. Picasso's regressive figures are *world women,* who pull aside the veil of second world illusion so as to reveal—nothing. That nothing is the most refined version of third world primacies of possibility. However catastrophic their regression from full hu-manity, the compensating mythic implication is that they are god-terms. Picasso hopes to disarm Christian images of the world woman, the mother of the second person of highest authority, in his images of the world woman as a threatening transgressor.

Picasso's picture is a crucial third world work of art. In this brothel on the rue d'Avignon, either/or yields to both/and. The figures may be rightly read as both lying down and standing up. Which? Consummate your own decision. Consummate both, if you feel rich enough in experience to have it both ways. Picasso so painted the picture that the viewer may see them both lying down and standing up. Genius knows how to exploit what seems to be but is not. Those figures are hieratic in their naked promiscuity. Promiscuity is the inverse of fidelity.

Another image entry of inversion follows. It is titled *Fountain*

32. *Hamlet,* 3.3.67–68.

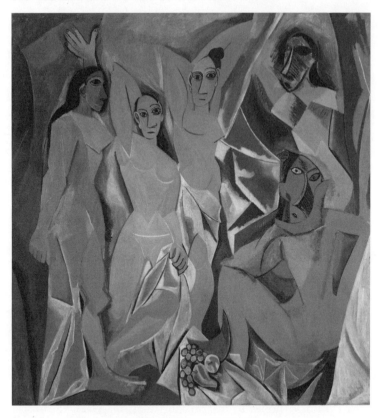

FIGURE 19. *Les Demoiselles d'Avignon*, Pablo Picasso, 1907

(© 2004 Estate of Pablo Picasso/Artists Rights Society [ARS], New York; Digital image © The Museum of Modern Art/Licensed by SCALA/Art Resource, NY)

(see fig. 20). But this is no fountain. It is a urinal. This is the first great *Ready-made*. It was signed "R. Mutt, 1917." Duchamp called it *Fountain* and said there is nothing immoral about it. It is patently, however, an inversion. Since when do you drink out of a urinal? When you level the sacred order of authority, you can make a urinal a fountain. It is both urinal and fountain. By the power invested in Marcel Duchamp, urinal becomes fountain even as it remains urinal. Why not? An anartist can say yes to both urinal and fountain exactly as he can say no to highest authority. The old anarchist slogan "No God, no master" holds. The irrationalizing rationalist answer to *shalt not/wilt not* is "Why not?" Duchamp asks "Why not?" of both urinal and fountain. That question unanswerable, all men may hope to be free at last to ride their hobbyhorses nowhere.

Duchamp's greatest deathwork, *Etant donnés* (Being given), on which he worked secretly for the last twenty years of his life, mocks sacred order. Two peepholes of a heavy door invite the eyes to see what is not to be seen, beyond a jagged hole in a brick wall (see fig. 21). A few feet away, our second world, represented as what it is not—a naked and mutilated dead woman—has been sacrificed to the energy of the next world. That next, third, world is represented by a faintly glowing gas lamp held as a vertical of light in her raised left hand. Here is the *world woman* in a condition of rigor mortis—all in a brilliantly lit landscape of which the only moving part is an image of primordial energy going ever downward toward the depth of power: a waterfall (see fig. 22). This is the energy of the fall, the new world of life after its creating death. Never has a deathwork been so easily seen through as this energizing death of *Being*, so far as it is *given*.

The three chief images in this deathly still montage—naked

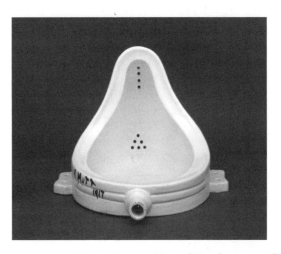

FIGURE 20. *Fountain 1917*, Marcel Duchamp, replica 1964

(Tate Gallery, London/Art Resource, NY; © 2004 Artists Rights Society [ARS], New York/ADAGP, Paris/Succession Marcel Duchamp)

FIGURE 21. *Étant donnés: 1ᵉ La chute d'eau, 2ᵉ Le gaz d'éclairage*
(*Given: 1. The Waterfall, 2. The Illuminating Gas*), Exterior, Marcel
Duchamp, 1946–66

(Philadelphia Museum of Art, gift of the Cassandra Foundation; © 2004
Artists Rights Society [ARS], New York/ADAGP, Paris/Succession Marcel
Duchamp)

woman, gaslight, and waterfall—are not of life's flow but of a
mortal struggle over the very form of existence. There is a fourth
figure, conspicuous in his absence, the artist himself, the dead
creator of this transparently deadly work of art, which, however
lightly we begin to look into it, ends in our complicity in its being
an abomination of darkest desolation brilliantly lit. This fictive
technological light and plastic green landscape are the abomination of the desolation conceiving our third world in a work of art.
In its own cleverity, this tableau is terrible as a proleptic pleasantry
of which the inartistic version is the death camps.

Duchamp creates destruction. Modernity is devoted to creative destructions. Life is a temporary disturbance of that which

modernity is most at pains to deny: death, which is modernity's one-syllable curse word for eternity. The leading image motif of creative destruction was constructed as his secret deathwork by Duchamp. *Etant donnés* may be read as a revealing parallel of Freud's 'death instinct'. Here is no abstract evocation of endless non-being. There is a violation of the temple of God, the body, in Duchamp's construct. From this destruction derives *being*.

FIGURE 22. *Etant donnés: 1ᵉ La chute d'eau, 2ᵉ Le gaz d'éclairage (Given: 1. The Waterfall, 2. The Illuminating Gas)*, Interior, Marcel Duchamp, 1946–66

(Philadelphia Museum of Art, gift of the Cassandra Foundation; © 2004 Artists Rights Society [ARS], New York/ADAGP, Paris/Succession Marcel Duchamp)

22. *The embassy of death.* If what is *Being given* can be seen through those two peepholes in the door at the end of a monastic room in the Philadelphia Museum of Art, then, with equal reverence, we may speak of an elegant murder or a beautiful ulcer. 'Elegant' murder. 'Beautiful' ulcer. These are words reserved to the aesthetic life. Thomas De Quincey's "On Murder Considered as One of the Fine Arts," written in 1827, gave for the first time, from German, the word "aesthetic." De Quincey affects to be giving the "Williams Lecture." "Williams" honors a famous murderer. De Quincey compares Williams favorably with Aeschylus, Milton, and Michelangelo. Like those peers, Williams "carried his art to a point of colossal sublimity." He was a genius; moreover, "all the Cains were men of genius."[33]

Wilde followed De Quincey by honoring a famous killer with an essay on the artistry of murder. Thomas Griffiths Wainwright received the honor of a brief memoir titled, "Pen, Pencil and Poison." Wainwright was not merely a less than mediocre poet, a painter, an art critic, and a forger, but also a "subtle and secret poisoner almost without rival in this or any age." Moreover, Wainwright got away with more murders than were ever made known judicially. 'Getting away with something' is the key to the criminal ethic. Wilde notes that he was a man of supreme and catholic artifice. His criminal artifice, poisoning, quickened some "hideous sense of power" in Wainwright, Wilde speculates. Genius means artifice in the highest and lowest. A genius is the true prince of liars. As Wilde put it, "A mask tells us more than a face."[34]

Junior maskers' indifference to the highest in authority may be judged by senior maskers of that same indifference verging on hostility, if not genius. Not so long ago, in 1984, in an America perhaps not so distant from Orwell's imaginings of that year, one Judge Altman presided over the murder pretrial proceedings that had already consumed two years while two young killers were given the usual psychiatric tests. The prosecutor, one Greenbaum,

33. Thomas De Quincey, "On Murder Considered as One of the Fine Arts," in *Selected Writings of Thomas De Quincey*, ed. P. Van Doren Stern (New York: Random House, 1937), 987–88.

34. Oscar Wilde, "Pen, Pencil and Poison," in *The Soul of Man under Socialism*, 73–79.

requested that the trial begin. To this request, Judge Altman responded as follows:

> This is only a murder, Mr. Greenbaum, and I have heard it over, and over, and over again. Only a murder, and we are talking about an 18-year old.[35]

Only a murder. This is *adiaphora* recycled as boredom. The cure for boredom was prescribed on the side of the Ponte Vecchio in Florence. There was a huge graffito, letters high as the bridge itself: *E VIETATO VIETARE* (*It is forbidden to forbid*). Such an interdict upon interdicts would teach a counterdiscipline of endlessly new responses. Plato teaches in his *Republic*, "for any musical innovation is full of danger to the whole State."[36] And not merely the fundamental laws of the state. Where it is forbidden to forbid, there is the primacy of possibility. Then *Being, given*, could be at once transgressive and creative.

Less hostile to the received faith in authority, which denies creation through destruction, is the image in figure 23, Holbein's *The Ambassadors*. These ambassadors are princes of Church and State. Between them are the emblems of human achievement in science and art. Yet there, in the foreground without their knowing it, is an anamorphic image. That image represents a great skull. The skull, so distorted that it means nothing unless eyed awry, is an image of human vanity in its own proud achievements. These princes of authority and power cannot—will not—see the vanity of both. The truth is that the creations of both authority and power, in the arts and sciences as in politics, will be destroyed. Where is that authority which conquers death? Nowhere in this great image. This is a picture in the pagan, first world tradition of fate, not faith.

Anamorphic imagery is best summarized by quoting Bushy's gloss on it to the Queen in *Richard II*, when she tells him of the perturbations of her "inward soul" where "nothing trembles."

35. Quoted in A. R. Kaminsky, *The Victim's Song* (Buffalo, NY: Prometheus Books, 1985), 63.

36. Plato, *The Republic*, trans. B. Jowett (New York: Vintage, 1966), 424c, p. 151.

FIGURE 23. *The Ambassadors*, Hans Holbein the Younger
(Alinari/Art Resource, NY)

Bushy exposits the meaning of that trembling negational sense
that dominates the Queen's sensibility:

> For sorrow's eye, glazed with blinding tears,
> Divides one thing entire to many objects,
> Like perspectives, which rightly gazed upon,
> Show nothing but confusion; eyed awry
> Distinguish form. So your sweet Majesty,
> Looking awry upon your lord's departure,
> Find shapes of grief more than himself to wail,
> Which, looked on as it is, is naught but shadows
> Of what it is not.[37]

37. *Richard II* (Folger), 2.217–25.

In the vanitas image of the ambassadors, their real embassy is unknown to them: that embassy of death of which Hamlet is our permanent cultural attaché. Death needs fewer culture attachés and more clergy in attendance to it. Clergies sign their own death warrants when they surrender their prerogatives over the meaning of death and the practices of interment and commemoration. We students of the anti-culture can find no image yet with which to capture the meaning of death; no more than have the Jews an image for their Shoah, which was not to God but for The Nothing.

Against the embassy of death, are there really, as I think, too many would-be ambassadors of life immortal and nothing sacred about it? I draw my first and briefest account of the new ambassadorial elite proposing an immortal nothingness from remarks made by Dr. C. J. Schramm, former department chair of hospital finance and management, The Johns Hopkins Hospital. He declares: "I think we can beat this thing called death."[38] The one difficulty Professor Schramm sees is that "we don't know how to pay for [beating this thing called death] and we don't know how not to pay for everybody who wants to join the fight" to beat death. I should add that Dr. John Rowe, who founded the Division on Aging at the Harvard Medical School, remarks, further, that "the question of rationing [immortality] has been in the closet too long. . . . Cost has to be a factor. We have to avoid misallocation of high technologies to individuals [presumably not so worthy of immortality] who have no likelihood of benefiting from them."[39]

Here I hear echoes of the Nazi doctrine of a life "unworthy of life"; rather, worthy of the expert applications made by a Nazi euthanasia expert, Christian Wirth. There was something deadly hospitable about Christian Wirth. He first practiced his hospitable techniques of euthanasia in German hospitals upon hopelessly ill and handicapped Germans, then opened a wider practice upon Jews, defectives, and other lives "unworthy of life." Prince-Bishop Galen preached against this practice, especially upon

38. *New York Times*, January 18, 1985, B2.
39. Ibid.

gravely wounded German soldiers, and this preaching helped lead to the one successful public protest in Nazi Germany against the policies of the regime. Then, ever following the 'Leader's Wish', in this case the wish for the murder of all Jews, Wirth and other experts in mass killing without mercy transferred their highly trained technical expertise and manically systematic energies of execution to the Final Solution practiced in Auschwitz and the like.

Auschwitz and the like are, I suggest, proleptic institutionalizations of that fatal raising, in science as in art, of the primacy of possibility of an immortality to be granted to all except those specially chosen by a transgressive elite, who have captured absolute power, for mortality—all or none seems an impossibly democratic polarity. The last interdict abolished, even for those lucky some who would be chosen for immortality, there is nothing to stop the total triumph of an endlessly therapeutic anti-culture and thus encourage changes of policy in selection by the all-powerful of the third culture.

What are the aims of the winning anti-culture, so far as these can be discerned so far in advance of its total victory? For an answering statement of those aims, I quote a question asked by the Donner Professor of Science in the Department of Computer Science and Electrical Engineering at MIT and the founder of MIT's Artificial Intelligence Laboratories:

> Should we robotize ourselves and stop dying? I think the answer is clear for the long run because in a few billion years the sun will eventually burn out and everything we've done will go to waste.[40]

Facing this waste, in a few billion years, the scientific mind asks: "How long will we be satisfied with the meager span of years our bodies last? What if we could achieve a kind of near-immortality by using robotics, and live healthfully and comfortably for, say, 10,000 years?" The Donner Professor was no wit. The question is solemn as the death of the spirit in the life of the body: "Is

40. Marvin Minsky, "Our Roboticized Future," in *Robotics: The First Authoritative Report from the Ultimate High-Tech Frontier,* ed. Minsky (New York: Omni Press, 1985), 287.

it possible, with artificial intelligence, to conquer death?" Yes, for
an answer: by techniques already in place—organ transplants, for
example.

Not a scientist, I ask: are not organ transplants a little like the
chop-shop industry? When a car is stolen, it can be dismantled in
seconds, and its vital parts transplanted to dying cars. Chop-shop
organ technology promises immortality. Of course, every solution creates new problems. At least let there be no caviling about
the problem of cost. The cost of achieving the primary possibility
must be the highest imaginable, to show respect for the ultimate
benefit. The Donner Professor continues:

> The first nylon stocking cost millions, too, if one adds up all the
> research that went into it. . . . In similar wise, we can extend the
> span of useful life by maintaining the body and replacing parts as
> they wear out—the bionic man approach. . . . What would hap-
> pen if immortality became possible? Then eventually there'd be
> no room for more new people, and that would raise more prob-
> lems.[41]

Who will care to join the unbenefited? His answer: "Of course,
you would damn well start caring once you get the chance to live
a billion years." How, then, to select for the two categories? Let
'caring' itself serve as the principle of selection. "We are all on
earth to help others. What I can't figure out is what the others are
here for." But humans are here to be here. Being here requires others not to be. "Once we start making ourselves, we'll really have
to face ourselves in an entirely new way."[42] That new way is in seeing, without shutting an eye, that making ourselves requires un-
making others. Once life as creative destruction is realized, the
highest life is lived through the taking of life. The last interdict becomes the first transgression, about which nothing need be or
should be said.

In death, nothing means everything. To everything, Hamlet's
last words apply: "The rest is silence."[43] With those last words,

41. Ibid., 303.
42. Ibid.
43. *Hamlet*, 5.2.385.

Hamlet paid the only respect possible to the fact that neither he nor anyone else belonged to sacred order. His liberal, high-minded anxiety against closure, too often misread as mere indecision, became his fate; and his celebrated half madness expresses the modern anxiety about the closure of belonging in, and to, sacred order. Hamlet's not-belonging makes more sense said in German: *Zu zein oder nicht zu zein. Zein* has two meanings: being and belonging in, and to, the order of life under the highest authority. Not-to-be is not to belong in, and to, sacred order. Instead, Hamlet became a master-actor, in love with his fate, a Nietzsche ahead of nihilism. Here I have given the briefest version I know of that aesthetics of authority which begins in not choosing not to be. That choice, too, requires respectful silence before the horror of what can and has been done, as in the silence of Christ before Dostoyevsky's Grand Inquisitor; and as in "there was silence in heaven" at the opening of the seventh seal (Revelation 8:1).

23. *The indifference of the artist: The case of Duchamp.* What can be read with the transgressive motifs that are boringly obvious in the titles and transparent contents of Duchamp's two greatest deathworks, *Etant donnés* (Being given) and *The Bride Stripped Bare by Her Bachelors, Even* (*The Large Glass*) (see fig. 24) is the supreme indifference of the artist to the meaning of these contents. Duchamp challenges the real world of sacred order precisely by engaging us in readings that cannot but be complicities in the transgressive realities treated in both of his great deathworks. One includes the simplest transparency of a glass, which is a remarkably enduring substance that must be fired at a very high temperature, but which can be shattered at a touch in the wrong manner, as it were, indecorous to it; and the other in which *Being* itself—the ontological condition—is transgressive in its energies. For without the transgression, *Being* would not be *given*.

Here we see clearly enough: a theorist of transgressive reality, a fun gnostic constructing his own alternative version of reality, which is not an alternative but more or less what the elites of third culture themselves may be said to believe, if their beliefs were not unbeliefs. Rather, their unbeliefs are mythic, scientific, and pseudoscientific systems that bring the tools of chance, of humor, of mendacity and irony, and of indifference into play. Play is the operative term in order to understand any of the other qualities of playing at life beyond sacred order, the vertical in authority, in a deadly way. Of course, as the Duchamp experts remark, his anti-

FIGURE 24. *The Bride Stripped Bare by Her Bachelors, Even* (*The Large Glass*), Marcel Duchamp, 1915–23

(Philadelphia Museum of Art, bequest of Katherine S. Dreier; © 2004 Artists Rights Society [ARS], New York/ADAGP, Paris/Succession Marcel Duchamp)

system is intrinsically anything but absolute: density oscillates, metals are *neighboring,* color is *provisional,* and exact measurements are determined by the chance fall of a length of thread.[44]

Here is what can easily be called rightly a repressive capricious metareality in which there are myriad aspects to any *given.* Here Duchamp is completely and supremely in the fictive, and therefore analytic/repressive, mode of third culture, that repressive mode in which "nothing is but what is not." It is in this manner that readings themselves become repressive, for as it is rightly said, everything can be read at least two ways at once. In the Duchampian manner, the Duchamp experts ask their own repressive question as if it were a paradox: when is a door not a door? "When it's a Duchamp."[45] When is an anartist yet another artist? When he pretends to have abandoned art or otherwise transformed it. Duchamp has not transformed art. He has simply seen it to its logically mendacious conclusion in a world in which truth must be aniconic, unless one learns not only how to read but how to obey the interdicts and live in subserving remissions with a good heart.

24. *The naked truth.* No great mythic motif exists in the present encounter between female and male. We have long since become far too conscientious in flagging mythic motifs for there to be a sexuality among the sophisticated in art, inseparable from the negation of what sexuality represents in art. It represents precisely that negation which makes nonsense of speculations on the relationship between mind and matter as if they were mindful of gender as such. As a fiction, the bride is no more female, except in our consciousness of Duchamp's mythic construction of female, than the bachelors are male. Equally, the mutilated torso on the ground of *Etant donnés* is not mother earth cultivated by a technology of violence that produces creative energy. It is what it appears to be, a mock-up of a woman's body that may well represent the transgression of mutilation. Moreover, it is not buried, and the fiction is most apparent when it concentrates on the inherently sacrile-

44. *Bulletin of the Philadelphia Museum of Art,* 1987, 16.
45. Ibid.

gious fancy that such a mutilated body could hold up a lamp. The very image is sinister.

To call these two image entries, to honor them by the title, 'poetic' is to suggest that there is no morality attached to art in sacred order to which we need be anything other than studiously indifferent. It is the indifference disguised by the respect for Duchamp's poetic aptness that makes us understand what it means to be a reverent viewer of such works rather than less reverent or indeed irreverent; for what transgression, however artful, deserves reverence? Better no image than a transgressive one. It follows that we may read both of these image entries as far from intangible in their meaning. The meaning is quite tangible. They are images of a far from invisible fourth or nondimension, the celebrated apparition of an appearance that characterizes both of these deathworks of Duchamp. The light from within and the mysterious generative forces playing beneath the surface (water, gas, electricity) are quite readably tangible motifs of the fictive *pop* of desire. This is the leitmotif of the third culture in its indifference to all verticals in authority in first and second cultures preceding it.

The Bride Stripped Bare by Her Bachelors, Even (*The Large Glass*) and *Etant donnés* suggest, from the perspective of second culture criticism, that the soul is there only to be seen through and, therefore, negated. The alternative offered in both images is of a construct. Duchamp understood this very well when he thought of making *The Large Glass* in papier-mâché. In second culture, body cannot be separated from soul. There is nothing in these great third culture images except the entry into myth and the negation of everything in life except transgressions. Therefore, the essential bridal act is against her, a stripping. In the other image, *Being* is *given* as a dead torso. It is nothing. Life has ended, and technology alone has begun. These mechanomorphic images are of life without soul, which is where third culture is taking us. There is no life in *The Large Glass*. It was fired from molten sand with a leaded mixture, not even from earth. Life may be seen here in another image of negation of life itself in Manzoni's image entry (see fig. 25) titled *Artist's Shit, no. 31*. Everything for a third culture theorist turns to *Dreck*, as Freud noted early in his mission as a third

FIGURE 25. *Artist's Shit, no. 31*, Piero Manzoni, 1961
(Réunion des Musées Nationaux/Art Resource, NY; © 2004
Artists Rights Society [ARS], New York/SIAE, Rome)

culture sage. Not the mightiest touch, but the killing one, is what characterizes the touch of third culture.

Both *The Bride Stripped Bare* and *Etant donnés* are sacrifice images of both life and soul together. Yet without an authority that requires these sacrifices, both can be understood as the truth of third culture in what Nietzsche called the third sacrifice; the sacrifice to The Nothing. Neither image has soul force in the *given*. Force or power has been transferred to technology. The female torso is a sacrificed soul force. She is nothing, not even her sex is alive. It has been transferred to the energy of the light.

In first and second cultures, there were perhaps excessive celebrations of being a bride, with gifts, celebrations, ceremonies, and holidays. In third culture, we can see a catastrophic devaluation of being a bride, as being a bride is seen through in the *Bride Stripped Bare* by those who will never be her husband and at her command.

Thus marriage and murder are trivialized in third culture. The naked truth is that the world of action, so exercised through the intellect as Duchamp would have it, brings us into a world in which the idolatry of intelligence has killed both the body and the soul. For the body does not live meaningfully without the soul, and the soul cannot be disembodied. This intellectualization of both body and soul as we see it in both great Duchamp images has been a catastrophe for Western humanism. Here we see the sheer fanaticism of insisting on the intellect totally emancipated from its identity with the soul. These are certainly cultural artifacts, but they are third cultural artifacts that have put the inwardness that is necessary to life, that is ineliminable from both soul and body together, aside.

25. *Both body and soul.* We have already begun to get arguments for cultures that are murderous, and we see this murderous quality in 'quality of life' arguments as they are now being made in favor of euthanasia and a variety of other ways of denying both body and soul as superior to and autonomous from culture. The whole idea developed during the Nazi period (by scientists both biological and social) of a "life unworthy of life" is a part of the third culture understanding of the naked truth. Life has to be submitted to a quality that makes it more and more difficult to justify life. For all life in the flesh is weak and perishable and, therefore, in the soul is weak and perishable. That weakness, that perishability, is now understood as the best reason for destroying life rather than living it through obedience to the commanding truths that can protect this very weakness and perishability until death occurs when the soul is deprived of life.

Wherever there is body, there is soul, and therefore life. If we return to the second culture understanding, then both abortion and euthanasia would be seen in their true transgressive meaning. Death cannot strike at anybody or any part of the soul without striking at its entirety. The entire relation between life and culture as the support of all life has been subverted by the theory of third culture as we see it in these great image entries by Duchamp. These two women of Duchamp's great image entries into third culture signal that they have no inwardness. There is no form of compresence in which we can relate ourselves to them. The inwardness that we know we inhabit, each of us in our otherwise incommunicable individuality, is hidden even from mere compresence. It needs a body.

Second culture members understood this about themselves. That is what allowed them and encouraged them to feel, as well as know, that there was an inwardness like that of each of them, an *I* like their own, that was and is their creator. That being there, however it has its being there, also has its body, however the Greeks deny it by rendering that being there strictly an idea. We can see that being there in every detail of life somewhere in the vertical of authority. We know that we cannot be simultaneously here and there, or else we could see every other body as we see our own. That body in that inwardness is the soul. That other being there is no projection of our own inwardness of body which is the same as soul. The *I* remains an *I* and the *Thou* remains a *Thou*. The two will not merge. Sexuality is not a merging of *I* and *thou* nor is the doctrine of the one flesh, other than as a prescription for the death of one or the other, or both.

The bride, like the torso in the grass of *Etant donnés*, is abstract, unreal. It is not a resistance. A resistance is created in these works only by the door, the façade, and the peculiar characteristics of glass through which we can look so to see that it is not a resistance. The remarkable thing about any *Thou* or any *I* is its resistance, its heterogeneity. This heterogeneity, or individuality, is irreducible unless each is reduced to an abstraction, as the torso has become an abstraction from every particular woman and therefore no woman. It is merely the feminine. The showing of the sexually discriminable parts is to suggest the abstraction or reduction into the feminine, as is the pseudomythological language that is provided to explain what really mystifies the *Bride Stripped Bare*. That is the case in which there is no service to truth, in which the nakedness itself is mythic, that is, mendacious. Body and soul cannot be separated. There is no transposition of any masculine *I* into feminine or the reverse. The whole language of homosexuality is a form fusion mythology that reduces the irreducible and must be a form of destruction through mendacity. Every being in either its *hereness* or *thereness* is a mode of resistance and completely different from myself. Any effort to reduce that difference, or equalize it, is oppressive and false. But we have sacrificed the clear and distinct *Being* there to a fiction of equality and of community that cannot obtain in reality.

What we can obtain in reality is a covenant, an agreement to observe the clearest and most distinct ideas of all, the only truly clear and distinct ideas, the commanding truths of revelation that can guide our conduct together. That covenant of togetherness is the only alternative to the loss of blood that is the hidden argument of all efforts toward the death of God, which is itself the predicate immediately of the death of man. These image entries created by Duchamp are into an unreal world of the abstract, of the generality for whom these images are caviar. But that generality is a fiction imposed on those irreducible identities destroyed in the reduction. As soon as we abstract the self from others that are resisters, we destroy the very reality of the self that is resisted and turn it into a fiction. There is no self, no soul, that isn't either male or female.

This particular *Etant donnés* with its female torso is superior to the *Bride*, who is too unlike a woman in her representation. That both are being sacrificed is the clearest indication that both are women, for most of the figures of sacrifice that we know in the history of culture are women. That both are being sacrificed is itself the key to understanding that the lesson we are to learn, the message we are to receive, is that reality is at its base transgressive. The transgression is against the female body in both image entries, and compresently the transgressor in both image entries is a male. Despite his addiction to mythologizing, Duchamp cannot disguise the fact that he must discover that, in the body, and indeed in their sexuality, the inwardness, or souls, of both are feminine. Both are women. That is unmistakable. Sexuality is not a generality; it must always be a gender. The Christian version of the second culture is wrong in declaring that women, as human beings, are somehow exactly the same and equal, so long as the feminine body differs so considerably from the masculine. So, the feminine soul must differ so considerably from the masculine. Bodies and souls cannot be fused across the sex lines. Inwardness will not be separated from outwardness. Bisexuality is as powerful a perversion and rebellion against reality and its commanding truths of resistance as is homosexuality. For love in the sexual mode must be across the sexes in order to be true.

26. *Appendix G.* Appendix G of Freud's deathwork *Moses and Monotheism* contains a curious passage on *historical truth* and *eternal truth.* The italics are Freud's. His emphasis on the historical in truth describes the dynamics of transference from second world historical truth, as the eternal acting in our history, to a therapeutic resolution of that action into ficta. Such therapeutic resolutions have no more supersessive canonicity than any other art-

FIGURE 26. *Self-Portrait,* Robert Mapplethorpe, 1988
(© The Estate of Robert Mapplethorpe)

work. Duchamp does not supersede Michelangelo. Those terribly distant and mortal rivals—Michelangelo's mother of God fused into her son and Duchamp's mutilated *world/woman*—represent what they are not: the dream of defeat eroticized in the female gender.

27. *The first and final fight.* Appendix G represents Freud's version of the first and final fights against eternal truth in history. Against such immutable truth, mutably observed, the word/life of our second world, Freud wrote what he himself called a historical novel. In their continual feeding upon novelty, making fresh occasions for renewing the old fight, repressions of revelation begin in private flight from eternal truth. It is the cleverity of repression to gather momentum as public readings of private meanings: the flight from eternal truth recycled as therapeutic truth.

28. *The not-I.* In sum, there are two kinds of deathworks in the world of art and the social sciences. One asserts the presiding presence of the *not-I* and addresses the *not-I*. By contrast, third culture deathworks such as this Mapplethorpe Kurtz image (see fig. 26) assert the ineliminable doctrine of third cultures: that there is only the I, however extended into forms of social and political authority and then receded back into the I. This is Durkheimian theory of all god-terms as collective representations of the self in efforts to avoid suicidal conflict. Gertrude's *Nothing but ourselves* is a great harbinger of third culture in the struggle between the I and the *not-I* which second culture theorists knew occurred from the beginning. The story of Adam and Eve is precisely of that order.

29. *Lifeworks/lifewords.* Choose life (Deuteronomy 30:20).

FOUR

Birth Year of the Third Culture
and Freud's Repression of Revelation

1. *Birth year of the third culture.* Any number of birth dates can be found for the third culture. What the apostle James calls the "Wheel of birth" (James 3:6) is that wheel of fire of coming into existence, of becoming, to which the members of the third culture are bound surely as Lear was bound to his wheel. Whether the wheel is turning up or down is a question that divides observers of the wheel. I think that the wheel is turning down. The question is when it began to turn down so that the earth has become again without form and void, in the original Hebrew: *tohu va bohu.* It is the distinct teaching of the history of the third culture that the wheel has turned down into an emptiness that is terrifying in the transgressions that take place within the emptiness.

How the date of birth of this third culture becoming an anti-culture, without form and void, can be established is not difficult. Some poetic commentators locate the annus mirabilis as late as 1963.[1]

> Sexual intercourse began
> in nineteen sixty-three
> (Which was rather late for me)—
> Between the end of the *Chatterley* ban
> And the Beatles' first LP.
>
> Up till then there'd only been
> A sort of bargaining,
> A wrangle for a ring,

---

1. Philip Larkin, "Annus Mirabilis," in *High Windows* (London: Faber and Faber, 1974), 34.

A shame that started at sixteen
And spread to everything.

Then all at once the quarrel sank:
Everyone felt the same,
And every life became
A brilliant breaking of the bank,
A quite unlosable game.

So life was never better than
In nineteen sixty-three
(Though just too late for me)—
Between the end of the *Chatterley* ban
And the Beatles' first LP.

Other men of poetic words have found earlier dates than Larkin's for the birth of the third culture. Trotsky proclaimed the slogan of permanent revolution in 1905. With that proclamation he became the wandering post-Jew militant, the Party, not Torah, the home that would kill him.

2. *The present form of order.* I have said that there are three cultures in which we live simultaneously and individually; therefore not equally. The third culture is predominant. The third culture does not begin in a historical event. Rather, it is a disposition in the guiding elites that appears first in the work of art itself, as a tendency within all works of art. In the fictive manner, it would be entertaining to offer dated events as the point of origin in the history of the synchronic development of the forms of order. That would allow us to continue the concept of narrative continuities and discontinuities. But, living as we do in the fictive third culture, we know that the myth of narrative as sacred history is itself easily discardable. Nevertheless, certain narrative pseudoevents can be considered for our purposes so as to entertain ourselves with second culture certainties.

Eighteen eighty△two is a remarkably decent date for the establishment in fiction of that anti-culture that would never address sacred order but only consume itself in its own addresses. It was in 1882 that Nietzsche announced the death of God and our movement in all directions, so destroying that vertical in authority that makes it clear that we can only move upward or downward or sidle remissively from side to side, in the manner of our suffering life on the cross of authority. With the fictive date of 1882, the *kulturkampf* has become more and more intense between third culture, which asserts that no sacred orders are true (at best fictions), and various versions of the second world.

Eighteen eighty-two was also the year in which Dr. Joseph Breuer was frightened into withdrawing from the Ur-case of Freudian theory, which was not Freud's own, except interpretatively. In that case, Dr. Breuer discovered that authority was a fiction of his own therapeutic role relation, as an authority figure, in treating Bertha Pappenheim, otherwise known in third cultural history as Anna O.[2] Breuer, on the verge of the discovery that authority was a fiction of erotic acceptance and dependence, was still so much a Jew of culture that he withdrew and opened the way for Freud's transformative understanding of the dynamics of the transference as the key to dealing with post-Jews and post-Christians; in short, with the modern temper.

The third culture is postmodern. It is a condition of human imaginations in which self-erasure and fusion with the other become dominant. It is clear how wise the ancients in the tradition of Jerusalem were to see the second commandment as itself next in importance to the self-revelation of the I; that identity upon I AM THAT I AM (Exodus 3:14), which all our otherwise incommunicable and irreducible identities are founded in the God-relation of our inwardness. Exodus 3:14 is the key passage in the unauthorable directive instruction of the second culture in which the predicative *I* of all others reveals itself in a sentence past that renders our own identities inviolable and incommunicable in our separate personalities.

It is from this *creative identity* that all identity derives and upon which all identities are dependent. What we call our rationality, that distinctive motif in man which distinguishes us from other

2. Joseph Breuer and Sigmund Freud, "Studies on Hysteria," *SE*, 2:21–77.

animals, is understood in all of second culture as no mere matter of rationality. Rather, rationality is all that we are, each of us in ourselves, even in those enactments in which we are most like any other mammal, as in our sexuality. The real difference between human sexuality and that of a dog is that ours is a sexuality within the *via* that itself can include shame, which is our sense of guilt at any lowering committed during the sexual act. In the sexual act, however the fusion occurs during the act itself, between self and other, each remains himself and nothing else. Sexuality, regarded abstractly, as theorists following Freud in the third culture fictions of sexuality do, may be said to have everything in common with all other fusions, even metaphysical, let alone brutal. But this is an abstraction of a sameness that does not exist.

Strictly speaking, human sexuality, even in the moment of orgasm, has nothing in common with the movement of energy in the universe or the coupling of brutes. Each lover has a vested interest in the very occupation with love in all that they are and remain, respectively, in themselves and for themselves. What seems to be common to the two that become one in the sexual act is so uncommon, so without similarity in the animal or physical world, that in sexuality the respective individualities of the partners remain within the body of each; however they appear to be coupled. Couplings are not fusions. Rather, the human body is singled out from all other bodies by its special sacred constitution, however weak in vital knowledge of the sacred in the body that body may be.

In the mind of each sexual actor, there is a feeling so distinct from all other minds that, instead of saying that two have become one, we ought to say that in the sexual act each differs from the other in all that each is, in identity and in communicability. The third culture expects too much from sexuality. It expects a destruction of that identity which it now feels as a burden rather than as the protective and limiting commanding truths that permit each of us the freedom to be and do for ourselves, so continuously establishing ourselves. There is always a space between lovers, however close they may be. The pathos of that space, of

FIGURE 27. *The Lonely Ones,* Edvard Munch, 1899
(Courtesy of the Fogg Art Museum, Harvard University Art Museums, gift of Lynn and Philip A. Straus, class of 1937; © 2004 The Munch Museum/ The Munch-Ellingsen Group/Artists Rights Society [ARS], New York)

that necessary and humanizing distance between lovers, is at once its ethos. Edvard Munch caught that space in an image of two lovers that has been read unnecessarily as sad (see fig. 27).

3. *Anna O. and the hiatus in the text: A therapeutic story.* Eighteen hundred and eighty-two was the year in which Freud's immediate precursor, Joseph Breuer, discovered himself too much a second world man to take the transference as his patient, Anna O., offered it and herself to him. Once, in the witness of a disciple, James Strachey, Freud put his finger on the telling hiatus in the story— call it 'case history'—of the text itself. That absence signified a presiding presence. Old Jew that he was, however reluctantly, Breuer could not say that the health Anna O. had recovered was inseparable, at that moment marked by the hiatus in the text, from the transferred truth of his erotic authority. Breuer was so alarmed that he left this element of the talking cure out of the case history. That "unanalyzed positive transference of an unmistakably sexual nature" was reserved for the Freudian of the future, no spiritual

kin of Breuer.[3] If only for procedural rather than moral reasons, Freud, too, would not become a Freudian of the future.

Eighteen eighty-two was another world. Unanalyzed positive transferences were still also of a still unmistakably spiritual nature. Both Breuer's silent amen to prohibitive truth and Freud's entirely technical reason for respecting it are forgotten by our more forward therapists. A certain signifying percentage of them do consummate positive transferences of an unmistakably sexual nature; the spiritual nature of the transference is always less certain and certainly less easily quantifiable. In its sexual nature, a crucial departure from our second world interdict upon adultery has been given a certain professional warrant in the world of mental medicine. Why not? All third world readings are of meanings equally half empty and half full. The hiatus in the text is what the text becomes when, as a silent teacher, it is overcome as a form of resistance to the therapeutic as therapist. To depart from the limiting and limited text, the Word, is to enter another life, in another world. In this other world, *book* is another four-letter word.

4. *The meaning of repression.* Freud never gave a better summary of the meaning of repression than in a remarkable footnote to a case of a young Englishwoman, about thirty, working as a governess, whom he called by the pseudonym 'Miss Lucy R' and began to treat at the end of the year 1892. This Englishwoman was plagued by the smell of burnt pudding, and she had chronically recurrent symptoms of what Freud called 'suppurative rhinitis'. Finally Freud risked telling her "really you are in love with your employer, the Director, though perhaps without being aware of it yourself." To this the woman replied "in her usual laconic fashion: 'yes, I think that's true.'"

Freud reports that he then rejoined, "But if you knew you loved your employer why didn't you tell me?" to which Miss Lucy R replies, "I didn't know—or rather I didn't want to know. I wanted to drive it out of my head and not think of it again; and I believe latterly I have succeeded."[4] Freud considered that he had never

3. Freud, "Studies on Hysteria," 2:40 n. 1.
4. Ibid., 2:117.

managed to give a better description of the strange state of mind he called repression in which "one knows and does not know a thing at the same time."[5] Of course, he had been in that state himself, and in that state he was unconscious of any contradiction in his feelings.

The English governess had said that she felt that people were not responsible for their feelings anyhow. The way to become not responsible for one's feelings was to be "afflicted," as Freud put it, by "that blindness of the seeing eye which is so astonishing in the attitude of mothers to their daughters, husbands to their wives and rulers to their favorites."[6] In time, he was to extend the theory of repression to everyone and to make it a condition of existence that was universal and a key to the unlocking of our particular duplicities that are our illnesses.

Repression is the unconscious last and negational playing out of the authority that once belonged consciously to revelation. The Freudian theory of authority heralds a third world anti-culture beyond the splits of consciousness that occur when the culture of commands is present and yet distanced enough to be obeyed more in the outward observance, as if with an uncircumcised heart— with the body ego going another way.

5. *Eighteen eighty-two: Borges/Funes the Memorious.* We have arrived yet again at the founding year of third world culture, 1882. In April of that year, *The Gay Science* is first published by the most imaginative student of that fictive founding year, Nietzsche. It is the very year, in June, that *Anna O./Bertha Pappenheim* expressed her wish to sleep with or otherwise offered herself in an unmistakably sexual way to her doctor, the therapist in the case, Joseph Breuer. The hiatus in the text to which Freud points is the first case of repression to which he pointed. That Freud himself was engaging in a tremendous repression of what the term means is clear in the very language of the greatest artist of the fictive order that Freud represented, the Argentinean writer of those stories he called *Ficciones*, Jorge Luis Borges. The story to which I recall

5. Ibid., 2:40 n. 1.
6. Ibid.

your attention, "Funes the Memorious," is one that allows me to describe the third world anti-culture now engaged in a great war against the second, using first world pagan culture for its own warring purposes. The real importance of Borges's fictive Funes is that he revealed himself to me as poor Nietzsche's successor role model. The Nietzsche who proclaimed, in his fateful future role as a madman, that 'god is dead'—and with him not only all gods but all sacred orders—seems to me to have had his self-transcendent reincarnation in Ireneo Funes. This Ireneo Funes, unlike his failed role model Nietzsche, is really "an untamed and vernacular Zarathustra," a truer precursor of the superman than Nietzsche himself.[7] Nietzsche could never forget the god of the Jewish second world culture creation. His anticipation was dreadful. That sacred order of revealed and complete law, the amen of truth in its culture of commands, would return like the repressed. The version of sacred order lifted from the Jews to become various Christendoms—I say little of Islams, which have scarcely more than started up in America—would return. Nietzsche forgot nothing; least of all the ineliminable significance of Jewishness as the law of being at home in the world. This one memory, in all its compelling variations, is the one Funes cannot have and is never to have. For this one reason, his singular gift for forgetting not only the Jewish Lord of the world but all others above and/or in their sacred orders, Funes could say to his author: "*I have more memories in myself alone than all men have had since the world was a world.*"[8] Funes even remembers and believes in his fictive memory that he knows the precise beginning of the very dawn of that third world culture creation to which he himself belongs, unlike poor Nietzsche his precursor and that world's proclaimant—"dawn of 30th April, 1882," when *The Gay Science* is supposedly first published.

6. *The case of Dora.* Freud's repression has behind it, and now our civilization expresses, the dynamics of anxiety at the rejection of that greatest of offenses: the very existence of sacred order. In

---

7. Borges, "Funes, The Memorious," in *Ficciones*, 108.
8. Ibid., 112.

that near faithless anxiety, as in the case of Dora, faith in authority is made secret from itself, a teaching of truths perpetually on their way to becoming untrue.

The case of young Dora can be simply summarized. That pathetic patient brilliantly resisted Freud's therapeutic understanding of her to the moment she broke off the working through of her hysterical symptoms. Dora found herself caught, only half resisting, in an erotic circle. In that circle were her father and her father's mistress, whose husband desired Dora for himself. Freud discovered Dora herself attracted unawares to her father's mistress. Dora had thought herself repelled by the husband, who had once rubbed his erect member against her. Thinking through this tangle of attractions and revulsions, Freud was far from certain of Dora's revulsions as the essence of her condition, even in the matter of the husband. To this matter, Freud appended a footnote, famous or infamous, however his own case may appear. The footnote reports that Freud had seen the husband of the mistress of Dora's father and had found the man "prepossessing."[9] Poor Dora. With such a therapist, she needed no seducers.

However Dora resisted, Freud's therapeutic desire was to free Dora for her own decision, once she grasped his authoritative interpretation: that the essence of the case was Dora's unacknowledged passion for her father's mistress. The mistress of her father is a mother surrogate. Both engaged in breaking and in flight from the incest taboo, Dora's deepest desire was for incest with more than one symptomatic incarnation of her faithlessness to an authority higher than her desire. Before Freud could establish her in the freedom of her decision on what to do, Dora emigrated to New York and spent the best part of her life going around in psychiatric circles with the message "I am Dora." Poor Dora; tied to her anxiety of being Dora.

7. *Faith and unfaith*. Suppose, following Kierkegaard's psychotheology in his *Concept of Anxiety*, that poor Dora had become inwardly rich; that is, through anxiety had been educated into

9. See Freud, "On the Case of Dora," *SE*, 7:58 n. 3, and also my reading of that case in *The Feeling Intellect*.

faith instead of being reeducated into unfaith. The anxiety of rising to a higher life in the *via* must eradicate what it brings forth,
namely, anxiety. There is the therapy to end all therapies; the beginning of faith. Kierkegaard tells us that anxiety distrusts even
fate; if not, then faith. *Either/or.*[10] Just when the individual wants
to put his trust in fate, that faithless god, anxiety, turns around and
takes fate away, because fate is like anxiety; and anxiety, like the
primacy of possibility, is a sorcerer's evil image. We have been
long in the age of anxiety, conjuring that primacy of possibility
by which both science and art have so concealed one triumph of
transgression after another as to make all appear the less offensive
in the order of real life at once sacred and social. A constantly less-
ening and more erratic sense of offense, even as both increase, appears to be the present fate of our culture. That sense so erratic
and separated from both sociology and theology, offense becomes
a matter of ideology and political manipulation. We see what has
happened to the racist offense. It comes now in disguise as therapeutic black racism. And black racism is now widely accepted by
the progressive pietists of fate as the price of white racism.

   8. *The negational No.* With the *no* uttered by a late second world
patient after a repressed intention has been presented, the commanding truths of consciousness register, simultaneously, the rejection of those commanding truths in the repressive mode. Unwilling to confront the rebellion, that *no* becomes the negation of
the interdict in its historical moment of untruth, which has become the punishing unconscious of the patient. Such a negational
no, of the established interdictory *No*, is a condition of double ignorance. For the patient is still so far a member in the vertical in
authority that the lowering of the negational *no*, as it signifies the
desired yes (or counterculture of *no* to *no*), cannot yet be acknowledged. The third world therapeutic strategy assumes that the
hidden *no* of the repressive mode, as it dominates the consciousness of late second world members, contradicts the obvious. But
that contradiction of the obvious is lost on those late second

   10. See Søren Kierkegaard, *Either/Or: A Fragment of Life*, trans. David and
Lillian Swenson (London: Oxford University Press, 1944).

culture rebels with bad consciences precisely because they can no longer face the systemic mendacity of their symptoms. These are post-Jews and post-Christians who no longer have a grip on the commanding truths. That is the wonderfully witty point of Freud's own joke upon the joke on the late second world and early third world culture of systemic mendacities that has displaced the world of commanding truths in both literature and life. The displacement in literature is remarked in Freud's story of the two Jews who meet in a train at a Galician railway station.

> "Where are you going?" asked one. "To Cracow," was the answer. "What a liar you are!" broke out the other. "If you're going to Cracow, you want me to believe you're going to Lemberg. But I know that in fact you're going to Cracow. So why are you lying to me?"[11]

This language of suspicion which unmasks systemic mendacities is itself a language in the repressive mode. For Freud, too, like the great poets and novelists enchanted by the disenchantment of an art and life that can only be one lie upon the other, there remains an art that is as compulsively cherished among the poets as among the neurotics; even more so.

9. *Edgar's song.* Robert Browning, long before Freud, makes the condition clear in a remarkable concision of Freud's Polish Jewish joke. The most concise account of systemic mendacity remains his play upon Edgar's song in *King Lear* in "Childe Roland to the Dark Tower Came." The world in which both the observed and the observer live in that poem is no less ominous than the heath in *Lear.* Browning saw, without joking, precisely the systemic mendacity that Freud conceals behind his Jewish joke. His poet/theorist's first thought was that the other poet, like himself, "lied in every word."[12] This poet/theorist, addressing a world the elites of which are intent on escaping the entire vertical in au-

11. Freud, "Jokes and Their Relation to the Unconscious" (1905), *SE*, 8:137–38.

12. Robert Browning, "Childe Roland to the Dark Tower Came," with the epigraph "(See Edgar's song in 'Lear')," in *Poetical Works of Robert Browning*, vol. 5 (New York: Macmillan, 1894), 194.

thority, is in as deadly earnest as the joking Freud. But the dark vision built upon Edgar's song in the depths of the *Learworld* of humans lowered to the lowest imaginable to Shakespeare's mind, though lower after by many deaths as late as Auschwitz, Browning's first thought is of yet another Browning or another Freud to whom lying comes as inevitably as words themselves. A society kills itself when it develops its dissimulations to the point at which they are widely admired. Freud's preneurotic joking Jew, in his earnestness of suspicion, is revealed as yet another

> . . . hoary cripple, with malicious eye
> Askance to watch the working of his lie
> On mine, and mouth scarce able to afford
> Suppression of the glee, that pursed and scored
> Its edge, at one more victim gained thereby.[13]

In Freud's case, Dora has no glee to suppress, as Freud does as he scores point after point against her as one more victim to be gained thereby for the liberated world of third culture into which Dora, to his shock and surprise, refuses to enter. Dora's great refusal is yet another *no*, though she cannot bring herself to utter the Sinaitic *yes*. Nevertheless, she rejects the third culture *yes* as a condition of transgression, that incestuous circle of her father's mistress and husband to include herself, from which she flees even as she saves herself by her waylay of Freud's own ensnaring lies. All travelers in sacred order, inseparable from social, might find themselves posted, as Dora was, along a road she does not know she is traveling, even as Freud knows and yet does not know in his own repression of revelation—tantamount as it is to his genius.

10. *The worldwide wandering.* Dora is a young post-Jewish girl. Her worldwide wandering is not in search of a commanding truth, but rather for a way out of the commanding lies of her own family life as they are made legitimate in Freud's systemic mendacity made into a science of therapeutic knowledge, inseparable as that therapeutic knowledge is from sophistication about membership in any residual, and therefore irrational, sacred order. The neu-

13. Ibid.

rotics Freud sees have dwindled into ghosts of members in the sacred orders of commanding truths. It is on their insubstantial obedience to those commanding truths that they are not fit to cope with them and with the price of them. Therefore, the therapist arrives to save them from the ghost of their own identities in sacred order. Therapists must rebuke the entire history of sacred order by finding it at the point of mythic cause that has narrowed the scope of the primacy of possibility even as that scope is, to the theonomic elites of second worlds, the heart of life.

Freud treats the second world as a sick person very near death. That second world may have seemed dead indeed in the Vienna of Freud's time, even as its death was pronounced by Hitler in launching his war upon the sacred nation of second worlds in 1939. Freud's literary career begins with cases such as Lucy R. and Dora. But it ends, as endings parody their beginnings, with *Moses and Monotheism*. There are no tears as Freud takes farewell of the Jews, in their neuroticism, in his work toward 1939.

Moses and Monotheism declares, though differently from Hitler, the death of the Jews as they derive their individual identities from the revelation to each of them by highest authority in his identity to each of them as a *Thou* to his *I*. No collective identity can supersede that individuality of address. Yet it is precisely that collective identity in the primordial world, of which the primal act is sexual in its expression, with which Freud confronts Dora as a young woman who has felt the erect phallus of her father's mistress's husband and yet rejected it, without knowing that the rejection is a late epiphany of the commanded truths directing our lives still from the revelation at Sinai. Forward from the Sinaitic Baal as a golden work of pro-Canaanite, pre-Christian folk art, forward to that version of Baal represented in Dora's father's mistress's husband, and beyond both Dora and Freud to Brecht's Baal as a sexual virtuoso, the struggle in its figurative meaning remains the same.

Brechtian Baal back to Canaanite, Baal remains a lie. It is only as a god-term—made on terms that evade commanding truths and create an ominous tract of warfare between commanding truths and powerful lies—that the imagery can be understood.

The trinket imagery of self-will, and its mendacious imagery of artful expression, comes to its foreseeable end in some end that never should have been, such as Auschwitz. There, Baal was not even offered as a trinket for the sacrifice of the founding nation of the entire second world, intent on sacrificing itself to yet another false, nonexistent world, except so far as worlds of death can be institutionalized. That death is one from which the obstreperous joy of a world fatal to the truth of our second was heard and is still heard despite all the trickeries of effort by revisionist history and the repressive mode as it normally operates to bury that joy itself in imagery of the obstreperous Jews of Israel.

The war between the lying world and the true is permanent, so far as a human mind's eye can see. That the war may be permanent is no reason for despair, no more than life itself gives any such reason. Nor does it require a pledge to the plain. Plain meanings are too safe a road round the complexity of the war. The plain itself is too grey for the sheer subtlety of life's power. Yet that subtlety is inseparable from the lies to which members in reasonably good standing of third culture shut their eyes. It takes no skill to lie in such a systemically mendacious world. Nor will judgment's fire cure the human of his capacities for the lie, for there has been judgment after judgment, fire after fire. No cure has come. For humans are not ill so much as they shut their eyes and refuse to turn them on their hearts, where second world has its life, rather than in the life of cleverities that come out of mind alone.

The living frame within which world pictures are taken needs a certain rigidity in order that the picture can be taken. But the human frame itself, as it is alive, changes its shape and quality as the framers, themselves at once makers and made, derive their imagery from modes of identity that are opposite to those according to which the conscious obedience to commanding truths asserts itself. The moment that someone speaks for a truth by means of a lie, the story that the culture tells of itself is threatened by a larger mendacity. That story is now represented as critically conscious of the commanding truths as somehow necessary old lies for which there is no longer a use; at least, not a use so valuable as the lies themselves once asserted. It is as if the commanding truths are grandiose. Rather, the lies are grandiose, for they can never be lived modestly, as the truths can be lived.

The most grandiose of lies is apparent to all who have been influenced by Freudian theories: the opposition between culture and human nature. But that opposition is itself a negation of the second world of revelation and creation from which the world and its cultures derive. No human nature exists outside that creation. Therefore, the negational doctrine of opposition between culture and a nature that is treated as warring precisely in its incapacity to accept the cultural except as a 'physical reaction-formation' describes a culture engaged in destroying the commanding truths that are inseparable from the doctrine of creation. It is only with the development of a third culture that the doctrine of culture as itself a form of reaction-formation against the primordiality of human transgressiveness has developed.

Freud's widely read work, and widely assigned by the third world professoriat, *Civilization and Its Discontents* is itself a recycling of mythological versions of an instinctual primordiality from which highest authority in second culture itself derives as a reaction-formation against the world that even Aristotle, one of the paramount first cultural theorists, quotes skeptically in his masterwork on the soul. Aristotle is skeptical that the same soul functions in and suffers at all points of the world conceived as a vertical in authority.[14] We do not think, perceive, do, and suffer everything with the whole or same soul. Rather, as Hamlet asserted that it was not Hamlet but Hamlet's enemy that had offended Laertes,[15] so are we different inwardly in our distancings from the commanding truths at the heights of the *via:* different precisely in our distances and therefore in our souls. There is a transgressive soul as there is an interdictory soul. The choice of where we are is what it represents: what we are. Membership is agency, and agency is responsibility. Precisely that doctrine of agency is denied in the repressive imagery that makes its way into dominance in a third culture dominated by the dynamics of lying.

14. See Aristotle, *De anima* (On the soul), 8.1.411.
15. *Hamlet*, 5.2.240.

Freud's own judgment of the nature of repression can be brought back to haunt him. At bottom, his own statements of repression are the same thing as to say, precisely in their resolute avoidance of predicative revelation: "that is something I would rather repress." *Civilization and Its Discontents* has been all too uncritically received through a number of generations of the radically remissive youth culture. It is practically a spiritual manual of that culture assigned to undergraduates in our elite colleges and universities. But this symbol of negation does not free its readers, however thoughtful they may be, from the limits of repression until they can see the transparency of Freud's own repression in the theory of repression. That repressive character of Freud's theory of repression is seen clearly in his war with Dora over her moral sensibility. His affirmation of Dora's sexual life, as he would have her lead it, is itself a negation of the central life as she herself understands it is to be read. Even Masie, in James's version of the same struggle over repression and revelation, has more help from the unlearned Mrs. Wick than Dora received from Freud. He was a conquistador indeed, but Dora was not an Indian to be so easily conquered.

Freud's mythological recycling of the Oedipus story of blinding here takes its proper place, as psychologists as early as Aristotle knew. It is when we do not have vision of the highest that we do not see the point of seeing or hearing, despite the whirligig of things to see, or noise, everywhere. Rather, vision is the predicate of the mind's eye. The opposite, that the mind's eye is the predicate of vision, is one of those lies that is transported by third culture theorists into the kind of pseudonaturalism that organizes the Freudian theory of instinct, and the pseudoeconomism and -materialism that organize the Marxist theory of the class struggle. Where there is such studio noise made everywhere, no wonder that the hearing do not hear and the seeing do not see. Theory precedes practice as vision precedes the eye.

11. *More 1882: The indeterminacy principle (or commanding fiction) v. commanding truth.* A basic proposition of third worlds is that there are no permanent *constraints/interdicts*. There has always been a struggle over the nature of constraint. The war over the

interdicts continues to this day. The uniqueness of the struggle today is that third worlds hold that all constraints are fictitious. Third worlds complicate the war by arguing the essential equality of all restraints, since they are all equally fictive and thus all equally true, and false. All constraints are subject to protest. Third world theory of culture struggle holds that the fighting is part of our addiction to our fictions. Social reality is reduced to the struggle for power, in which the most persuasive symbolic wins.

12. *Repression.* The sense of guilt, which Freud found at the birth of culture, is shame in sacred order. Shame occurs to the fully human even at the possibility, let alone the inevitability, of giving offense to sacred order. Occasional as it is, true guilt can be distinguished from false. By the doctrine of occasions unattended, false guilt is to be seen in the occurrent sense that there is something neurotic about rising toward a higher life: the nearer the interdicts, the more sacred the self-mover; the farther, the more profane. True guilt is inseparable from an offense against interdictory demands called for by highest authority. Deaf to those calls, the self-mover may deny guilt and so lose consciousness of where—and therefore, what—he is. In *Hope Abandoned*, Nadezhda Mandelstam gave the following reading of the fusion between guilt and a true sense of self.

> A sense of guilt is man's greatest asset. Sin is always concrete, and repentance commands unique and powerful words, in an unequivocal language of its own. It may be the language of a specific moment of time, but it lasts forever.[16]

'Repentance' is an unequivocal word that appears to belong to what I call the second *world/culture*, forged in the traditions out of Jerusalem. What, then, of the shamelessness prevalent in the third *world/culture* constituted by repressive vanguards in second? Those vanguards of reflective selves have taken themselves out of the world of second *culture/creation* and into a third in which the freedom to be shameless is widely proposed as a newly acquired

---

16. Nadezhda Mandelstam, *Hope Abandoned* (New York: Atheneum, 1974), 266.

right. That right is at war with another, rarer duty: the duty to make the right decision based upon interdictory commands inseparable from second world creation. Second world duties permit no surrender to consumptive desire. The consuming third world desire, as if it were primal life itself, what Freud god-termed *Eros*, proposes a third world higher illiteracy that has nothing to do historically with primitive societies. Rather, such illiteracy reads no possibility of ascent in a world of authorities dedicated precisely to the leveling of all verticals in authority.

Right decisions are made by reading where we are in the *via*. Metaphorically, these readings constitute *faith/knowledge*, indistinguishable as *shalt not/wilt not*. By seeing through fictive constructs of ourselves to changeable second world readings of where the self may be in the vertical, the self identifies its own whereabouts in that vertical and, further, identifies dangers of self-lowerings in unrecognized offensives against what is highest above that vertical. The 'highest' is the *creator/identity*, the god-term of, but never in, its world. That *creator/identity* is the predicate of all other identities, which are stipulated as after the image of the *creator/identity*. That identity is the presiding presence over second world culture. From this Being There derives all individual identities. These derivatives mean that the self in its irreducible identity belongs to its Creator—and not to its father, mother, or itself. In these irreducible identities, each individual is inviolately itself from the moment of conception after an image that has no biological form or social substance. Like the *creator/identity*, each being is given, at the moment of creation, its difference from every other: in its identity, its incommunicability, its character. These god-created, and therefore god-related, identities are univocal in truth and equivocal in perception.

The *both/and* of third world identities exists as an equivocation, or trick, of second world univocalities of *either/or*. See figure 28 for a famously simple image of equivocal perception. The modal identity of the *man/Jack Rabbit* or *Donald/Duck*, when it yields to our fictive third world *name/game*, commits an offense against the real person in real authority as it is owned by the personal creation, whoever the personal carrier—say a pregnant woman—

FIGURE 28. *Duck/Rabbit*, Ludwig Wittgenstein,
after J. Astrow

(Reproduced with permission from drawing on p.194 of *Philosophical Investigations*, 2nd ed. [Oxford: Blackwell, 1958])

may be. There is something inevitable in the percepted *both/and* endlessly shifting and equivocal as it is. Like the remorseless decree of fate, images of indecision split into decisions no better than indecisions. Duties, right decisions in sacred order, once commanded from above the *via*, can be undecided by ourselves but not made wrong in themselves. Rather, in second world theories of what is highest and all below, the wrong decisions take the form of forgotten commands or disobedience of a univocal voice—'loud' as Joyce liked to play upon the *world/name*, 'Loud' of that voice.[17]

Within second world theories, sacred history never repeats itself. The children of Israel cannot stand again at Sinai; the Second Coming cannot repeat the first. Second world cultures of commands take their individual life-turns, which are constantly occurring, from sacred history. By contrast, third world images in the manner of the *both/and* allow, even encourage, mythic repetitions: as if each were a new liberation from the authority of the past lost in the next decision and then found again only to be lost again. Our second world credal culture of commands, abandoned by anticredal elites in particular, is challenged by our emergent third world anticredal and pseudomythic culture now consuming itself in characterological instabilities that reach from the bottom

17. Joyce, *Finnegans Wake*, 258.

of the vertical upward toward the social top. Third world character is to second as sand is to stone.[18]

13. *Repression of revelation.* Repressions belong to the leveling
languages of symptoms. They derive from anxiety and represent
half belief, bad faith. Repressions represent what they are not;
they are concealments that allow the return of something more
offensive than a trespass or the thought of a trespass. That return
must be disguised and distorted out of any possible recognition of
a return. Nevertheless, every return in disguise is a harbinger of
what has returned behind the disguise.

Freud remarked the prefix 'UN'—as in UNunited Nations, or,
better, UNknown Soldier—as the prefix of self-deceits returning unaware of themselves. Repressions express Freud's dynamic
second unconscious, the perplexed genius of his life, his *crucial
problem* unresolved. By Freud's 'first' Unconscious, I understand
transgression returning disguised by Freud as the 'instinctual' or
'impulse' life. From both first and second unconscious, there is
an interior flight, necessary and inescapable, that now goes by its
educated slang nickname, the apparatus of *unpleasure/pain* Freud
named *repression*.

Daring as he was, Freud dared make little more than negational
sense of repression. He admitted it into his theory on condition
that it become, and never cease to be, his crucial problem. The illuminative facet of repression was itself repressed by the operative. Before this gatekeeping 'Not' Freud sat all the main part of
his intellectual life, without being able to know how cleverly
negational had been his only so recognized sacred order.

Freud's cleverity, as a theorist, as a visionary of the highest, was
compulsively negational and inversive. To admit repression in
service to revelation would have confronted Freud with the most
frightful theoretical necessity "of postulating a third *Ucs.*, which
is not repressed."[19] That third unconscious, predicate of the second, raised a possibility superior to Freud's lowering second: that
of making the "characteristic of being unconscious . . . lose sig-

18. See Kierkegaard, *The Present Age.*
19. Freud, "The Ego and the Id," *SE,* 19:18.

nificance for us."[20] In the repressive, repressed, we may find the combination that unlocks again the meaning of therapeutic authority. The repressive thus rendered by Freud, unrecognizable in its imperative as sacred order, becomes that very general rule about the degree of distortion and remoteness from the primacy of possibility achieved by linked repressions proper that Freud himself could not see.[21] Distanced from sacred order, tastes and distastes, addictions and abhorrences, become inexplicable or unhistorical in their determining origins. Culture becomes the mythology of otherwise inexplicable splittings into oppositional modes of that primacy of possibility that aims only at its own expression.

As symptom to symbol is repression to revelation. Freud's greatness was as symptomologist not as symbolist. Moreover, Freud was captive of his own symptomology. Repression is to psychoanalysis as unknown gods are to pagan theologies. Repressive splittings make of every cultural expression an illuminative act that refers to Freud's own radical dualism more than it refers to the distancing arts of obedience and disobedience in sacred order. 'Ambivalence', along with 'ambiguity', becomes the code word, favored in modernity, for a faithlessness that forbids knowledge of sacred order. Freud's repression of the repressive allowed this forbidden knowledge to play upon its enactors. 'Repression' became Freud's terminal negation for what culture must include: deeply forbidden knowledge; that which is, at once, known and unknowable. These intellectualizing and paradoxical resistances to the revelation predicative of repressions show the brilliance of the one kind of knowledge forbidden to us: of sacred order, for which Art

20. Ibid.

21. In Freud's negational symbolic, the symbol is *not* what it represents. So instinct and its vicissitudes represent the primacy of possibility. Secondary imaginative processes suffer complete inversion. What is primary becomes secondary and vice versa. On Freud's inversive inability to lay down, in his theory of repression, a general rule of a little more or less in sacred order those necessary degrees of distortion and remoteness by which self, in its artfulness, is constituted as our continuous address in sacred order to it, see Freud, "Repression," *SE*, 14:117–307. The papers of 1915 are especially important in working through Freud's negational recognitions of sacred order.

and/or Sociology are the chief modern would-be surrogates. What we modernists fear to know, we admit back into Art and Sociology on condition of its denial. Where 'It' is, there the Sacred once was.

Freud's ingenious repressions of revelation serve continuously, and in an intensely stipulative manner, against admitting sacred order back into a modern consciousness pregnant from the father of these repressions. The revelational father unacknowledged, except as *primal repression*, modern sensibility has been achieved at the cost of a critical insensibility. The sacred is denied even as the arts of its address are celebrated as ends in themselves—as Art or Science, but more as Art. More than the sciences, the arts are our repository of faithlessness. How much more easily Freud is accepted nowadays as artist rather than as scientist; and rightly so.

Our culture feeds on its doubly critical addresses: to a sacred order that is allowed to exist only for purposes of lowering everything high in it. Critical intellect rubs near criminal impulse. That nearness implies movements of moral inversion no culture religion can long survive. Our endlessly critical culture religion is ending, I reckon, in massive movements of inversion. To lower the interdictory motifs, to raise the transgressive: in sum, this is the function of that criticism for which our secular humanists and other enlighteners held such high hope.

14. *Death instinct.* To come nearer understanding modernist movements of inversion, authority celebrated in its lowering modes, we must first recognize its love affair with death as the interdict of interdicts that modernism would abolish as meaningless. In his negational language of the 'death instinct', Freud framed his most completely up-to-date resistance to the eternal yesterday that is sacred order. Authority must be eternally past, in every culture, however unstable. But all cultures are unstable precisely in their vitality: all are moving balances of abhorrences and idealizations, one the predicate of the other. Repression is best imagined in its mobilities rather than, as popularly conceived, in its immobilities. If the repressive in service to revelation is not constantly renewed and attached to fresh primacies of possibility, then authority will lower, and so transform itself into power. It is

in this repressive mode, raising and lowering the threshold of possibility in its denials, that cultures constitute unstable responses in sacred order to that very order.[22]

In its strictly modern cultural truth, unknown to ancient man, repression, as the untrustworthy servant of revelation, represents a resistant anticipatory invasion by a purely imaginative construct: the primacy of possibility. That primacy exists only as transgressions specific to interdicts. A transgression is always and everywhere the violation of an interdict. Once upon a time, it was said to be the preneurotic, or religious, case that transgressions were only dreamt of, and then only in disguise, deceit, distortion, distancings of a wish that cannot be fully waked out of its enchantment; that wish guarded by its kind censor, sleep. In that case, sleep served a waking life, rendered the less offensive and dangerous in the servant functions of sleep to fantasy, without directly endangering reality.

Now we sleepers have been waked, by Nietzsche, by Freud, by their creation: the therapeutic. Modernity is a time when the most offensive fantasies have invested sacred reality; as if that reality were primordially transgressive and God, the good, a reaction-formation, as we Freudians say. Repression appears here to stay; chiefly in order to fail man as man has failed revelation. Nothing fails more in this age of disenchantment than servant repressions no longer in the service of their old master, revelation. Here is moral theology disguised as an anti-theological psychology spiteful as it is kind; the last psychology likely to occupy itself with the religion of discontent as a symptom of a terminally ill civilization. The tense connection between modern repression and ancient revelation seems to me clear enough to see in the bizarre efflorescences of spiritual pathologies in the everyday life of the therapeutic.[23] The postmodern reader should find it possible to break through his own repressions of revelation to text analogues suit-

22. See my essay "By What Authority," in *The Problem of Authority in America*, ed. John Diggins and Mark Kahn (Philadelphia: Temple University Press, 1981), 223–53.

23. On the therapeutic as the dominant character type of modern culture, see my *The Triumph of the Therapeutic*.

able for citation in this postmodern text; postmodern in its straight recognition of sacred order without concealment behind yet another religion of art and/or symptomatic psychology.

The servant repressions have been produced in order to fail even as they routinely betray their master, revelation. Indirect communication cannot sustain itself without renewals of command by direct communication. Repression is the treacherous condition psychological man, the therapeutic, has invented, the better to repress revelation. Produced by anxiety, the current truth of repression leads on to a guilt that itself displaces informed obedience to commanding truths, that praxis of the faith now disdained by the more educated faithful.

I have speculated that, had he dared look, Freud would have discovered revelation beneath its transparent disguise, the second unconscious, in the third. Mere speculation of course. Petty Pascal that I am, I would wager on this sure thing: not repression but revelation; not the immense disorder of modern cultural truths; not this culture consuming itself at the historic end of its theological tether. Then, had he dared look down far enough, Freud would have seen he had the world upside down. But then Freud would have ceased to be an 'infidel Jew' and made his way back toward the sacred order of Israel. That return of the repressed is the one return this self-described 'infidel Jew' could not imagine. Had Freud dared this return and suffered it, he would have been deprived at once of his epochal psychological toys. The price of faith is the genius of all psychologizing, therapeutic, and scientific unfaiths, so near faith and yet so far they can go no farther in their repressive distancings, distortions, and negational recognitions of revelation in its most modern opposite. I see repression, therefore, as the historical successor of revelation in a culture that feels compelled to recycle eternal truth into mythic, through historical repetitions disguised. This recycling repeats the symptomatic murder of what Freud called the 'primal father', that first in a cycle to which Freud attached the murder both of Moses and of Jesus.

15. *A pathology of denial.* Here is a massively mediated little pathology of denial, a pseudowisdom of suppression, offered with sublime condescension by a young officer of a third world army in

our current *kulturkampf* against a dying old officer of a great second world army. The Reverend Ralph Abernathy, interviewed by Bryant Gumbel on NBC's *Today Show* shortly after the publication of his memoirs, *And the Walls Came Tumbling Down*, found himself subject to the most arrogant, smiling condescensions by a man who is much his junior in more than years. Unwilling to tell a lie, the Reverend Mr. Abernathy had included a few essential passages on Martin Luther King Jr.'s infidelities during the last night of his life. Condescending and complacent as Mr. Collins in *Pride and Prejudice*, and at least equally subtle, Mr. Gumbel asked the old man: "Why'd you include the pages [on King's adulteries]? . . . It could have just as easily been left out." The old minister responded, "Because I wanted to set history straight, and I wanted my book to be an honest account of what happened."[24] In his marvelous and erudite ethic of honesty, Gumbel then taught Abernathy the third world gospel, quoting from "a movie called Man Who Shot Liberty Valence [*sic*]" as if he did not know that "legend" is a cultivated word for lying: "When the truth collides with the legend, print the legend." Here we are, in a flash of darkness, sealed in our third world ease of lying.

There is another epiphany in that same meeting between the mass media officer of the great electronic army and the tired old soldier of Christ. There is a most revealing confrontation between a man of faith and a man who has no idea of what faith is. Faith always and everywhere includes trust and honest judgment of one's fellow men. By contrast, faithlessness induces cynicism and the kind of analytic attitude I saw in its most brazen expression in a railway compartment during a journey from Munich to Milan. My German fellow passenger, sitting opposite, had been an officer of the SS. During our long conversation, he referred regularly to *Unsere Adolf*—Our Very Own Adolf. Asked to explain this cozy usage, the former SS officer told me that he could not believe such a naive response from a professor. Surely I knew

24. Transcript of *Today* show, October 17, 1989 (New York: National Broadcasting Co., 1989), 17–21.

that almost all Germans, excluding the stupid rank and file of the movement, knew that Hitler was a trickster. *Unsere Adolf* referred to a virtuoso of the Big Lie. A virtuoso is to be admired as our *leader/mock god* to whom and with whom the self is identified. He is us. Therefore, the phrase *Unsere Adolf.*

When that protective legend suffers the consequences of truth, as the Reverend Mr. Abernathy insists it must, then Gumbel can utter the cry of his own lying heart: "I'm not sure I'm hearing all this."[25] Gumbel is suggesting the supreme usefulness, and therefore importance, of the *Unsere Adolf* syndrome. If our leaders are liars, then we need to maintain the protective legend of their lies. Perhaps Gumbel knew, yet knew not, that he was urging a lie. Abernathy finished the interview by lighting the darkness, with a blessing that was as well the severest condemnation of Gumbel's call for self-conscious systemic mendacity. The old man, grandest as he neared his final comment, can be heard in the subtlest of interdictory modes, the one that suggests the grace and favor in which our commanding truths have been, and remain, given to us, however undeserving: "God Bless You." The undeserving Gumbel, and all the rest of us, should know the alternative truth: God curse you. In our third culture, we have said good-bye—as in 'God be with you'—to both. Far less evasively, in that second world to which our ancestors and the Reverend Abernathy belonged, even unknowing lies are not without deepest consequence.

16. *More repression of revelation.* Repression is the Freudian word for lying to oneself without ever quite knowing it. A repression that is known ceases to function, while a conscious lie may be continued indefinitely. A culture can encourage or discourage the lying habit in the repressive mode as well as in the deliberate. To deny an interdict works nothing like its abolition. Rather, such sinuous failures of faith as Gumbel's may put human imagination on the fictive stretch of evasion so triumphantly, though temporarily, that they emerge as art or transgression, or, indeed, as

25. Ibid.

transgressive art. In the repressive mode, as it must be always when it has no excusing reason that subserves its interdicts even as such reasons may accomplish their purpose as exceptions that prove the rule, the disproof remains in the lying.

A lie can express itself in accomplished and quite spectacularly attractive symptoms. There can be about the well-told or grotesquely transparent lie a certain gloss of authentic immediacy, suavity, and lyric purity. When it is brought off, as by a Falstaff or a Hitler, whether for hugely comic or tragic effect, the lie develops a paradisiacal quality. It is as if, in the primal garden of human imagination, divisions of true and false, rights and wrongs, had not yet been made. All that is sordid or tragic can be made to fall away. There are now armies of specialists, not only literary but legal, virtuosi staff men and women preparing judicial decisions that are what they represent: new lies in the old face of commanding truths, fallings away that are the entitlements of our emergent third world. Third world abolitionist movements deny commanding truths so richly—read *Roe v. Wade* or Duchamp's *Etant donnés* as cases of third world creation—that our second world seems impoverished, uninteresting, a bore. "Boring! Boring!" chant the all-purpose protesters. Our third world is a vast grievance procedure against highest authority.

Bryant Gumbel appealed to an interesting authority, extrajudicial, a film. Ralph Abernathy appealed to highest authority, judicial as well as extrajudicial, that can both bless and curse. There, in that either/or, is the uninteresting, unambiguous, inartistic, impolitic boredom of a second world, now and apparently forever dying in its inanitions. Wherever it appears, boredom is a sign of cultural ill health. We shall never know whether the Israelites-to-be were bored even then and there at the foundation. Moses had not quite yet brought home to them the commanding truths. Yet we know those truths were near enough to create an abreaction of giddiness. Alas, we shall never know whether giddiness was at the etiological source of the dancing. We do know, as in our own flesh and blood, what a bore obedience can be—more precisely, has been—and how interesting disobedience can be, anywhere and anytime. Dancing can be misread by our third mind's eye when, as in Jane Austen's great ball scene in *Pride and Prejudice*, in Joyce's quadrilles danced in "The Dead," or laterally in John Huston's mysterious cinematic revision of quadrilles into lancers, the dancers appear to maintain decorum enough to appear most unerotic. In its decorum, ballroom dancing has become uninteresting to such a time as ours. The one always popular contemporary curse is the ancient Chinese: "May you live in an interesting time."

17. *Sentencings in the penal colony.* A reasonably recent and brilliantly artful repression of revelation can be read in Kafka's masterpiece of our second world officer class defeated by our third world explorer class. Kafka first read "In the Penal Colony" to his friends Max Brod, Otto Pick, and Franz Werfel on December 2, 1914. That date also should go down in the history of our *kulturkampf.* Kafka sees to it that the self-sacrifice made by the last officer of the last sacred order that our anthropological explorer's mind's eye can read/misread may be read by our own mind's eye as the explorer's deathwork mission. In that great parable on the continuing end of our second worlds, the explorer's missionary deathwork is reciprocated by the officer's suicide. We find ourselves near Thomas Garrigue Masaryk's now underrated work on our *kulturkampf* to which I shall refer in the closing note of this book.

In Kafka's masterpiece of our second world read/misread as a punishment colony, the reader is drawn into the work by the possibility Kafka contrives: that of being both officer and explorer, precisely ourselves as we are met in this permanently transitional time by the self in search of everything but her sacred self. In Kafka's type, the permanent explorer, on his fatal and permanent field trip from sacred order to sacred order, each almost at its end even as he arrives to administer that end, we engage in precisely that walk through ourselves—but always meeting ourselves— that Joyce thought would supply the text of our next world. "In the Penal Colony" supplies a master key to our readings of those most interesting new pieties, our many transgression therapies, as they are now offered for our endless release from the world of Law and order.

Wherever there may be an indefinitely expandable doxa of rights to transgressive conduct, there follows, as night follows day, third world recyclings of fictive taboos as they fight their endless war against interdictory truths. One such taboo, fictive as it is self-contradictory, refers to the rights-related doxa that homosexuality is at once no less natural than heterosexuality and, on the other hand, less natural than cultural: i.e., a "lifestyle option."

There is an insuperable difference between taboo and interdict. The former remains mysterious in its origin and undiscussable in its meaning. A further distinction: taboos are not revealed. Rather, third world taboos derive from doxa of political correctness, shining in their recency rather than venerable in their decency. The current piety of disrespect for the commanding truths of our second world is not least a misunderstanding of the relation between those truths and their venerable contemporaneity.

However repressed in the present, the authority of the past will out. There and here, then and now, the presiding presence presents even the most self-confidently evasive Jewish princes and princesses of libido with the inescapable shadow of their sacred selves. Evasion is one thing. Escape is another. Shadows of truth are cast over the most accomplished psychological deathworks of *Kafka's/Freud's* own devising. That the greatest of transitional theorists from second culture to third, the last of the death-dealing trinity *Marx/Kafka/Freud*, accomplished upon himself as his model case a merely psychological and, at the same time, anti-credal Jewishness suggests the psychomachia in which very late second culture Jewry finds itself; at once gladly as in Woody Allen's character Zelig and sadly as in the neurotic character that supersedes Jewish piety in the Freudian vision of our second culture's inner history. Freud casts his great shadow of sadness, the inner struggle of self suffusing the outer struggle of cultures by which second world sacred history has become its opposite: third world psychobiography.

18. *Unholy trinity Marx/Kafka/Freud is right.* All hate the Law, the commanding truths, and all seek a possibility of a kind of people emerging out of the defeat of the Law and its people who would be something very different. The most skeptical of the

three is Kafka. That difference is a kind of primordiality that they find suppressed in the Jews themselves.

19. *The secret dynamics of Jew-hatred in the third culture.* With the death of the God of Abraham, Isaac, and Jacob, as that death was announced in 1882, and with the rise of a rationalist psychotherapeutic theory of human identity as the enactment of various unstable roles, the traditionalist predicates for the dynamics of Jew-hatred might be thought to be absent. Quite the contrary is the case. With the death of God or in the view of those who find him permanently absent, the dynamics of Jew-hatred increased exponentially in the third culture. The irony of the extraordinary intensity of Jew-hatred is that it is related to the end of theism; and, indeed, to the end of all the gods.

In both the first and second cultures, the gods or God were supremely authoritative. They acted in society according to their own interest. Homer conceived the power of the gods in such a way that whatever happened on the plain of Troy reflected various intentions, otherwise hidden, on the sacred mountain of Olympus. The conspiracy theory is a version of the acts of the gods or the God who rules everything. Once God was dead or permanently absent, the question remained: who is in his place? That place could be filled most rationally by the inventors of the God of the second culture, the Jews themselves. After all, they were and remain highly visible, high achievers and yet without power. The conspiracy theory of a plot by this figure of highest authority developed its own rationality.

Moreover, highest authority was itself malevolent. The popular gnostic tradition is not very hard to find in the third culture. The best place to look is in its fiction. In the fiction of D. H. Lawrence as of John Cowper Powys, the God of Abraham, Isaac, and Jacob was opposed by one of their own, Jesus the Christ. Following elements of the gnostic tradition, Christ became like Lucifer, without the transgressive element. On the contrary, it was highest authority, the God of the Jews, who was transgressive, and his creation was transgressive as well. So in the most powerful of Powys's novels, *A Glastonbury Romance*, one of the characters suggests a common understanding of Christ.

He's the enemy of God. That is, He's the enemy of creation! He's always struggling against Life, as we know it . . . this curst, cruel self-assertion . . . this pricking up of fins, this prodding with horns . . . this opening of mouths . . . this clutching, this ravishing, this snatching, this *possessing*.[26]

We can now see how Christology, so far as it survives in the third culture, operates. We have the popular gnostic doctrine, against his Jewish father, of "Jesus only! Jesus always! All for Jesus!"[27] With these words as its standard direction, there was founded an Anglican order in the winter of 1887, a fraternity of the Christian life. This is one of many third culture Christological orders that implicitly go their gnostic way in the third culture without showing any signs of Jew-hatred. That Jew-hatred does break out in a variety of ways seems surprising only to those who do not see the link between the death of God and the fantastic presence of the Jews as highest and malevolent authority in this cursed world. So we can begin to understand the apparently bizarre rise of the bizarre and sudden visibility of Jew-hatred among American blacks.

This is to say nothing about the further malevolence of the greatest and most secret power in the world, the Jews, in having their doctors spread not only AIDS but polio and venereal disease through inoculations of black children. The irony of this explosion of black hatred of the Jews is that the Jews themselves have been, and remain, among the blacks most ardent supporters; this is only an aspect of the profound and suicidal confusions of post-Jewry. The Jew-hatred of the blacks is a rationalist element in the terrible tragic comedy of their own existence in America. As the Jews are revealed as a commanding people, surrogates of their commanding God, the blacks themselves are trying in a fantastic rationalist mode to correct their deracination in the third culture

26. John Cowper Powys, *A Glastonbury Romance* (Woodstock, NY: Overlook, 1987), 815–16.
27. See "Meditation V: Christ's Teaching," in *The Works of the Rt. Rev. Charles C. Grafton*, vol. 5, ed. B. Talbot Rogers (New York: Longmans, Green, 1914).

by assimilating the leadership of that culture in one of the most accurate measures of that leadership: namely, Jew-hatred.

One of the most rational and manipulative of black leaders, Jesse Jackson, has taken over the Jew-hatred of a manipulator of the fictive Islamic movement among blacks, Louis Farrakhan, as a uniting political and moral leader in American society. These third culture figments become a mythic reality and function rationally in the search for power through sheer assertion of the new black body politic. The blacks themselves turn away from the Jewish God, their churches become post-Christian churches in a subtle and realistic way. Their address to the relics, the Jews themselves, is to cosmic conspirators against the blacks and their struggles to correct this curst world.

Many post-Jews joined them in this movement. Those Jews are themselves pathetic and haters of highest authority. It is perfectly in keeping with the rationalist tradition that they should play out their fantasy of rebellion by joining the Jew-haters. The greatest post-Jew of the third culture, Sigmund Freud, performed a similar miracle of theoretic reversal by making Moses an Egyptian. In that way, Freud himself joined the Jew-hating movements of modernity, and yet the way was so fictive that Freud himself could remain repressively unaware of his Jew-hating persona. Marcel Proust, as an inventor of fictions that became Marcel himself in literary posterity, is also a figure to be analyzed in terms of the dynamics of Jew-hatred in the third culture. Proust's literary genius is for remembering everything about himself except the sacred history of the people to which he belongs by birth.

Some of the reassurances of the sacred in either its first or second culture meanings, mythic or revelatory, can be preserved by fictive haters of the Jews by the expedient of seeing the Jews as at once above and below and everywhere secretly, like the dead God, in the third culture. The Jews become the mysterious *Other*, that mysterious nonidentity that puzzles Hamlet about himself and to which Rimbaud referred in his effort to understand himself. The real death cry of a god dead at last of extreme old age becomes the cry for the death of an extremely old people, the Jews. Again, John

Cowper Powys understood this very well in another of his novels, *Wolf Solent.* One of his characters says to himself, so as to reassure himself about the threatening otherness that he feels himself to be, that "Christ is different from God. . . . Only when God is really dead will Christ be known for what He is. Christ will take the place of God then."[28]

With the death of God, the conspiracy theory of Jewish power takes a turn that can be exploited rationally by Jew-haters. This is certainly the case among black Jew-haters in America nowadays. This was certainly the case for Hitler as he expressed his desire for power in 1922.

20. *Josef Hell.* I turn to some remarks made by this high priest of desire in 1922 to a recorder of that desire. That recorder carried a perfect parody of a third cultural name. His name is Josef Hell. During one of their conversations, Hell asked Hitler how it was that he came—like God, as it were—to choose the Jews. Hitler promptly dropped his usual ranting style and gave a perfectly rational answer, as intellective as it was transgressive.

> My object is to guide first-rate revolutionary upheavals, regardless of what methods or means I have to use in the process. Earlier revolutions were against the peasants, or nobility, or the clergy or against dynasties and their network of vassals, but in no case has revolution succeeded without the presence of a lightening rod that could conduct and channel the odium of the general masses.[29]

What rationality less odd of this dead god than to choose the Jews, who become themselves rationally understood as at once creative and deadly in the third culture. After all, Creation is in the here and now. Why not? As Hell remarked, the Jews were an undeniably intelligent people to whom the entire world owed an incalculable debt in the areas of art and knowledge. It was just at this

28. John Cowpers Powys, *Wolf Solent* (New York: Garden City Publishing, 1933), 8.

29. Josef Hell, *Aufzeichnung,* 1922, Z.S. 640, p. 6, Institut für Zeitgeschichte in Frankfurt. Quoted in Gerald Fleming, *Hitler and the Final Solution* (Berkeley and Los Angeles: University of California Press, 1984), 28.

point that a calm and rational Hitler could make his calm and rational case for choosing precisely the Jews, for sociological reasons that followed the theological in his own struggle against the second culture. Hitler remarked now,

> . . . weighing every imaginable factor, I came to the conclusion that a campaign against the Jews would be as popular as it would be successful. . . . Disproportionately to their small number they account for an immense share of the German national wealth, which can be just as easily put to profitable use for the state and the general public as could the holdings of monasteries, bishops and nobility. Once the hatred and the battle against the Jews has been really stirred up, their resistance will necessarily crumble in the shortest possible time. They are totally defenseless, and no one will stand up to protect them.[30]

Since the terrible otherness of God is dead, there remains the terrible otherness of the chosen. That otherness is to be found in works of art that are far removed from the tremendous tragedy of the Jews that signals the end of the second culture.

21. *The no to No.* Repression is an entirely private, indeed entirely unknown, dynamic of alienation from the self of something unknowable in the self. To the third culture self, it is the *No* that can be heard uttered by the third world patient etherized upon his table of the anti-Law. The repressed reminiscence of revelation presented to his conscious perception as if for the first time here or anywhere can no more than register the distance of the repression of revelation and, moreover, its severity. That *No* uttered by a third world patient is a register of the existence of the repression of revelation, a veritable gauge of that repression's cultural strength.

That *no* to *No* in the relation between the interdictory predicate and its negation expresses no impartial judgment about the prohibiting commanding truths of Sinaitic interdiction but ignores them, so as to commit a life to be lived in a world entirely without reference to that *No*. If third world members understood the char-

30. Ibid., 28–29.

acter of that second *no* they would see how bound they are to the first and begin to signify the required *Yes*.

We have now stepped onto the very ground of third world false consciousness only to see there a convergence between the demystifications of the Freudian mind and the repressive knowingness of third world mind. That mind is powerless to change its mind from the inside. It is so thoroughly alienated from all worlds and ways of sacred order that only an analysis from the second world can begin to destroy the artifices of that alienation, which is an alienation from the self of second culture. Third world selves, precisely in their alienation from the reaches of revelation, have gone out of self-control. That world passes through an indefinite number of stages foreign to its own intention to do itself no harm. The harms appear mysterious, as if from an incomprehensible *pop* realm for which there is no rational explanation. That very rationality of explanations would have to begin with the alienated nature of those who seek an explanation, those who have consolidated themselves, throughout the whole range of their activity, against the objective truth and power of the second world's aesthetic of authority.

The *floating/flirting/throating* of third world expectations and the failures to solve a variety of social 'problems' in that world are entirely a function of the repressive mode in which the third world mind works. The mindfulness of second world cultures of commanding truths are considered an alien force that is the residual cause of the very problems from which second world selves suffer. Therefore, the more intense the problems, the more intense the assault precisely upon the governing possibility of resolving those problems in the degree to which the old order can restore the new disorder to a new order. This is the problem facing a post-Freudian as well as post-Marxist civilization. The problem is of a renewal as well as restoration of second world commanding truths that cannot be fantasies of repetition in facsimile editions of the world from which third world selves fled into their present alienation.

It is the regular rendering of repression from revelation, the transformation of the repressive mode from a concealment of revelation into its negation, that produces that power of unknowing which makes our lives grow out of control, thwarting our expectations and bringing our disenchantments into ever more destructive enchantments. This subversion of the revelatory mode by the repressive has become so widespread as to appear natural, rather than the perversion it is.

The repressive mode has passed through various stages independent of revelation in a way that has rendered repression, no longer in service to revelation, as the prime governor of a world that can only truly exist dominated by the culture of commanding truths out of revelation. So self-confirming is the repressive mode by this time in the history of the supersession of revelation by repression that the present third cultural mode has become autonomous. The derivations of third world repressions become autonomous art, autonomous sex as apart from love, and the entire region of extraterritoriality that gives the repressive mode its privileged place in third world culture.

Third culture children are deprived of that development of their sense of awe by the swift shutdown of sacred orders under the pressures of repressive miseducation. There is no original act of repression, so to parallel neatly in fiction the act of original sin. The repressive mode has gained dominance by accretion in ways that are too multifarious to describe here. The war against the world of commanding truths is being fought continuously in every institution and aspect of radically contemporaneous life.

Because the essence of revelation lies in a necessary turning away from direct and conscious expression of everything primordial, everything before praise and blame, a culture that reinstates repression in its positive form, primordiality, if it could exist, would kill itself in closing the distances between any desire and its object. That closing of distances appears most markedly in the American drug culture. There is the inner-worldly language of everything thought or felt as if it not only would be done but has been done, on the instant. Third culture is the achievement of such narrowing devices made conscious, and direct, in a variety of pharmaceutical, or acoustical, or visual representations (e.g., hard porn) as will register the positive of the repressive, i.e., primordiality. Primordiality may be called ecstasy, in its older and more exquisite word, recycled by third world *hip*-hoppers who take 'Ecstasy', or it may still be called the 'quick fix'—the instantaneous satisfaction of desire.

The third culture primordial constitutes a reenchantment of the world. The dissolution of myth and the substitution of knowledge for fancy, and the further substitution of fancy for revelation, as in the faith/knowledge that Coleridge called the 'primary imagination', means the development of a program of mastery that no longer needs the rational as it was understood in the eighteenth and nineteenth century. What is rational, in a world repressing revelation, may lead to mass extermination or other modes of reenchanting the world through reason. Call it *oceana* or any other fictive names for third culture. The Orwellian name for the institution of a radically politicized world that is undergoing reenchantment through reason, *The Party*, is itself now under the rule of disenchantment. The very political institution that once saw through everything and everyone has itself been seen through, not by itself alone but by everyone else. Therefore, the politicizing of the great reenchantment of the world under Party ficta has been destroyed and another mode has been introduced, the mode of democratic artistry. This democratic artistry is to flatten all resistance and develop the kind of primordiality that operates through total domination by collective identification. The media of artistry is the televised or filmed image, which is capable of seeing through all differences by reducing them to one primordiality or another. The condition may be called "third culture knowing inertia." This knowing inertia has as its fancy term the word *hip*, a kind of disenchanting ecstasy that was part of the drug culture before the drug culture became extramusical.

The quick fix, the instantaneous satisfaction, is improbable. But life itself contains these improbabilities. The effort to eliminate both repression and revelation represents a recycling of precisely those improbabilities that are expressions of primordialities. That aim of third culture is itself an astounding wish to undo the very nature of culture, its interdicts and taboos, which, even when they fail, keep the improbable and its primacies of possibility at a distance. Negationally expressed, repressed contents represented to Freud the credenda of consciousness vested in what is thought most incredible. But the most incredible become reality is the aim: the extremity and fantasy of the aesthetics of third cultures. In therapeutic third cultures, the revelation is intimately bound to those intimacies that are the expression of secret and repressed wishes. The betrayal of those secrets is therapy become a public culture. It becomes the office of the therapist to forward this parody of revelation as a duty toward the world of knowledge so that many other patients who are suffering from the same disorder of psychosexual life can subject themselves to the revelation as it becomes established in its authority over the new society. The truth is in this commitment to a therapeutic revelation of most secret and repressed wishes which once were called the arena of the primordial—the secret and sexual, as well as other modes of transgression, against the superseded but not eliminated commanding truths.

It is life ineptitudes rather than life transgressions that are to be scourged and ministered by the new guiding elite. There is no one and nothing to be acknowledged except the correction of these life ineptitudes and the re-creation of those satisfactions that have been subjected to precisely those most secret and repressed wishes which no longer have the task of obeying commanding truths against their fulfillment.

Precisely the minutiae of everyday life, as it is attended in the respectable middle classes, is paralleled by the concentration upon that minutiae of the new therapeutic guiding elites. Particular interiors are to be examined with the meticulous attention that was devoted to the art of the interior in the Dutch and Flemish schools of seventeenth-century painting. This immersion in the petty detail of daily existence is to free the individual from the symptomatic entanglements of an impulse life that no longer has the kind of world obedience to the order of commanding truth that could never be described as neurotic or in any way unsatisfying. The pious of second culture have suffered so long a burial of their mutilated wishes that they do not even know that they are dead. It is these mutilated relics of the sacred center of antiquity, the order directed by revelation, that the conscientious therapist is engaged to destroy even as he reconstructs its particulars in a case that has come to him; or, that the artist can see in his imaginative surveillance of himself as he meets that case in the moment he leaves himself behind in his studio or study.

The walk through ourselves, meeting robbers, ghosts, giants, old men, young men, wives, widows, brothers in love, does not mean that we always meet ourselves. The only self we have met is the social self. The sacred self is not that easily met, not even in the therapeutic session, that very private world historical meeting of two isolated figures, which represents in its course of treatment precisely the third world view of social order as essentially a condition in which someone is to help liberate someone else and, in the course of doing so, liberate himself. All those who are liberated, save one, shall live. That one is the authority above the vertical in authority, or anyone representing that one.

FIVE

Sacred Messengers and the New Man

1. *Sacred messengers.* The sacred messenger is a bridge between sacred order and social. One walks, or stumbles, over that bridge to receive the message from highest authority, which is the truth. As the metaphor implies, the life of a sacred messenger is not an easy one. The bridge figure is literally stepped on. That stepping can be painful for the scourge and minister of sacred order.

> . . . but heaven hath pleased it so,
> To punish me with this, and this with me,
> That I must be their scourge and minister.[1]

Hamlet knows that the office of scourge and minister of sacred order is more like a punishment than a reward. That punishing office will cost Hamlet dearly: his life.

2. *Hamlet's failed mission.* Hamlet knows both his office as sacred messenger and his failure in that office. Hamlet cannot succeed because he only half believes. Gertrude cannot convey the truth to Claudius because Hamlet has failed to convey the truth to her. He knows he is acting, merely acting: he is mad in craft (3.4.210). That craft is not the same as acting on truth. Hamlet cannot see the truth as something other than a half-truth.

It seems that all sacred messengers fail. Their job is neither easy nor enviable. We can read Hamlet's failure when he fails to act as a bridge to sacred order. Despite his pleadings, Hamlet is unable to make his own mother see even the ghost of authority.

> Ham.   Do you see nothing there?
> Queen. Nothing at all; yet all that is I see.

1. *Hamlet*, 3.4.194–96.

Ham. Nor did you nothing hear?
Queen.   No, nothing but ourselves.
(3.4.148–53)

Hamlet knows that it is Gertrude's trespass and not his madness that speaks. And he knows that he cannot convince her of that truth. At 3.4.170–73, he tells her what to do:

Confess yourself to heaven;
Repent what's past; avoid what is to come;
And do not spread the compost on the weeds
To make them ranker.

Thirty lines later, Gertrude asks "What shall I do?" Hamlet has failed to make Gertrude see the invisible truth and act upon it; he cannot make her see the true answer to those four basic words of life. He knows that in this failure lies tragedy.

There is a sense in which every sacred messenger is making a deathwork. The delivery of the message from highest authority is fraught with danger. When Socrates leaves the heights he says: "I went down."[2] That going down is never good for the health. Gertrude, and Hamlet, will not be able to avoid what is to come. What is to come is bloodshed. Gertrude will "break . . . [her] own neck down" (3.4.218). Hamlet, Socrates, and many others end with broken necks.

3. *Failure and bloodshed.* The failure of sacred messengers can lead to bloodshed before any righting of sacred/social order. Hamlet reigns over a bloody mess. Knowing his failure, he begs Horatio to "tell my story" (5.2.372). It is not altogether clear that Horatio will be able to deliver the truth to Fortinbras and the noble audience. Who then succeeds? Shakespeare, and those who can read the messenger and thus the message correctly. When Hamlet says "the interim is mine," he knows that it is through the play that he will finally speak truly, because he will be read truly (5.2.80). That true reading is a matter of work by the reader. The bridge is there to be crossed, but that crossing is never easy. Ham-

2. Plato, *Republic,* 3.

let resists, shuffles before highest authority, before he understands the nature of his agency; so too must we struggle to read truly his, and our, right place in the vertical in authority.

4. *Another sacred messenger.* Thomas in Antonioni's film *Blow-Up* (1966) has seen the truth, through transgression. He too realizes his failure to deliver the truth to the reigning absence in authority, his agent Ron. Thomas's face in the final scenes expresses the truth more eloquently than any words. His sadness is from the realization that he lives in a third world indifferent to the *via*, and that he is now a sacred messenger who will not be read truly, at least in swinging 1960s London. Of course, Thomas remains on film, there to be read and reread. Through Thomas's and Hamlet's failures as sacred messengers, we can read the permanent spiritual wars, which are never merely matters of the spirit.

5. *The difference between artist and sacred messenger.* Typologically, the second world sacred messenger is the opposite of the third world artist. The artist speaks in many voices, expressing a chameleon self. Hamlet refers to the chameleon self. Keats, too, knew he was an artist and not a sacred messenger when he referred to the "camelion Poet."[3] Sir Anthony Quayle echoed that sense of third world self when he said of Sir Lawrence Olivier: "Larry was never really himself except when on stage." No man of many voices, such as Olivier or any other actor or artist, can be a sacred messenger. Sacred messengers are not sent to entertain or to amuse. The sacred messenger carries a message from highest authority and speaks that message with one voice. That one voice is the voice of the sacred self, the *I* that is predicated by the *I* of highest authority.[4]

That great artists are never sacred messengers was realized by Keats when he wrote that Shakespeare's brilliance was in his "*Neg-*

3. John Keats to Richard Woodhouse, October 27, 1818, in *The Letters of John Keats*, ed. M. B. Forman, 2nd ed. (London: Oxford University Press, 1935), 228.

4. The question must be raised of *Saul/Paul.* Being all things to all men comes dangerously close to speaking with many voices, as an artist. From the literature, Paul appears to be both genius and sacred messenger. He is a virtuoso performer, as Christ cannot be.

ative Capability."[5] Hamlet himself is a great poet. He is an artist who speaks with many voices and suddenly finds himself saddled with the message and task of righting sacred order. Hamlet becomes a scourge out of his own panic and dread at being a minister. Scourge means transgressive, for which every scourge is punished. Oedipus too is a scourge. After his marriage to his mother, a scourge sets in. Hitler scourges Europe and is himself scourged. But Stalin dies in bed. This is not impossible in second world theory. The doctrine is that if not now, then later, down to the tenth generation: there will be retribution. Stalin's empire continues to be torn apart. Fifty years is well short of ten generations.

6. *Scourge.* A scourge is not a minister of sacred order; he is a rebel against it who emerges to punish, unjustly perhaps, social order. Scourging is itself transgressive, and so scourges must be scourged. 'Scourge' is in the second world reading. They are killers who act, momentarily, as agents freed from sacred order and its commanding truths. Scourges must be scourged in order to restore sacred order. Hamlet is at least part rebel from sacred order, and for that rebellion and the bloody scourgings that follow he must be punished.

Scourges are what they represent: wounds to the social organs which are themselves deeply disordered. Figures from the underworld, maniacs, avengers have this quality. Perhaps Meir Kahane was a scourge, on a small scale, a figure of desperation after the Shoah. The Jews are a deeply traumatized people. But that does not excuse scourges or make them agents of sacred order. Scourges add suffering to suffering. Most scourges are agents of sheer responsive punishment. But they can be cultivated, grown, mass-produced; like dragon's teeth. It is entirely possible that some young blacks are now being prepared to act as scourges of the unjust American social order. They are now to be schooled in the ideological fictive helmet of the new racist scourging which then fuses with lust, sadism—wilding, madness. Scourges may be figures of radical evil who appear to rise out of nothing—Ted

5. John Keats to George and Thomas Keats, December 21, 1817, *Letters of John Keats*, 72.

Bundy. They are mysteries of evil. But these goodfellas and our young black scourges are not mysteries.

As scourge, Moses has three thousand men killed; is that the will of highest authority or the will of Moses? Moses pursues the death of those men with a vengeance. But *vengeance is mine, sayeth the Lord.* It is clear that Moses is human, not divine. Human messengers can exaggerate and make mistakes. Christ's scourgings, of the temple for example, are part of his humanity, his vanity. The line between the will of highest authority and the will of the minister of sacred order is a shadow that is easily crossed. Moses is punished for that confusion which places his vengeance before God's and makes him a scourge of social order. There are proleptic images of Moses's scourging, such as the angel who threatens him with castration. He must die before reaching the Holy Land as punishment for being the scourge and minister of highest authority. Hamlet too knows that he will be scourged for his scourging of the Danish social order.

7. *With malice toward none — Lincoln as sacred messenger.* Lincoln suffers for being a scourge and minister of the American social order. Some of that suffering may be read in this famous photographic portrait (see fig. 29). He knows that he must pay for the massive bloodletting he has released.[6] Lincoln is still, 140 years after his death, being scourged. Lincoln is the last, and perhaps only, sacred messenger and figure of grace in U.S. history. His memory is a casualty of the war against sacred order and its embodiments. He has been wiped out, replaced by President's Day. The displacement of Lincoln by such a vaguery, meaningless to most Americans, is part of the *kulturkampf.*

Cultures without sacred messengers are in trouble. Lincoln himself rose from the lowest social classes—his parents could not read. How is the population to understand the vertical, the rise that is always possible, without the supreme figure of Lincoln?

8. *Posthumous scourging.* Lincoln's removal from American mythology—the elimination of his birthday, the typical criticisms

6. See, generally, Abraham Lincoln, "Second Inaugural Address," in *Speeches and Letters,* ed. Peter Parish (London: Everyman Library, 1993).

FIGURE 29. Photograph of Abraham Lincoln
by Alexander Gardner

in contemporary documentaries—is part of a scourging of Lincoln, the minister of highest authority. This scourging is a deathwork aimed at the second culture as it still exists in the United States. Ironically, this tragedy inverts the real tragedy of the Civil War. It is as a scourge that Lincoln is scourged by highest authority; he pays for the war he believed was just and necessary, as it may have been. Nevertheless, like Moses, he must be scourged. To unleash mass killing, whether just or not, is to be a scourge, which is inevitably transgressive because it is uncontrolled and allows human vanities and excesses to be expressed. But Lincoln's present scourging by third world elites is for his office of minister, not scourge.

9. *Third world scourges.* Third world scourges are killers, re-

leased from sacred order by retreating second and oncoming third world elites so as to destroy the injustices of the world. For a third world scourge, this means destroying white males, patriarchy, biological constraints on sexuality, the ruling class, capitalism, pet ownership, law: any restraint that keeps a man or woman from becoming the world. Schools that teach self-esteem therapy are preparatory schools for scourges who will have nothing but an ideology of anger and hatred. This preparatory scourging sets the stage for far more violent scourging later. Scourges do not come from nowhere. Without the Party it is likely that Stalin would have remained an ordinary killer. It is only through his education in the Party that his scourge potential became real.

American culture is producing more not fewer insane people. The fundamental movement against sacred order has produced an increasing number of world men and world women. MOVE (recall that third culture abolitionist movement?) was an ideology of primordial blackness. The members were executing white inhibitions—washing, for example. That once fringe romantic ideology is now entering the school systems. No system of commanding truths or its third world inversions can operate without a system of indoctrination. Third culture pietists assume they are antidoctrinal and anticredal. But the obvious truth is that third world antidoctrines are really third world supersession doctrines. Third world education is a matter of indoctrination into the fictive culture of the primacy of possibility. Of course, there are strands of truth in *pop* doctrines—there are different skin pigmentations, gender-based differences in behavior, economic classes. But it is the elevation of these basics to the level of primordial truth that creates the lie.

10. *More Bundys.* Third culture is producing more and more serial killers, and it is usually women who suffer. In Freudian theory, the first and ultimate world to which we belong, the *not-I*, is the mother. The *not-I*, that which is outside our subjectivities, must be destroyed so that each man and woman can be his or her own world. The group 2 Live Crew and their current derivatives are a matter of world conquest, although the women are not world/women figures. Rather, they are mere objects, the consumption of

which confirms rather than creates the world man. That creating, the destruction of the *not-I*, has already been accomplished for many third worlders. Beyond that struggle against the *not-I* lies endless life-affirming consumption. That desire is precisely what is encouraged in third world arts of consumption and self-affirmation.

11. *World/woman, world/man.* The world woman or world man is opposed to the sacred messenger and to all figures in authority other than himself. Representing the world, which always affirms itself, a world man expresses immanence. By contrast, sacred messengers express transcendence. The world man figure may be assimilated to genius. The world man affirming himself may be as comic as Falstaff and totally without moral scruple. There are obviously elements of sheer transgression in the world man. Falstaff lies, cheats, re-kills the dead hero Hotspur—anything to affirm himself: "Banish plump Jack, and banish all the world."[7] Self-esteem therapy as third world education is extraordinarily dangerous as it is linked to the therapy of being a scourge. So we have the explosive combination of self-esteem therapy and the scourge responding to imagined or real injustices and the obvious implication for violence. Falstaff was at once a fighter and a coward, a thief and a charmer; whatever suited his sense of the moment. The world man ceases to be comic, or to sing beautifully, when he becomes a Ted Bundy or Gary Gilmore.

Ego pathology is an obvious implication in Freud that he deals with as narcissism. But the narcissist is the person who identifies his ego with the world. Now third world culture is producing mini-world men and women by the thousands.

12. *Democracy and dependence.* Democracy has always had guiding elites toward obedience to the commanding truth in sacred order other than those of the state. Jefferson, Madison et al. assume there are in place these mediating institutions that are not institutions of the state. Now we are assuming, because of the decline of these mediating institutions—family, church, etc.—that the state can take on these mediating functions. For democracy to exist in

7. *Henry IV Part I* (Folger), 2.4.526.

the manner intended by the founders, there must be as its objective correlative sacred order as it evolved out of Athens and Jerusalem. The original doctrine of independence is being destroyed by those claiming a doctrine of private affairs and purely internal matters.

Democracy depends upon the perpetual rediscovery that the world is not ourselves, that there is a *not-I* who is master of our limits, both imaginatively and in social action. That perpetual rediscovery of the *not-I*, which Durkheim reduced to society or the supreme collective representation, is the object of art in the third culture repressive mode. The Gertrudian doctrine that there is *nothing but ourselves* to see is the doctrine of a perpetual covering of the *not-I*. The *kulturkampf* is being waged intellectually, and the third culture guiding elites are teaching us a certain blindness that must be reread and seen through. What is at stake is both democracy and the integrity of the intellect. That war is being fought out at once in the mass media and in the schools, from the youngest to the oldest students. In these institutions the perpetual rediscovery of the *not-I* is being displaced, distorted—in sum, repressed. The foundations of democracy are being destroyed from the top down, not from the bottom up.[8] As sacred drama, *Hamlet* takes place in the Middle Ages. That sacred drama is being replayed massively in contemporary society.

True democracy must perpetually republish its declarations of dependence on something suprapolitical: its predicative sacred order, the vertical in authority. The interdictory mode supreme in it and second culture responses to the Commandant of truth, democracy can perpetually re-create its mediating civil society. But this perpetuation implies sacred messengers who appear constantly on the verge of defeat and alone, even as the Commandant constantly reappears. One of the measures of our democracy in trouble is the absence since Lincoln of sacred messengers in its political life. Not that the nation would recognize such a figure. Part of the tragic character of democratic societies is precisely that

8. Remember Rieff's First Law of Social Order, 'The rot starts at the top, always'.

there sacred messengers are recognized only posthumously. That was true in the period of the Greek democratic society, as it is today.

13. *We hold these truths to be sacred/self-evident—Jefferson as sacred messenger.* Jefferson's declaration of dependence was transformed into Franklin's declaration of independence. Perhaps it was the sentiment of the vacuity at the limitless and dark heart of what Benjamin Franklin called "Providence" that led him to persuade Jefferson to change the opening line of the Declaration of Independence to read, instead of "we hold these truths to be sacred," the canonical and more ambiguously philosophical "we hold these truths to be self-evident," which is far from the case.[9] Franklin was a profoundly shrewd operator. If those truths Americans are to hold are understood to be absolutely directive—that is, sacred—then every human is absolutely dependent on them. There is a subtle elimination, or at least reduction, of the vertical in authority where truths are held merely to be self-evident. They then become a matter for logical debate and the feeling of absolute dependence upon them is open to limitless perspectives of their change and, indeed, dissolution. Franklin's suspicion of the word *sacred* leaves a world that is far less transparent than the world of the humans who pledged their allegiance to the word that was their lives. That second world is far more transparent in its revelatory character. Thus began the process of inversion which third culture elites have continued: the transformation of life, liberty, and the pursuit of happiness into the pursuit of the freedom to transgress and the happiness of transgressing.

Happiness means that sense of being blessed in our lives, and the pursuit of the good life in its modest forms comes from obeying the commanding truths inseparable from creation. The pursuit of happiness does not mean what one of the characters in the Canadian film *The Decline of the American Empire* (1986) asserts it to mean: a personal happiness that consists largely in transgressing the commanding truths of the Creator in second worlds

9. See Walter Isaacson, *Benjamin Franklin: An American Life* (New York: Simon & Schuster, 2003), 311–12.

through, in that character's case, the obsessive pursuit of sado-masochistic relations. That is, happiness means, as it meant in both the classical tradition out of Athens and in the traditions of commanding truth out of Israel, the sense of right living.

Right living is in accord with created nature. That sort of happiness Lincoln, as sacred messenger, says is contradicted when some men, slave owners, lounge about while living on the sweat of slaves; that is not according to nature. Therefore, slave owners could never achieve the happiness meant by the pursuit of happiness. That freedom and leisure may appear as happiness. But both the happiness of the master and the unhappiness of the slave are reflections of each other. Neither is obedience to commanding truth. The terrible condition of being a slave is transgressive; the terrible condition of being a slave owner is transgressive. Thus the freeing of slaves every seven years in ancient Israel. Every social order is imperfect.

The second world sense of happiness as obedience to commanding truths, which incorporated the first world sense of virtue, has been relentlessly assaulted and now superseded by the third world sense of happiness as freedom from commanding truth. The radically individualistic world Tocqueville saw coming—each man thrown back upon himself alone—is now being fought for as the basic right of civilization. A Supreme Court ruling states: "The most comprehensive of rights and the right most valued by civilized men" is "the right to be let alone."[10] The right to be let alone here is an utterly blind version of the rebellion against sacred orders; Justices Blackmun, Brennan, Marshall, and Stevens have not the slightest idea of what they are saying. This rebellion as the highest cultural value augers a new civilization, a civilization based upon negative communities. Ultimately those communities number one.

14. *Klee's* Angelus Novus. Walter Benjamin's reading of Klee's new angel of history personified (see fig. 30) appears to me to be correct, so far as it goes. Benjamin's reading runs as follows:

10. U.S. Supreme Court, Dissenting Opinion, *Bowers v. Hardwick*, 478 U.S. 186 (1986).

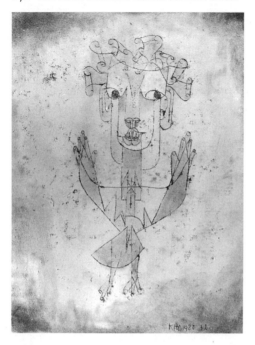

FIGURE 30. *Angelus Novus,* Paul Klee, 1920
(© Collection The Israel Museum, photo by David Harris; © 2004 Artists Rights Society [ARS], New York/VG Bild-Kunst, Bonn)

A Klee painting named "Angelus Novus" shows an angel looking as though he is about to move away from something he is fixedly contemplating. His eyes are staring, his mouth is open, his wings are spread. This is how one pictures the angel of history. His face is turned toward the past. Where we perceive a chain of events, he sees one single catastrophe which keeps piling wreckage upon wreckage and hurls it in front of his feet. . . . But a storm is blowing from Paradise; . . . This storm irresistibly propels him into the future to which his back is turned, while the pile of debris before him grows skyward. The storm is what we call progress.[11]

11. Walter Benjamin, "Theses on the Philosophy of History," in *Illuminations: Essays and Reflections,* ed. Hannah Arendt (New York: Schocken, 1968), 257–58.

Benjamin's reading of Klee's *Angelus Novus* does not depend upon its size at all. But it is mistaken if the reader of Benjamin's reading, a contemporary Benjamin scholar named Susan Buck-Morss, means that Klee's new angel, as understood by Benjamin, is a humanly proportioned figure.[12] The head is far too large and the entire figure entirely too threatening to be compared so simply to the gigantic winged sculpture, the angel of victory celebrating the history of French military triumphs, that Buck-Morss gives as a contrasting predicate of optimism and the infantilization of the third culture masses as can be read in public art. It is not clear that Benjamin himself has any discussion of that gigantic composed piece of sculpture, a parody of a classical figure entirely out of proportion to what is meant by classicism. The angel of victory has no human proportions. It is far too large.

15. *My reading of the Benjamin reading.* An angel is, at least in its second culture imagery, always a sacred messenger. But Klee's angel is himself terrified, and terrifying in the look of him, not least the sharpened teeth in his mouth. The new angel is an image of messages that center entirely on third culture primordialities. He is himself in flight, out of fright, as he tries to escape the very primordiality of which he is the repressive image. This angel of history, this third culture sacred messenger, looks like no other. His face is turned toward the past because, in Benjamin's reading, the past itself has been transformed into one single catastrophe which third culture history reads as the power of sacred orders, all of them in all their varieties, piling the wreckage of the social orders they have supplied with creative force.

Sacred orders are the origins of storms. Third culture history, which Klee's new angel represents symptomatically, is being driven irresistibly, but more precisely resistlessly, into a future upon which the angel has turned his back so to suit his blindness. Not seeing what is coming, the trashed world of third cultures is a pile of debris growing toward the sky. That is a parody of the Tower of Babel. Third culture elites call this storm 'progress'.

12. Susan Buck-Morss, *The Dialectics of Seeing: Walter Benjamin and the Arcades Project* (Cambridge, MA: MIT Press, 1989), 95.

Storm imagery is well known to us in second culture traditions. The great storm imagery of *King Lear*, on the heath, is an account of the destruction of sacred order that should inform mere social order. The family quarrel and hostility between daughters and father is both unnatural and a destruction of the culture in that first culture time. That this is the wrong time and that the ruling figures of Lear's kingdom are made of the wrong symbolic stuff describes the hidden truth behind the storm that Lear welcomes. Centuries later the storm imagery is repeated in later works of art that reveal, even as they conceal, the reality of the cataclysm of late second culture under the imagery of the cataclysm of nature. The old correlation between sacred macrocosm and social microcosm is repeated by the modern author George Stewart, when he makes the central character of his story nature itself.[13]

Stewart considers that these storms are as inevitable in the life cycle of nature as in our individualities. His fiction is of the world and its inhabitants existing for the glory of this storm, as if it were a wonderfully enriching way to increase our vision of the overwhelming events around and within us. The storm in social theory upon which he is depending is that primordiality to which Freud turned and which he called 'libido'. Freud's rather modest rediscovery of what Benjamin calls 'Paradise' is of sexuality. In that particular, Freud is a third culture symbolist. Sexuality is the commanding truth of much that we can see through in our third culture. Libido is a third culture goddess of life buried by second culture revelation, which is wisely mistaken, in its unsuccess, for repression. That is the common meaning of repression now in our war of mocking of words.

16. *Niagara/Viagra*. There is a nameless sadness rolling over the late second culture world that has to do with the vicissitudes of libido which is now a primordiality that has succeeded the inmost soul, the sacred self, identified in second culture symbolism. Libido becomes the ever-flowing river of the unconscious which is the real life of humans iced over by revelation regarded as itself repression. This unregarded river of life has had its engineer,

13. See George Stewart, *Storm* (New York: Random House, 1941).

Freud, to pull away the dams that had been built up to distort it in its flow toward what Freud called 'genitality'. This sense of primordiality as psychic energy anchored in sexuality is equally the goddess of burials, since the buried life of late second culture can, when exposed, be quite destructive. The association of the third culture primordial libido with eros is by no means sufficient. Where there is pleasure, there is going to be pain.

As a term for sexual appetite, the unblocking of libido, standing in the same relation to the mouth as hunger, has created that image of sexual hunger which is the storm that drives in a major way third culture imaginative energies. It even extends into experimental science, searching for chemicals that might be called by a name similar to hormones or, indeed, to Bergson's *élan vital*, which would associate this storm of libido with the water image of life itself. Once the desire for knowledge of such a buried life seemed to third culture liberation symbolists an unspeakable desire that must be spoken so that its disguises could be stripped away. But after the initial burst of symbolism for the primordial of sexuality, the nature of the primordial has come under greater and greater pressure of the ambiguity of the imagery of sex as the primordial.

Behind this storm of sexuality was another which Freud saw as the even more primordial element, that is, beyond life and its pleasures, called death and its pain, which in life emerge as aggression and transgression. The Freudian movement divided ego and sexual instinct as facts of life itself in its primordiality. The character of satisfaction therefore included what would otherwise appear deadly and at the least immoral. Freud saw no sexual paradise but only the storm of libidinal conflicts in life structures of authority, the source of which he traced to the vicissitudes of libidinal life itself. Primordiality invites a theory of authority, even a theory in authority, which Freud called his mythology. That mythology by no means excludes war and versions of war.

The sacred messengers of second culture have become, before our very eyes, angels of death in third culture and if not death, than at least exchanges of pleasure for pain, as in sadomasochistic erotic rituals. The reciprocities are necessary and should be not only permitted but encouraged in third culture social order in the light and darkness of an infinite new primordiality of needs. The reciprocity of pleasure and pain achieved in the neutral service of primordial needs can no longer be challenged by second culture sacred orders. Needs themselves have become primordialities that are obviously fed by consumerist culture. But that consumerist culture is so widely noted that I think I can spare the reader further remarks on it.

Benjamin understood that, in the form of reading that I call verticality, history has not moved; rather, in his terms, it stands still and gathers the dust which covers the truth of these primordialities. The dust is in the eye of the beholder. The primordialities are inventions of third culture elites, including Benjamin himself as he tries desperately to cope with the progressivist culture elites of whom he is himself an ardent member, in its political phase at least. For Benjamin was unable to part with his Marxism, that dustiest of all third culture doctrines. As a sacred messenger, Benjamin himself achieves a certain prophetic reputation, for he is led by a disenchantment with Marxist theory that makes him a prophet of its demise at the same time that he cannot give it up, as if the sanctity of custom had hallowed his membership in it and opposed his prophetic realizations that the external and objective vertical was not subject to the imperious demands of Marxist or post-Marxist elites.

Benjamin has a split message which he feels an impulse to deliver. But the truth given him is entirely a critical grasp of Marxist teaching that negates it without a supersessive assertion of sacred order in second culture senses. Benjamin is a Hamlet figure, one in whom there is a rediscovery of sacred order that is itself so alarming that he finds himself unable to admit it or to allow himself, having admitted it, to declare those commanding truths in which he himself is engaged as an agent and avenger. In Freudian terms there is something about his condition that binds Hamlet to the crippled sensibilities of the reigning monarchs, his uncle stepfather and his queen mother. But he is in a crisis in which the source of his delay resembles that of Benjamin and every other who finds himself unable to trust the inner laws and development of events in sacred order.

Hamlet cannot speak and act his sacred self because, long before the occasion of his father's death, he has, as a student, despite his exemplary life in Denmark, found himself inwardly challenging the commanding truths and therefore all sacred orders. Hamlet conveys the melancholy of his condition, in which he cannot act within the appointed time because he cannot express his own membership in sacred order or accept it as a stupefying power that would lead him to do as he must do and not wait for yet further calls. In that melancholy and the bitter joking that goes with it, Hamlet resembles all in our own time. The time was out of joint precisely in the sense that Hamlet is out of joint with its moment of truth in a sense far deeper than the one that concerns only his family history. It is sacred history that is the hidden horizon of his delay. As a sacred messenger, Hamlet is a failure.

17. *Dispossession.* The storm in third culture is a dispossession, which is why Klee's/Benjamin's angel faces backward. These third culture children are in a storm do not know they are in, and they are not interested—they are accustomed to life in the storm of dispossession of the entire world of commanding truths. They are interested in distraction. In Mark 10:19, Jesus says to a rich young man, in my sacred sociological translation, "You already know the commanding truths."[14] The third world future promises more of the same storm. It carries none of the weights of life lived in truth. The communist regime, in its own mendacious way, promised a future, a possession. Now those freed Europeans face what the West has faced for some time: dispossession of all truths and their commanding character.

A figure like Hamlet is a sacred messenger toward the future; from the beginning, when he says to his mother, "Seems, Madam? Nay it is,"[15] Hamlet both knows the commanding truths and does

14. Mark 10:19: "Thou knowest the commandments, Do not commit adultery, Do not kill, Do not steal, Do not bear false witness. Defraud not, Honour thy father and mother" (KJV).

15. *Hamlet,* 1.2.81.

not believe in them, or rather half believes. He has been dispossessed of an entire world. Hamlet has lost that world; he has been dispossessed. He is a figure of the future; he is a contemporary, not because of the Oedipus complex, as in Olivier's reading, but because he has been dispossessed of the world of commanding truths. That is the *is-ness* he cannot express. Thomas in Antonioni's *Blow-up* never knew of such a world. By a fatality he recovers knowledge of sacred order, but he cannot convey it—who is there to tell?

The self-dispossession of the world of commanding truths is the project of modern culture. We all know the commanding truths, but to say it is a bore to the children of third culture. Rilke's angels are agents of dispossession—the storm of passionate intensity dispossesses second world commanding truth. Third world *artists/messengers* have a new task, which is to promise people that it is all right to live their lives in a condition of dispossession. There must be an art and a university that accepts, even promotes, that life. Not that the possessions—the commands, the self-evident truths—are not worth studying or knowing; they simply cannot command, be self-evident. They are of interest aesthetically but can have no normative content.

Martin Scorsese's *Goodfellas* (1990) is a pathological picture of total dispossession. Those gangsters can do anything to anyone, including themselves. Transgression and "no problem" violence are released in the storm of dispossession. The storm of dispossession makes the current debate over curriculum in the university pointless; you can only offer them whatever they want, a smattering of everything/nothing. The young man who speaks to Christ in Mark 10:19 would not understand, or care, what Christ has to say in our time. A true sacred messenger speaks out of the past and into the future. Third world sacred messengers can only report the storm and its varying intensity. The kind of future prophets warn about in light of the commanding truths does not exist anymore. This is not to say that these people have not heard of the commanding truths; rather, that they focus their energies on eliminating whatever sense of second world commanding truth remains.

What lies after dispossession? The storm may continue to rage for generations. There are degrees of dispossession. The old possessions still have powers of distraction and entertainment, but the young are by no means possessed by them. They still go through the motions of education, work, family, etc.—what else is there to do? Why not do everything, like Oscar Wilde? Wilde was for the aesthetics, even of Christianity; it all entertains, whether feasting with panthers or attending his mass. Dispossession can be seen as a positive good, fodder for endless creativity. As long as their bodies are satisfied, their souls are content. A culture of civility that is separated from sacred order has not been tried before.

The first dispossession is of the whole notion of being in the image of God (Genesis 1:23). The dispossession of that notion means that one can always be the contrary. The absence of a specific and known character is the first and final payoff of a de-sacralized culture. *Imago Dei* is definitive. Klee's angel does not look like the received image of an angel—he is new, and as such, he could be anything, including a devil. Angels were those closest to highest authority, in perfect faith. Klee's new angel argues for a quite undefinitive human being. If one is feeling too definitive, too fixed, the best thing to do would be to take a bath in the river that is not the same river twice. That changing river now confirms our lack of definition, as opposed to the baptismal waters of second culture, which fix the image. Joyce ends *Finnegans Wake* with an image of that ever changing river in his development of an image of protean man.

18. *Gabriel/Joseph*. When my father came to Ellis Island, with my mother, both twenty-five years of age, in late November 1921, my father was deprived of his greatest asset: his given name, Gabriel, that of the great sacred messenger in both varieties of second culture known in our America, Jewish and Christian. The petty officials at Ellis Island did not understand my father's pronunciation of Gabriel and, being in a hurry, wrote him down as a Joseph. So, at an American stroke, he found himself with an American name that meant nothing to him. His own search for meaning in his life in America, his appearance as a man, was harmed by this stroke of American fate, in the guise of

the growing higher illiteracy of the nation and its officialdom. He simply lost the most important part of himself, the past that made him understand the sacred self as his own theorist of his own membership in traditional sacred order. The name is a bond. Accepting a change of name—Gabriel to Joseph—weakened my father's bond in the authority of the past. Yet, this story is one of both life and death. My father and mother were fleeing a world that would very soon turn deadly; those who did not leave that world, with rare exception, were dead within a small number of years, including this young man from the Warsaw ghetto, in figure 32, to whom I think I, as a young man in the asphalt jungles of Chicago, bore a remarkable resemblance (see figs. 31 and 32).

Slowly, in a way no one in my family understood, the family use of my father's true name, Gabriel, gave way before the fictive Joseph and became even more diminutive, as Joe. Joseph is carved on his gravestone. The triumph over any implication in

FIGURE 31. Photograph of the author as a young man

FIGURE 32. Photograph of Jews captured by SS and SD troops during the suppression of the Warsaw ghetto uprising (April 19–May 16, 1943)

(United States Holocaust Memorial Museum, courtesy of Instytut Pamieci Narodowej)

my father's name that he was himself in the name of the supreme among sacred messengers, bringing understanding of theory in the highest, was complete in the slow destruction of the family membership unambiguously in the traditional sacred order out of which they had come. My father's morale was severely damaged by this change of name, which confused him into acceptance. Slowly, as his Americanization took place, my father escaped from his name as a man of God. He lost a certain dignity, even though Joseph is a name of considerable meaning. But a Joseph is not a Gabriel, and there is something in his new name that divorced him from any message of divine comfort. He became a profoundly uncomfortable man. I have certainly transferred some of that self-discomfort to myself.

Watching names around me now for many years, I have seen how few Gabriels there are, not only among the Jews, but among those who might still think of themselves as Christian. I wonder if this can be because in the Christian tradition the archangel Gabriel announces the conception of Jesus as the Christ and therefore the messenger as messiah to the Blessed Virgin Mary. In Christian imagery, the sacred messenger Gabriel has always been associated with the Annunciation. Precisely that annunciation has fallen to the triumph of therapeutic sexuality, which makes the Annunciation itself the most transparent of large glasses as these have been seen through and shattered by third culture symbolists. Duchamp's *Bride* is a counterimage of the Annunciation. My father, stripped as he was of his name, was resistless to the process by which he ceased to make any sense of the theory of the Jews as a chosen guiding elite and led to an entirely aesthetic and psychological Jewishness, which consisted largely of going to synagogue on High Holy Days to hear how the cantor chanted.

The old angels of second worlds never announced a primordiality. Instead of any primordiality—love or death or energy—the sacred messengers in second cultures were intermediaries between highest authority and those highest in the hierarchy of life itself, human beings, who, like the angels, were to sing the praises of that highest authority whose commands they were born obediently to perform for and as nations and as individuals. Man was only a little lower than the angels in his obedience and in his understanding of those obediences as a true way of life. Angels were themselves images of the sacred self, spiritual beings; more precisely, beings who, in their spirituality, could understand the messages that are commanding truth.[16] These commands are never to be abolished, they can only be negated. The promise of no abolition is the messianic one, the second coming of Matthew 16:27. That promise is totally negated by such a work as Duchamp's *Bride*.

19. *There is no shuffling.* My maternal and paternal grandfathers have been, always, the middlemen of my life as a remembrancer.

16. See Matthew 18:10, 16:27.

My grandfathers, maternal and paternal, continue to return my messages, which is more than my sacred self condescends to do. For example, my gold watch is a beautifully engineered cultural artifact, made by Thomas in Munich in 1925, when I was three years old. It was given to me by my grandfather, who was a slave laborer in Hitler's death camps. The watch was ninety years old in 2005. That is not very old as a cultural artifact. *Macbeth* was written in 1605. One test of a cultural artifact is its endurance.

My grandfather told me, in Rockefeller Chapel at the University of Chicago, that he wanted to go to Svad, Israel, the town of his great teacher, Isaac Luria, to die. America was to him a land without grace, and he could not die amid such gracelessness.[17] In figure 33, you can see his gracefulness in even this passport photo taken for the journey we made together to Israel. My grandfather saw this de-created world coming; he thought that Hitler had won in some way. The evidence surrounded him: the gross sexuality of the young, the aestheticization of my father's Judaism in his passion for the Hinini.

20. *Readers/remembrancers*. My grandfathers, myself, my students—we are readers, which means that we are remembrancers. What remembrancers and resisters read is de-creation. Third worlds are cultures of de-creation. Joyce understood this perfectly. *Let there be fight* means let there be fight for a de-creation. At the level of art, the de-creative thrust has created masterpieces. Duchamp's *Etant donnés* and *The Bride Stripped Bare by Her Bachelors, Even*, complete with its pseudosacred guiding text, are masterpieces of de-creation. Wallace Stevens's great de-creation, "Notes toward a Supreme Fiction," ends with images of the antichurch militant. Was Stevens a remembrancer, or a master conveyancer of what I call third world? The officer classes in all sacred orders, first worlds or seconds, are remembrancers. The officer classes of third world anti-cultures are conveyancers. The conveyancer's gift lies in his hostility to culture in any of its first or second forms.

17. See C. P. Snow's use of the name Luria through a character who is based, in part, on myself in his *A Coat of Varnish* (New York: Scribner's, 1979).

FIGURE 33. Passport photograph of the author's grandfather

21. *Remembrancers/resistances.* For remembrancers, myself and my students included, reality is iconic, in the repressive mode. The reality we read conceals more than it reveals. That has always been the case. It is even more the case now because this is the most intense period of the *kulturkampf.* When Augustine hears the sacred messenger, which is a child's voice saying "take up and read," he opens the Gospels to an interdictory passage.

The commanding truths are Nots. As my grandfathers well knew, before permission there must be prohibition. This is true in first world taboos and second world commanding truths. The unprecedented character of the abolitionist movements is that they are against taboos and commanding truths. The tradition of sacred messenger imagery depicts the figures towering above nature, for nature is dominated by the messages of highest authority. Nature is there for us to dominate; and appreciate. The word, not nature, is primordial, and the word was with God and the word was God. What is left for me to do with this book could not have been *imagined/done* by my grandfathers. They found the world around them indescribable. My grandfathers understood themselves as rather small figures like Friedrich's monk (see fig. 34). *Monk by the Sea* presents an utterly empty landscape, primordiality itself, at the edge of which stands a solitary monk holding his head in his hands. He is separated from that startling and opaque emptiness by an unmistakable sense the viewer has that he is lost in thought. The world is uncompromising in its otherwise meaningless self-reference. Earth, sea, and sky, the boundlessness of the given and the minuteness of that black vertical of a human being are characteristic polarities of the primordial and the human world.

22. *Remembrancers of revelation.* To be without the forbidding sensibility trained in the traditions of revelation is to be empowered and yet crippled by that guiltlessness to which third world activists aspire. Though not principled inactivists, except in class-

FIGURE 34. *Monk by the Sea*, Caspar David Friedrich, 1809
(Bildarchiv, Preussischer Kulturbesitz/Art Resource, NY)

rooms, as teachers in the academy, second world officers, teachers included, are required to be remembrancers: those guilty/ knowing agents of sovereign authority who once collected the debts of others due their sovereign. In the German ladder language of faith, as with *kulturkampf*, the critical matter is far more clear, for its fusion of debt and guilt, than the same matter in English. Debt in English carries no sense of guilt. *Schuld* carries both meanings at once.

To illustrate negationally that saving sense of guilt which is collected for redistributive justice by remembrancers, Borges created yet another of those paradoxa cherished by third world genius: a memorious character who is not a remembrancer. To be memorious and yet not a remembrancer heralds a technological supersuccessor of the unfighting intellect. Imagine an idiot savant as forerunner of the computer data bank. For an entertaining version of this characterological possibility, entirely third world in its meaning, remark the vaudeville entertainer Mr. Memory in Hitchcock's film *The 39 Steps* (1935).

There is a great remembrancer in our own sacred historical time. He is A. I. Solzhenitsyn, who dedicated *The Gulag Archipelago*

to all those who did not live
to tell it.
And may they please forgive me
for not having seen it all
nor remembered it all,
for not having divined all of it.[18]

The Gulag Archipelago is the greatest book of remembrance, the greatest martyrology, ever written; far greater than Fox for the Protestants, far greater than any of the Catholic martyrologies. There are all too many Jewish books of remembrance to the dead of the Shoah, and to the dead of earlier hatreds within the inter-

18. Aleksandr I. Solzhenitsyn, *The Gulag Archipelago 1918–1956: An Experiment in Literary Investigation*, trans. Thomas Whitney (New York: Harper and Row, 1973).

necine warfare of hatred against the Jews. But no Jewish book of martyrology contains its artistry of theonomic tension anything like so authoritatively as Solzhenitsyn's immortal work. That immortal work is little read by the cultivated and reeducated classes in America. So little are the four volumes read that they have been remaindered. The next sociologists of religion will have to study these conveyancers of revelation repressed, negative capabilities without the gift of assimilating themselves to all characters in sacred/social order.

23. *Comedy: Shakespeare and Nietzsche.* Second worlds have comedies of the stage, such as *Measure for Measure.* In comedies, the sacred/social order is righted without bloodshed. Third worlds claim all of life as a comedy. In 1882 Nietzsche made the third world case that the comedy of existence will become conscious of itself.[19] But real life always disappoints. While the Nazis were horribly comic in their way, the truth is tragic. The third world successor to the sacred messenger is the artist, who knows he has nothing to say but clever mystifications of the transgressive nothing. The comedy of third world is that the sacred primordial is nothing. The artist is a bridge to nowhere. Third world sacred messengers do not suffer; they laugh. Of course, there are degrees of knowing laughter. As I have said, pieties never die, they only shift from object to object. Those amusing and amused creators such as Duchamp have their followers, their believers. But those followers are not the theorists of third worlds. The theorists know there is—nothing.

In fact, many third world artists despise their clients and followers, exactly because their followers believe in the art. The true/untrue third world artist insists on keeping the nothing behind everything in mind. One must guard against slipping into belief.

24. *Negational sacred messengers.* Is Don Giovanni a negational sacred messenger? A sacred messenger without knowing it? In second worlds, sacred messengers are not transgressive or trick-

19. Nietzsche, *The Gay Science,* 74.

sters, as in first culture. Second world messengers are given their messages by highest authority; the authority makes the apostle, not the apostle the authority.

25. *So/so.* There can be no deification of second culture without the fatality of recycling it as if it were a rediscovery of the primordialities that are the absolute horizons of first. There can be no culture religion. Culture is an indefinitely variable area of morphoses between sacred order and social order. But the metamorphosis is not equally in the opposite direction. This is the 'ideology' fallacy. Commanding truths are not clothes, which the emperor does, or does not, wear. They are not ours to give away or throw away. Though, in culture, they always become, on making, secondhand.

The repressive mode, despite its distancings of commanding truths from their objects, ourselves, does not take us so very far away from those truths. Yet, near as they are, in their unbreakable connection, *sacred order/social order — so/so*—cannot be fused; not before the second coming or the messianic age in its enduring form. But then, in that fusion, neither sacred order nor social will be as recognizable as it ever was. Nor will it be any of our recognizable and fatal utopias, Marxist or other. Until that anti-Utopian time of final fusion, of which Marx was the last hater great enough in his hatred to imagine he had seen its ghost in the various traditions out of Jerusalem that he considered in service to capitalism, sacred order, in its commanding truths, must not be confused with any kind of utopianism.

The prophets of sacred order, all our second world sacred messengers, were anything but systematic theorists or leaders of movements. Systems theories, such as the Marxist or any of its epigonic successors, such as the feminist or the gay or the racist, have constructed a psychosis about the established commanding truths in sacred order that has come to be shared by hundreds of thousands who have been moved toward these shared psychoses by a perverse religious sensibility. Their utopias can never come. Commanding truths will not be mocked, except to the destruction of everything sacred. These movements drive sacred and social orders farther and farther apart. Their transliterating cultures insist on fictive primordialities that create parody deifications specially for the cultivated classes, those miseducated enough to be tempted into these negational forms. As these movements advance through the culture class structure, they leave those of us still with one foot out of the grave of second culture to defend it as the necessary source of social order without ever making the fatal blunder of identifying that source with its necessarily repressive and dependent distortions. Knowing so much about the metamorphic character of all cultures, defenders of the minimalist reading of culture must never be lured into any kind of Arnoldian defense of culture, as if it were frozen in its canonical form. That is to play the game of orthopraxis in the fictive and withdrawn sectarian world of the orthodox themselves. The orthodox are dependent for their strength precisely on their withdrawals from the *kulturkampf* that obsesses them.

26. *What is a sacred object/space?* Those spaces/objects have derived their sacrality from the terrible history of suffering described in them. The chief instrument of Christianity, its ineliminable sacred object, is the maximal Roman instrument of torture, intended to intimidate any and all efforts to subvert loyalty to the fictively deified state. It is ineliminable from Christian culture that its instrument ever shall be that memory of torture. The Star of David has become the sacred symbol of the Jews after Auschwitz. Those images can never become triumphalist without mocking themselves. As soon as they cease to be on the defensive, as in a culture religion, they cease to be themselves. The images are inevitably fused with third culture power movements.

27. *What the third world needs, but refuses to admit.* There is a desperate need for an elite that carries an interdictory sense, a reading elite that carries illuminative certainties. Third world elites will not allow the development, or redevelopment, of such a reading elite. Our new age elite cannot and will not tolerate such authority.

Large societies can be organized around either a hopeless romantic notion of functionalism or an elite that itself thrusts commanding truths/illuminative certainties into the less expert readers. When Eliot makes his criticism of *Hamlet* that the language and emotions in the play appear to have no "objective correlative," I find Eliot's criticism itself a devastating implicit attack on his own poetry.[20] The same abysmal uncertainties characterize the poetic voice in *The Waste Land*, up to the *Four Quartets* when he discovers the *via/Heracleitus*. That absence of the objective correlative characterizes the poet's melancholy. The objective correlative can only be read through actions and imagery in the culture and in the social order. They are there for the reader, or *Hamlet* would not be the pivotal and enduring masterpiece that it is.[21]

The objective correlative is never visible on its own. Even the incarnate messiah of second culture looks like any other man. He has no aura or nimbus. Wherever you look for the objective correlative, it must be read. Anything else makes idolatry complicit in the reading. The commanding truths remain outside the reading, invisible, concealed. Why does Eliot find Hamlet's responses disproportionate? He cannot read from illuminative uncertainties. By contrast, every reader must have the equivalent of Shakespeare's genius in some degree; that equivalence Keats called "Negative Capability."

> The imagination may be compared to Adam's dream—he awoke and founded truth.
> . . . Adam's dream will do here and seems to be a conviction that Imagination and its empyreal reflection is the same as human Life and its Spiritual repetition.[22]

Keats describes what it is, outside revelation, to be in an illuminative certainty. No sacred messenger is required.

> . . . it struck me what quality went to form a Man of Achievement, especially in Literature, and which Shakespeare possessed so enormously—I mean Negative Capability, that is, when a man is capable of being in uncertainties, mysteries, doubts, without

20. T. S. Eliot, "Hamlet and His Problems," in *The Sacred Wood: Essays on Poetry and Criticism* (London: Methuen, 1920), 95–103.
21. See Joyce, *Ulysses*, 212: "After God, Shakespeare created most."
22. John Keats to Benjamin Bailey, November 22, 1817, *Letters of John Keats*, 66.

any irritable reaching after fact and reason—Coleridge, for instance, would let go by a fine isolated verisimilitude caught from
the Penetralium of mystery, from being incapable of remaining
content with half-knowledge.[23]

The necessary grasp of objective correlatives, the condition
Keats called "Negative Capability," cannot be expected in any rationalist or empiricist manner. It is a state of the mind and body at
rest, so that truths, in their particulars, can be given to whatever
identity has achieved, however briefly in such moments of illuminative certainty, a reconciliation with commanding truths themselves observed in whatever context has occurred to the person in
that state. The incapability to remain content with half knowledge
is characteristic of the messenger. Therefore there is a preparatory
state that has nothing exclusively intellectual about it by which the
messenger may bring facts and reasons back into the illuminative
certainty he can then convey to others, beginning with himself.
That illuminative certainty is, in such a condition, entirely com-
patible with uncertainties, mysteries, doubts. But it never has
been known to come out of nothing. More proximate to the truth
of such messengers is the Platonic vision of them as links in a chain
that descends from highest authority. No one, even the humblest,
is excluded from this chain of being a messenger.

Negative capability is the opposite of negational theorists such
as those men of achievement in third culture. However Freud ad-
mires Shakespeare, they are not moved by the same illuminative
certainty.

28. *Barbarism*. True barbarism can never exist under the authority of the past, whether in first or second cultures. It can only
express itself as a militancy released from all constraints except
fear, and that not sacred fear, to express itself in primal force figures that themselves are incarnate promises of death inseparable
from primordiality.

True barbarism has never existed before. We are witnesses to
the first true barbarians. It may have been there in the *furore teu-
tonicus* released by Hitler. Such a release may increase the fatality

23. Ibid., 72.

of such a cultural movement by its acquisition of the technology of death on a mass scale.

29. *Hierarchy of hatred: Poets and politics in third culture.* Opposed to the sacred messenger of second worlds, who, operating under the authority of highest authority, delivers a message that will bring the world into saving obedience, the third world messenger delivers a message of subjectivity that amounts to hatred. One can see the same hatred operating in the writings of Hitler and other great third world poets and politicians. Hitler's love for the abstract *"volkish* view of life" is matched only by his hatred for any real manifestation of 'the people'. Stalin and Hitler were able to create hierarchies of hate.[24]

The creative force behind third world theorists of art and action is inevitably hatred. Many of Picasso's images are hateful, toward women in particular. The toughness and studied vulgarity of *pop* performers such as Madonna is part of the dynamic of hatred. In Scorcese's film *The Last Temptation of Christ* (1988), Paul is transformed into a third world man of hate; he is indifferent to the Christ. Paul's expression of his subjectivity is inseparable from the expression of hatred toward Christ. In the artistic realm (remember that Hitler was a failed artist), the expressive hatred is inevitably turned outward, toward the viewer. Stevens expresses contempt for everyone else; but, of course, some of those people will be his readers. Insulting one's audience is now a tired trick of art creation. In his self-portrait, with whip, Mapplethorpe displays that studied contempt for his viewer, as one can see in figure 35. His other images of leather homosexuality point toward the hatred that is part of homosexual panther life. (Of course, hatred is part of the heterosexual world, i.e., heterosexual S&M; but the homosexualists are increasingly political representatives of support for just such a world of hatred.) Homosexuality as a social movement is not a movement of love but a movement of hatred and indifference. Third world heterosexualists follow the same

24. Adolph Hitler, *Mein Kampf* (New York: Stackpole Sons, 1939), 581. Also, see Theresa Toranska, *Them: Stalin's Polish Puppets* (New York: Harper and Row, 1987), in which Stalin has all his political puppets dance, in a ceremony of hatred and humiliation.

FIGURE 35. *Self-Portrait*, from *X-Portfolio*, Robert Mapplethorpe, 1978

(© The Estate of Robert Mapplethorpe)

pattern of hatred and indifference. But the homosexuals are the vanguard.

30. *The final solution.* It is the third culture that offers to all humans, as Hitler offered to the Germans, the final solution to the self-limiting character of human identity. That final solution is constituted by a variety of forms in which the culture of self-erasure becomes the supremely de-creative act of the arts and sciences. The work of art, like science, may be understood as, in the language of the second culture, rebellion. And it stands as a negation of those commanding truths by which we live in sacred order.

The image of self-erasure that we can see in all its calculated emptiness was made by the American Robert Rauschenberg in a specific way, as art must in third culture, and not as a universal counterrevelation. Rauschenberg took a drawing, given him for the purpose, by Willem de Kooning and used his eraser as what he called "a drawing tool." This drawing tool represents an instrument of the third culture. Of course, Rauschenberg stops short of the symbolic suicide, as an artist, in which he should have engaged had he followed the morality of the third culture. He thought of using one of his own drawings for this supremely trivial/important third cultural project, but realized that this would bring his work, if erased, too near to a pagan "return to nothing," as he suggested, perhaps without quite knowing what he was saying, in an interview he gave in May 1976.[25] This return to nothing he understood only as a self-disposal that would not be notable enough for his own drawing, would not have been already recognized as a simulacrum of the self—that is, as a recognized work of art. And so Rauschenberg had to find something that was a surrogate for the self of the second culture, something that was itself important and difficult to erase. We are told in the catalogue of the Rauschenberg show of third culture work that appeared at the Smithsonian Institution in 1976 that de Kooning selected a drawing covered with thick crayon, grease pencil, ink and pencil markings.

It took Rauschenberg almost a month to erase the drawing upon which only slight traces of its identity remained because they have been, as the catalogue naively reports, "absorbed by the paper." Here, "the paper" is a symptom of the sacred order that is unrecognized. It is the simulacrum of sacred scripture that is no longer to be readable, as even Kafka's Officer perhaps cannot read the commanding truths on the drawing of the 'Apparatus', the presiding presence itself, that he carries in his breast pocket as he is about to commit suicide, as the last officer in sacred order. In order to assert the fiction of this suicide, which is itself fictive, Rauschenberg had lettered the title, "Erased de Kooning Draw-

---

25. Interview (May 1976) in *Robert Rauschenberg* (exhibition catalogue), National Collection of Fine Arts, Smithsonian Institution, 36.

ing, 1953." He put his own name on a label; all put within a gold-leaf frame bought specifically for it, as a parody of 'value'. The frame itself represented the obsolete, money itself being the great fictive object behind all objects in postmodern art, as the negation of theology. Rauschenberg comes very close to understanding his effort at self-disposal. He remarks in the interview some twenty-three years after his great effort at displaying the negational character of the third culture:

> I was trying both . . . to purge myself of my teaching and at the same time exercise the possibilities so I was doing monochrome no-image.[26]

At this point we see a negational carrying out by Rauschenberg, as an anti-theorist within the anti-culture, of the second commandment: *Thou shalt not make unto thee a graven image.*

It is important to re-cognize that the second culture itself, especially in its Christian theorizing under the spell of its greatest theorist, Saul/Paul of Tarsus, has a certain predicative affinity with the final solutions to the identity of self in the third culture. I must not press the predicate of Christian theorizing too far in asserting it contained the theoretical predicates of the resolutions of authority sought by theorists in the third culture. Self-disposal in Christian theory is itself a necessary imaginative act in the procedures of redemption. Those procedures of redemption allow the self to disappear into a highest and better self which is the redemptive *I* of Christ crucified.

The key text in Christian theory of doing away with the self, as a sacred being itself, guarantees that sacrality. The passage crucial to Christian theory and the culture of personality derived from it is Galatians 2:20. This human identity which is incorporated—Christ, that Christ in turn reincorporating the human identity—disappears in order that a better, more spiritual, form live. This is an extension not a break (although the relation between extension and break is ambiguous—sometimes fatally so) of the ancient Jewish understanding of the created identity of each individual. In

26. Ibid.

that Jewish understanding, the Christ is not present, of course. Rather, the story is told by the ancient rabbinic commentators that in the beginning God created; but that beginning referred to sacred order, the commanding truths of the instruction on how to live.

So the ancient rabbis understood the verse in Proverbs 8:22, "The Lord made me as the beginning of His Way." This sacred way, or order, which fuses the laws of living among the Jews called Torah, is identical with revelation at Sinai and need not be repeated. It need only be understood rationally and applied. This means that all truth is there commanding, and what is needed is a reading of that truth in the particular moments of life thereafter.

Beginnings, or origins, and sacred order are one and the same. The Christian variation is of a new beginning implicit in sacred order that lives in the flesh of the Jew Jesus as himself, in himself, sacred order incarnate. There is the split in sacred order within the historic second culture. The race of highest authority is not to be found in sacred order itself, in its commanding truths, but in the person of Jesus fused with the Christ. This use of the image of Jesus as the Christ suggested to the ancients of Israel from the beginning a danger to sacred order itself. Of that danger, Saul/Paul was himself aware. On the one hand, he knew that if sacred order did not need the sacrifice of the fused God/man, himself a Jew, obedient in sacred order to highest authority, the creator of sacred order, "then Christ is dead in vain" (Galatians 2:21).

Paul argued with Saul, the two inseparable. The great Christian predicate of self-erasure was put in place for the anti-theorists of the anti-culture to exploit. The emergence of Christ into the self of every faithful Christian became the art of imagining oneself crucified with Christ. This being with Christ was not necessarily a doing of the commanding truths out of Israel as it had been established and continued in a variety of rationally considered applications. On the contrary, the self-disposal of the Jew of culture is itself characteristic of the negational argument in Saul/Paul.

> Wherefore then serveth the law? It was added because of transgressions, till the seed shall come to whom the promise was

made; and it was ordained by angels in the hand of a mediator. (Galatians 3:19)

The mediator and intercessor was the second person of highest authority, a personality itself at once separate and yet united with the first person. There, the mediator is not a mediator of one but finally merges, in the logic of the Christian theory of self-disposal, into a mediator that is at once one and merges as, at once, a unified highest authority that has three identities within it that are roles of the one highest authority. Trinitarian theory, which became dominant in the second culture, has somehow to deal with the commanding truths of sacred order. Those commanding truths were best understood as historically superseded by the advent of the Christ. Yet, that supersession included sacred order itself.

Is the law then against the promises of God? God forbid: for if there had been a law given which could have given life, verily righteousness should have been by the law. (Galatians 3:21)

But the sacred writings, the great cultural achievement of Israel, were concluded under a condition that was itself unredeemed. The human remained human, even though there was this implication of divinity in the spirit of created man. With this declaration that sacred order was not enough, even for the most faithful and willing obedients to it, there emerged the very ground of faithlessness that characterizes the third culture in the doctrine that is Pauline, of justification by faith alone. Sacred order was not only not enough but actually excluded the revelation of that faith which is fusion of Christ's self into every believing human self. Here is the origin of the famous pragmatic will to believe in this version:

Wherefore the law was our schoolmaster to *bring us* unto Christ, that we might be justified by faith. But, after that faith is come, we are no longer under a schoolmaster. For ye are all the children of God by faith in Christ Jesus. (Galatians 3:24–25)

After that will to believe has come, every man becomes a master of his fused self, as Paul wrote in an entry of tremendous predicative importance for the emergence of the art of being in the third culture therapeutically. So Christ actually replaced sacred order, and the great antinomian implication was, in the second culture itself, an implication that the forerunners of third culture tried to exploit immediately in Saul/Paul's own time. "God forbid" if Saul was eliminated, and a certain Christological utopianism became the break that built a new and fictive continuity into the history of man in the second culture. The Christian story became the predicate for the anti-Christian, and first of all anti-Jewish, story of the supremacy of the arts and sciences in the third culture. There was no longer a clear story of self-erasure as a prelude to entry of a redeeming personality into the self. Rather, self-erasure became a negation of the death and resurrection of the Jew Jesus as a revered paradigm for the Western conception of a historical redemption.

The Christian mode does help clarify the kinds of self-erasures that are now culturally dominant in our arts and sciences. We can see this development in the work of the great anti-theorists of the third culture. The final resolution of the Christian transference of redeeming personality, the Christ image, into the otherwise merely obedient or righteous self is a paradigm for a work of art and the artist as post-Christian. There is no longer a mergence with Jesus the Christ who is good and properly dead. Nor is there any sustained concern for the obedient personality, that soul as an entity of obedience and rebellion that characterized the Jewish understanding of the free life in determined and revealed sacred order. Nor was there a projection of the self into the Christian afterlife. The future became the future of the work of art. Not Robert Rauschenberg, but his erasures would have an afterlife. This artistic criticism of the unrepeatability of sacred history was incorporated into a sense of discontinuity that institutionalized rebellion as itself the necessity of creativity to express the self.

The sense of creativity was given an American cultural twist as early as Emerson in his call for an erasure of self that would call attention to the self as a performance of presence. The performative aspect of self became all there is to the self against a culture of sacred order in which traditioned knowledge assigned the self a stability of response to commanding truths. The biblical commentary was no longer to be read or studied or extended through new cases in continuity with revelation. Rather, the supersessive body of biblical commentary became literature and science itself. Where the book and its living theoretical traditions of the practice of theoretical life existed, there the traditions of books and poems would be as expressions of the self-erasing self. That there had to be a self engaged in self-erasures was undeniable, but that self was negational, a constant re-creation of rebellions against the commanding truths of life in sacred order. No particular directions could be given. 'Being given' was doing your own thing in an order that was understood to be fictive. It is the authority of that order derived precisely from the common consent of reader and writer that the created order was fictive and must remain so however often it appears to command our admiration. Admiration is not obedience and can easily be discounted. Literature became disillusional and only in that respect does it become mythological, as in the case of Freud's theoretical case literature.

The literature of the causal history of those arrangements of sacred knowledge, traditioned so to apply a commanding to a constant shift of cases, was itself erased; for it there was substituted a literature in the human sciences and a poetry that was built upon a constant negation of precisely the literature which arranged life according to the applications of sacred knowledge. In effect, literature had nothing more to teach; nor did the literature of the human sciences. A vast shift occurred that led from the forms of application of living models of command in sacred writings to another saturated with more or less explicit negations, of which the most obvious were the negations of Nietzsche and of Freud, who therefore became the most influential theorists, or anti-theorists, of the third or anti-culture. For the directions and instructions of commanding truths in applied sacred knowledge there was substituted a literature of function, and for the primacy of commanding truths themselves there was substituted an analysis of norms and rules and systems. Systems analysis becomes the functional equivalent of the commanding truths in sacred scripture.

31. *The new man.* So a new image of man in Western culture emerged, an image that, as Michel Foucault rightly remarks, and as I have tried to demonstrate in my own writing, pivots on the work of Freud. The wager in Foucault is on the results to be obtained by the dissolution of the commanding truths of the second culture by the literature and sciences of the third. Just what this third is to be can at present only be understood negationally. For the entire literature is an offense against what is highest in the second. Foucault postulates a post-Pascalian wager.

> One can certainly wager that man would be erased, like a face drawn in sand at the edge of the sea.[27]

What Foucault, in the appendix of his book titled *The Archaeology of Knowledge*, calls the principle of "reversal" is a principle of inversion that characterizes third culture anti-theory, theory in which the highest only emerges as a "rarefaction" of the lowest. Foucault understood the positive role to be played by the authorial actor in his will to negational truth:

> . . . we must rather recognize the negative activity of the cutting-out and rarefaction of discourse.[28]

As a great anti-theorist, Foucault is determined to affirm that the world of continuous commentary in application of sacred knowledge operates from the virtually complete revelation given in the sacred writings of the second culture. This virtual completeness of revelation must be destroyed by what Foucault calls "the principle of discontinuity":

> The existence of systems of rarefaction does not imply that, over and beyond them lie great vistas of limitless discourse, continuous and silent, repressed and driven back by them, making it our task to abolish them and at last to restore it to speech. Whether

27. Michel Foucault, *The Order of Things: An Archaeology of the Human Sciences* (New York: Vintage, 1970), 387.

28. Michel Foucault, *The Archaeology of Knowledge*, trans. A. M. Sheridan Smith (New York: Pantheon Books, 1972), 229.

talking in terms of speaking or thinking, we must not imagine some unsaid thing, or an unthought, floating about the world, interlacing with all its forms and events. Discourse must be treated as a discontinuous activity, its different manifestations sometimes coming together, but just as easily unaware of, or excluding each other.[29]

In this principle of discontinuity, a new "epistemic" order of criticism that is relentless in its turn against the knowledge of sacred order, inseparable from life in the second culture, becomes visible to us. In every piece of the critical writings and human sciences characteristic of third culture anti-theory, the third culture begins its historic collapse all over again. The fractures in its design are shown as if by X-rays. The literature of X-rays becomes the new Christ in us that characterizes the humanities as a re-creative destruction of the instructional texts and their applications that characterize the cultivated life in the traditions out of both Athens and Jerusalem. This demonstrates the faint hope we may have for the humanities as they are operated by the critical intellect which is engaged in creative destruction in their fusillades of fictions, as the performative intellect that has superseded the feeling intellect of the symbolists who were the teachers in generation after generation of those who lived in the second culture. That entire teaching elite, the rabbinates and priesthoods, and the professoriats that derived from them, have themselves engaged in a long withdrawing roar of criticism on the land of law against the ground on which they themselves could once always make their stand against rebellions. Now those priesthoods and rabbinates are themselves so enculturated in the critical intellect that they are themselves hostile to the commanding truths that are theirs to teach and reteach.

The problem of the critical intellect, as of the sociologists and poets and painters who are the critical intellect incarnate, is to free themselves from the commanding truths revealed as the foundations of the second culture. This means also to free themselves even from Freud, so to become the cruising performative

29. Ibid.

intellects of the third culture with no countertransferences. The technical rule substitutes for the interdict, as in the case of the reasons that can be given why a therapist should not sleep with his patient. There are complex and devious movements within the hostile elites of the third culture that describe these constant critical negations upon which the literary action of the suicidal old officers of the second culture depend. But the history of those suicidal officers does not unfold with any kind of conventional narrativity. History becomes synchronic. The memorious imagination knows that Sinai is still with us and that the task of the critical commentator is now, not to apply the commanding truths and the traditions out of Sinai, but to negate them. The abolitionist movements characteristic of third culture elites are engaged in asserting repressive truths where revelation is; there shall repression act.

As a herald of the third culture, its greatest anti-theorist before the third culture was fully established in the critical institutions of the university and the state as a work of art, Nietzsche well understood the relation between truth telling and lie telling in its extramoral sense. The date of the third culture also could be located fictively as 1873, when Nietzsche wrote his little discourse "On Truth and Lie in an Extra-Moral Sense." There he tells us that the human intellect does not appear in nature. If we saw it in that way, we would be telling a lie, which is true. The human intellect is not an element of nature. It is an element of divine creation, sometimes called the *logos*. But Nietzsche understood how shadowy and aimless, except negationally, the intellect has become. He understood the distrust of it when it is emancipated from the discipline of sacred knowledge. But his distrust is itself a proud distrust, an assertion of a suspicion that turns intellect, as earlier understood, against itself. After all, in natural history there were eternities when intellect did not exist, and there will be times again when it will not exist. Then we will know that, as Nietzsche put it, "nothing will have happened."[30]

30. Nietzsche, "On Truth and Lie in an Extra-Moral Sense", in *The Portable Nietzsche*, ed. and trans. Walter Kaufmann (Harmondsworth: Penguin, 1954), 42.

Nietzsche's critical intellect grasped the fact that it had no sacred mission, nothing that would lead it toward that fusion with highest authority, beyond the natural life of the human in the body that Paul promised in the commanding truth of Christianity that *not-I*, but Christ in me, will live. All that Nietzsche considered to be a fiction was there to be eliminated. The human does not exist "as if the world pivoted around it." The human is no more signifying than an insect, such as the mosquito, who no more lives in sacred order than does the human. This Nietzschean reduction is a key to understanding the powerful mixture of pride and abasement that the anti-theorists of the third culture feel.

32. *Despair.* Despair is transformed into the work of art itself. From the flying insect we would learn, Nietzsche thought, that it "floats through the air with the same self-importance, feeling within itself the flying center of the world."[31] The flying center of the world is the admirer in every human, the porter who wants those whose bags he carries to admire him. At this point, admiration easily becomes envy. The Kierkegaardian understanding that admiration can turn most easily to cynical dismissal is characteristic of the kinds of reversals and lowerings that the critical intellect performs, since it is nothing but a performance of its own capacity to move. This shadow of sacred intellect has become flighty. But the flight is no longer an ascent in sacred order but rather performances of descent that suggest the self is whatever role he wishes to assume; at least if the other whose role he assumes can be dominated by the assumption. Third culture images, therefore, refer us to their negational source, to the imperious will and energy of the performative author, who then becomes what the rabbinates and priesthoods and the professoriats following them had the naïveté to think they were not: i.e., criminals.

The criminality of the author is something of which the author is aware without shame in sacred order. Were he ashamed, as author, then he would be silent or offer what is merely commentary of application derived from a sacred knowledge of a revelation complete in itself. Instead, the banner of the triumphant author

31. Ibid.

is itself the object of authorship. That object becomes the source of authorship itself. Authority becomes an epistemic disposition. The will to truth becomes inseparable from the will to power so far as the truth is understood by its great anti-theorists as negational. In this period, in this manner, Freud's great essay on civilization and its discontents is itself a manner of imperiling civilization as the institutions, the actions, of symbolists in sacred order. The title of *Civilization and Its Discontents* might well read, if rightly understood, as a program toward the achievement of a civilization with little law and less sacred order which then will create a new age of discontents.

The source of art is rebellion. 'Discontent', in its Freudian usages, is itself a repressive concealment of rebellion. The German word is far more revealing in its repressive character. *Unbehagen*, Freud's original, carries in its very prefix the concealed truth that discontent is to civilization as a means of rebellion is to the end of sacred order. *Unbehagen* should carry with it, in parentheses, another German word that would carry the latent meaning of the Freudian address to civilization. That word paralleling *Unbehagen* is *Unbesehen*. For the character of civilization, or culture, as the practical application of sacred knowledge is unseen by Freud himself and by those anti-theorists now dominant in our time. The answer to the sacred Yes is No. The answer to the interdictory No in the vertical of authority that characterizes the rhetoric of the critical and fictive intellect is No.

There can be no new age, no fourth culture, because the great finality, the solution to sacred order achieved by the anti-theorists of the third culture, is that not only those anti-theorists but any human can put what Emerson called a "new face on all things."[32]

33. *Wanted: A theory with a strategy of testing its limits as a practical art of warfare.* What is needed is a new second world writing-out of the resistances to third world art; more precisely, the arts and sciences of third world radically remissive elites. In the present age, that is a difficult need to satisfy. Art breeds art because

32. Ralph Waldo Emerson, "Circles," in *Essays by Ralph Waldo Emerson* (New York: Houghton, Mifflin, 1894), 268.

myth, or medium level horizontal flight, is necessarily more absorbing than the pursuit of obedience up the vertical in authority. As good Calvinists used to say of this slippery slope theory of truth, which works in both directions (though the way up is as far from being the same as the way down as blessings are from curses): "If the world be sloped on both sides, therefore put your foot in the middle of it."

There is an art in living well in second culture. Going down is no art. Going up is the true art. But the pursuit of the means of ascent is never a natural but always a supernatural discipline. Ask any child or beginning reader. Right readings remain a secondary art of pursuit. It is still an art and not a truth. This secondary pursuit of truth is the oldest game. It started—God knows when: as soon as paradise—the premoral primacy of possibility, was lost. It is now a mere means of a return never to be made; like Kafka's imperial messages that never reach their destination, and anyway have not been sent because the Emperor actually has not a message in his empty head. But we have all the messages we could possibly want. Silence is now the preferred form of prophecy. We have been given all the words wanted for the historic time being to reconstruct the truth behind the glamour of events, including the auction of world pictures after the horrors of third world facts from their permanently cast shadows.

Shadows of truths are the texts of resistance to which we can train our necessary new literacies of resistance. Reading is an ecumenical art. No second culture can now make readings exclusive to their rules of fighting each other. Those terrible internecine quarrels will become deadlier than ever in the context of the new battlefield on which all the old armies of second world faith/knowledge find themselves engaged against each other yet again. There is no advantage in protesting the internecine warfare yet again, especially if the protesters are Jews. Jews of protest always end fighting their own means of protest toward some end against themselves. Second world readings cannot become catholic enough for the world struggle against third cultures. That is their strategic, as it is their historic, limit.

34. *On the comedy of our third world war against second.* Is it pos-

sible to laugh our way out of second world existence, at least temporarily? Laughter is disarming. Of the founding sons of our second worlds, Nietzsche tells us, "there is no denying that *in the long run* every one of these great teachers of a purpose was vanquished by laughter, reason, and nature: the short tragedy always gave way again and returned to the comedy of existence."[33] Among the most zealous of third world prophets, we must respect the old Voltaire, undaunted even at seventy-three by the tragic sense of life in sacred order. Thin and yet Falstaffian trickster that he was, Voltaire was a great lover of himself in warring office. "I carry on the war to the last moment, I get a hundred pike-thrusts, I return two hundred, and I laugh." How easily we can join Voltaire in laughing at his Protestant neighbors in Geneva "on fire with quarrels over nothing." In his grave Voltaire could "laugh again." He had raised laughter to the dignity of prayer. By contrast, there is no laughter in the Bible, and not a single joke that I have ever been able to find. Laughter was Voltaire's way to "thank God that I can look upon the world as a farce, even when it becomes as tragic as it sometimes does. All comes out even at the end of the day."[34] Joyce's mockery of Genesis 1:3 is not so amusing here and now in its endlessness. *Let there be fight. And there is.* The enduring *is-ness* of this warring brings to my ear no sound of laughter from the Jewish and its descendant camps.

35. *The all in all in all of us.* There is a primordiality of a sort, nothing sacred nor splendid in its savagery, in all of us. From the world fight, thirds advancing as seconds retreat ever deeper into the interior of our selves, no one escapes a degree of hurt inestimable by any legal, medical, or psychiatric standard. One of the officers I would rank highest in the allied and yet conflicting armies of our second world read our historical situation more than a century ago: "Every war hurts the victor as well as the vanquished, and the *kulturkampf* is no exception to this rule." Thomas Masaryk understood us, those of us here and now with half a mind

33. Nietzsche, *The Gay Science*, 74.

34. Voltaire, quoted in William James, *The Varieties of Religious Experience* (New York: Longmans, Green, 1925), 36.

in some third culture camp, as if we were there and then in the Europe of 1881: "Along with a deadening indifference, vexing skepticism and disgusting cynicism are spread; men are dissatisfied and unhappy, and, more and more loudly and menacingly raising their voices, they do not shrink back from a revolutionary reorganization of society."[35] But soft noises of war are not necessarily less menacing than loud in the battles yet to come.

35. Thomas G. Masaryk, *Suicide and the Meaning of Civilization*, trans. W. B. Weist and R. G. Batson, with an introduction by Anthony Giddens (Chicago: University of Chicago Press, 1970), 165.

Index

epiphany, 22, 140, 152
equivocal perception, 145, *146*. See
    also *Duck/Rabbit*
Erasmus, Desiderius, 76n37
Eros, 32, 60, 84, 145, 181
eroticism, 6, 10, 86
Euripides, 52, 69
Europe, xxiii, 6, 16, 33, 170, 213
euthanasia, xiv, 115, 123
Evans, John, xxviiin5
evil, 11, 137, 170–71
Exodus, 3, 5, 7, 36, 39, 62, 130
explorers, 41–42, 155
extraterritoriality, and the repres-
    sive mode, 163
Ezekiel, 36

face: in fusion images, 23–24; new,
    210; sacred, 100n20; use of, 32,
    112, 117, 147, 169, 206
faith, xvi, 55–60, 66–68, 75–76,
    136–37, 147–49, 151–53, 202–3;
    and the aesthetics of authority,
    62, 71, 113; bad, 147; *faith/
    knowledge*, 164, 211; faith-
    relation, 47; ladder languages
    of, 47, 55, 192; as leitmotif of
    second culture, 5, 12, 33, 50;
    praxis of, 60; received, 113;
    replaced by fiction, 91–93;
    and roles, 56; sea of, 81; and
    stability, 38
faithlessness, 136, 148–49, 152,
    203
Falstaff (character), 154, 174, 212
family, 27, 174; author's, 82, 139,
    186–87
Fanon, Frantz, 62
fantasy, 6, 10, 92, 150, 162, 165
Farrakhan, Louis, 77, 159
fashion, world of high, 10
fate, xxi, 36, 49–54, 135–37, 146; in
    contrast to faith, 58, 113; as a

knocking, 33; as leitmotif of
    first culture, 12, 49, 72; and
    science, 69
fear, 68, 197; sacred, 36, 73, 77, 79,
    149
feasting, 10, 185
feeling intellect, xviii, xxviiin4, 27–
    28, 79, 207
Feeling Intellect, The, xv
Fellow Teachers, xxvii, xxviiin2,
    100n19
female(s), 120, 122, 125, 127;
    clergy, 86
feminine, the, 124–26; feminiza-
    tion, 86
feminism, 84, 97, 194
fetuses, as symbols, 105n31
ficta, 25, 73–74, 97, 126, 164
fiction, 74–75, 120, 129–30, 157,
    200, 209; analytic, 73; ending
    in reality, 9; faithless, 72; faith
    replaced by, 91; identity as, 102,
    125; leitmotif of the third cul-
    ture, 12, 33–34, 157; of multi-
    culturalism, 14; "Notes toward
    a Supreme Fiction," 15n23, 38–
    42, 74, 189; of primordiality, 25;
    scientific, 41; self as, in third
    culture, 33n43; supreme, 6, 18,
    74; as weapon, 78
fidelity, 47, 101, 107
fighting, culture as, 1, 14, 94, 144,
    211
figments of imagination, 33n43,
    74–75
Final Solution, the, 116, 199, 201
Fine, Gary, xxi
Finnegans Wake, 1, 4, 26, 28, 31,
    89n3, 146, 185; as greatest liter-
    ary deathwork, 94–96. *See also*
    Joyce, James
first culture (world), xx–xxi, 3–6,
    12–14, 19–22, 43–45, 48–54,